W9-BSW-906

SOUL MAKING

OTHER BOOKS BY ALAN JONES

EXPLORING SPIRITUAL DIRECTION
JOURNEY INTO CHRIST
LIVING IN THE SPIRIT (coauthor)

SOUL MAKING

The Desert Way of Spirituality

Alan W. Jones

1817

Harper & Row, Publishers, San Francisco
Cambridge, Hagerstown, New York, Philadelphia
London, Mexico City, São Paulo, Singapore, Sydney

Scripture quotations are from *The New English Bible* © The Delegates of the Oxford University Press and The Syndics of the Cambridge University Press, 1961, 1970.

Acknowledgment is made for the following: "The Rowing Endeth" and "Jesus, the Actor, Plays the Holy Ghost" from *The Awful Rowing Toward God* by Anne Sexton. Copyright © 1975 by Loring Conant, Jr., Executor of the Estate of Anne Sexton. Reprinted by permission of Houghton Mifflin Company; excerpts from "For the Time Being" and "In Sickness and In Health" from *W. H. Auden: Collected Poems*, edited by Edward Mendelson. Copyright © 1976 by Edward Mendelson, William Meredith, and Monroe K. Spears, Executors of the Estate of W. H. Auden. Reprinted by permission of Random House, Inc.; excerpts from "Little Gidding" in *Four Quartets*, copyright 1943 by T. S. Eliot, renewed 1971 by Esme Valerie Eliot. Reprinted by permission of Harcourt Brace Jovanovich, Inc.; exerpts from "Wilderness" in *Cornhuskers* by Carl Sandburg, copyright 1918 by Holt, Rinehart and Winston, Inc., renewed 1946 by Carl Sandburg. Reprinted by permission of Harcourt Brace Jovanovich, Inc.

FIRST EDITION

Library of Congress Cataloging in Publication Data

Jones, Alan W.
    Soul making.

    Bibliography: P.
    Includes index.

    1. Spiritual life—Anglican authors.   2. Love (Theology)   3. Soul.
I. Title.
BV4501.2.J5854   1985   233   84-48222
ISBN 0-06-064182-7

87 88 89 RRD 10 9 8 7 6 5 4 3

In Memoriam

Stephen F. Bayne (1908–1974)
and
Edward Augustus Jones (1901–1952)

Contents

Preface   viii
Introduction   1

I. THE INVITATION TO SEE
1.   Children of the Desert   19
2.   The Christian Neurosis   35
3.   Death in the Desert   60

II. ENTERING THE EMPTINESS
4.   The Gift of Tears   82
5.   The Fiftieth Gate   107
6.   Love: God's Wild Card   124

III. THE CALL TO JOY
7.   Love and the Making of a Soul   143
8.   The Three Conversions   159
9.   The Soul Maker: The Holy and Undivided Trinity   185

Epilogue   206
Notes   210
Index   217

For the garden is the only place there is, but you will not
    find it
Until you have looked for it everywhere and found nowhere
    that is not a desert.
                            —W. H. Auden, *For the Time Being*

Preface

The two men to whom this book is dedicated bespeak its origins. Stephen F. Bayne was a bishop in the Church of God: an urbane, intelligent, and compassionate man of deep spirituality to whom I owe double debt. First, I value his example of simplicity and directness in dealing (with grace and integrity) with the complex issues that face the world and the church. He was a diplomat, and managed to be one without losing his soul. Second, I had the honor of occupying the Chair of Ascetical Theology at the General Theological Seminary in New York City that bears his name.

My father, Edward Augustus Jones, died when I was twelve years old. He was no diplomat, but a rough-and-ready sort of man—a skilled laborer—who had little time for the church. I remember two things about him: his love of the truth (he hated lying or any form of cant), and his infectious and earthy sense of humor. He shared, with Bishop Bayne, an enviable integrity. He only went to church for baptisms, weddings, and funerals. I remember one family wedding in a little country church in East Anglia. I was, at that time, a choirboy and a "serious" believer. My father had fortified himself with a pint of beer in the local pub. When he came down the aisle to sit with us he was in a cheerful mood, so cheerful in fact that an officious verger came over to our pew and asked him to be quiet! "Miserable bugger," my father said in a stage whisper. At the time I was amused, shocked, and ashamed all at once. When I look back, I realize that the church was, for him, a group of such "miserable buggers" and that's why he hated to go. That he was in his heart, along with Stephen Bayne, one of the true believers, I have no doubt. Both men have helped me become and remain a believer.

Kingsley Amis wrote,

All sorts of people are uncomfortable in a universe where there seems to be nothing supernatural, nothing beyond this life, no undiscovered forces, no God. I sympathize; I find it none too cosy myself; but I do wish there were a little less eager, cruising credulity about. I wish too, quite vainly, that such people, other people too, would face a little more squarely what is entailed by believing, or believing in, something.[1]

Neither Bishop Bayne nor my father ever succumbed to "cruising credulity." Both have inspired me to "face a little more squarely what is entailed by believing."

I owe a word of thanks to the Department of Theology of the University of Dallas and to the Anglican School of Theology of the Episcopal Diocese of Dallas. I am grateful to The Rev. Dr. Peter Phan of the University and to The Rev. Dr. Lynn Bauman of the Anglican School for inviting me to deliver the Gorman-Garrett Memorial Lectures in November 1983. These lectures are the backbone of this book.

As always, I owe a great deal to my friends—not least my family (my wife Josephine and my three children, Lena, Charlotte, and Edward). They provided the basic stuff of which this book is made. In a sense, it is as much their book as mine. The making of a book, as with the making of a soul, is a cooperative enterprise that takes a lifetime—at least.

Introduction—
Angels of God: Believers and Unbelievers in the Desert

Call the world if you please "The vale of Soul-making."
JOHN KEATS, Letters 1819

This is a book about how human beings are made. It is concerned with the ancient task of soul making. In order to discuss how we are made, I have to write about love. I feel inexperienced and ill-equipped to do this, except in one respect. Even though I am not much of a lover, I do know that I am loved. This is a statement of faith the effects of which, from time to time, spill over into my experience. One of the side-effects of knowing that one is loved is the desire to tell others— and to tell them in such a way that they are included in, and not excluded from, the circle of love. How do I write about love without sounding unrealistic and sentimental? How do I write about the making of a soul without lying about it? As we shall see, human beings are not made overnight. Nor, indeed, is the process ever finished. The word "soul" is a metaphor for this process of transformation. We are, as it were, more or less "human" insofar as we are in the "school of love." The only qualification required of pupils in the school is the willingness to wake up.

Jacob Needleman suggests that the process of waking up is seriously hampered by the tendency to view the human person or the "soul" as a finished product. The twin traditions that inform the way of believing to which this book is dedicated (those of psychoanalysis and the desert) both insist that there is an unfinished quality about human beings that is both tragic and glorious: tragic because the openness and freedom of human identity is hard to bear; glorious because the openness and freedom corresponds to our deepest desire. Many people (perhaps most people in and past middle age) think of themselves as in some way *finished*. And on the finished entity we place impossible demands. For example, we are told that we must love everyone—an absurd and impossible command if there ever was one. What believers tend to do, then, is to lay on themselves the necessity to love without first realizing that they have to learn slowly and painfully how to do it.

This is where the desert tradition can help. Desert believers understand that they are in a school of love. It is a good school, and they find themselves in kindergarten or in first grade. They also understand that there is no real loving without tears. They soon discover that learning how to love is the same as learning how to be. Since they tend to be clumsy pupils when it comes to simply being in the world, they are not averse to weeping.

Numerous jokes begin with the formula, "I've got some good news and some bad news." They go on to pass on a minor piece of good news, which is then vitiated by a disproportionate piece of bad news. They sometimes revolve around the hopes and claims of rival religious groups. For example, a messenger arrives at the Vatican, repeats the opening formula to the pope, and then says: "The Good News is that Jesus is coming! The bad news is that he's coming to Salt Lake City." The joke can be rearranged in order to please or offend whatever group has our attention.

This book revolves around such a formula, as does all talk about love. The good news is that we are lovable and we are loved (that is, we have a "soul," we have an identity, we are somebody). The bad news is that we neither know it nor believe it. To be sure, there are those who *think* they believe it, but, as we shall see, believers are easily deceived.

There is, however, one important difference between the good news/bad news jokes and the formula as it is applied to the Gospel. In the joke, the bad news is out of all proportion to the good news: in the Gospel, the good news is amazingly disproportionate to the bad. The Gospel begins with God's joy and delight in us. This book is about that basic truth and the various obstacles in our path to our accepting that love. Much in what follows may *sound* like bad news, and it is very important to remember that what undergirds the exploration of hard truths is the fundamental one of God's love for us. Much of our believing has to do with the issue of discernment.

We often ask ourselves the questions, What am I to do? How am I to be? The Cistercian writers of the twelfth century (St. Bernard of Clairvaux, 1090–1153; William of St. Thierry, 1085–1148; and Aelred of Rievaulx, 1109–1167) took our basic and inalienable dignity as their starting point. The purpose of life was to discern our true worth and to know the One who bestows it. Indeed, the life of virtue (the answer to the question, "What shall I do?") was simply the desire to discover the author of our dignity, and know more and more fully that we possess it and thus give glory to the giver. This is certainly good news.

The 'bad news' is that we are always in danger of suffering from a sort of spiritual amnesia. When we forget our dignity (our true worth), we forget the source of that worth. Sin is a sort of willful forgetfulness of how great and wonderful we are. It seduces us into thinking that we have to be our own creators, that we have to be the fabricators of our own souls. It lays upon us terrible burdens. Ironically, one of the ways by which we are encouraged to forget our true worth and are seduced into trying to build up our own "dignity" is in the practice of religion.

BELIEVERS WHO ARE INTOLERABLE AND UNBELIEVERS WHO ARE INSANE

And if the good news is true, why are its public proclaimers such assholes and the proclamation itself such a weary used up thing? . . . As unacceptable as believers are, unbelievers are even worse . . . [The unbeliever] is in fact an insane person. . . .The present-day Christian is either half-assed, nominal, lukewarm, hypocritical, sinful, or, if fervent, generally offensive and fanatical. But he is not crazy. The present-day unbeliever is crazy as well as being an asshole—which is why I say he is a bigger asshole than the Christian because a crazy asshole is worse than a sane asshole. . . .The rest of my life . . . shall be devoted to a search for a third alternative, a tertium quid—if there is one. If not we are stuck with two alternatives: (1) believers, who are intolerable, and (2) unbelievers who are insane.[1]

This quotation from Walker Percy's *The Second Coming* may

seem an inauspicious way to begin thinking about love. But if we bear in mind that our fundamental starting point is God's delight in us, we can proceed with confidence. It is often best to plunge in at the deep end and begin with the worst. Such a strategy, admittedly, reveals a certain kind of temperament; but I find that I am in good company. Walker Percy is a Catholic Christian, a philosopher, and a humorous and moving story-teller. I trust his judgment, even when it is mediated through one of his characters. He presents an all too true picture of the current social scene in its secular and religious aspects.

I am one of the believers and therefore (along with Percy) one of the assholes. I should add that I am both glad and proud to be a believer, even if it also means accepting Percy's far from complimentary description. It is important that I make this clear at the outset. I *am* a believer, but I find it increasingly difficult to feel at home with my fellow believers. I feel disarmingly at home with many of my "unbelieving" friends, and seriously out of step and tune with many who call and profess themselves Christians. I am confronted with Percy's two alternatives: the believers who are intolerable and the unbelievers who are in-sane. Like his character, Will Barrett, I am looking for a *tertium quid*, a third alternative. I want a kind of Christianity that can be embraced with both passion and intelligence. And in case the reader assumes that I am advocating some watered-down stuff, let it be known that I want nothing of "morality tinged with emotion." I want a gutsy, old-fashioned, demanding reli-gion with no compromise and no nonsense. I want a great deal.

Often, I feel that as yet, I have nowhere to lay my head. The heartiness of fundamentalist, charismatic, or evangelical brands of Christianity are unattractive to me, as is the legalism of certain brands of Catholicism and Protestantism. I have no wish to be judgmental. All I want to do is make clear some of the things I cannot live with.

I want to share with the reader my particular *way* of believing. This *way* finds that of the fundamentalist literalist far too ra-tionalistic. In spite of the fundamentalist/evangelical emotion-alist style, conversion for the literalist is largely a matter of rational effort. It's as if we have to argue ourselves into belief. John Mortimer tried to do just that when he was a boy at school.

In chapel he had sung the hymn: "Only believe and you shall see/That Christ is all in all to thee." He thought he would try hard to believe so that he would be able to *see*. "I dug my nails in to the palms of my hands, stood quite alone in the playground and forced myself to believe for at least ten minutes. Even so I couldn't see it."[2]

The young Mortimer, of course, was going at it all wrong. Yet the idea that we can argue ourselves into belief is still strong. That is why, perhaps, John Mortimer would consider himself an unbeliever. Yet when I read his books or see his plays I find myself in tune with a sensitive, humorous, and compassionate soul whose "unbelief" seems very close to my "belief."

NO BELIEFS OF MY OWN

My beliefs are not *mine*, they belong to all those who believe. I do, however, have my own *way* of believing, and while it is not peculiar to me, it is by no means universal. Some of my fellow believers find my *way* of believing very odd indeed. (This is one reason why I'm grateful not to be living under the Spanish Inquisition or in seventeenth-century Salem, Massachusetts. I and some of my colleagues are made of burnable stuff!) Of course I have friends and acquaintances in the various camps. I make no claim that mine is the right view or even the preferred one. I am simply looking for company in a world struggling to find its way.

THE DESERT WAY

I find myself at home in an ancient form of Christianity embodied in what is known as the "desert tradition." Not many Christians in the West are aware of this tradition. I suspect most would find it exceedingly peculiar, although many might find it surprisingly liberating and refreshing. Still more, those who call themselves "unbelievers" might be able to embrace a way of believing that opens their hearts without closing their minds.

What comes to mind when we hear the word "desert"? A dry and desolate place? A barren yet beautiful terrain? The desert wilderness is the place where nothing grows and where our very existence is threatened. Yet it is also the arena (which means, in Latin, "sandy place") especially chosen by God as the focus of his revelation. Thus the desert of which I speak is a desert of the spirit: a place of silence, waiting, and temptation. It is also a place of revelation, conversion, and transformation. A true revelation is a very disturbing event because it demands a response; and to respond to it means some kind of inner revolution. It involves being "made over," being made new, being "born again." The desert, then, is a place of revelation and revolution. In the desert we wait, we weep, we learn to live.

This austere and refreshing desert way of belief has a peculiar array of devotees. They have two basic characteristics: a heart and mind willing to pursue the truth wherever it may lead (and the ability to acknowledge that they may be wrong); and the kind of sensibility (which is the joining of the mind and heart) that is captive to wonder, mystery, and awe.

TWO THEOLOGIANS

The Roman Catholic "believer" Karl Rahner and the Anglican "unbeliever" Don Cupitt are two very different followers of the desert way. The latter has been characterized and caricatured as an English theologian who doesn't really believe in God. I find myself taking issue with most of what he has to say, but I am struck by his uncompromising honesty and his willingness to face the unknown. Unfortunately, he doesn't let on that he knows anything about the desert tradition. He does, however, know a place that is very much like it.

In his book *The World to Come*, Cupitt speaks of our need to accept the gift of Hyperborean faith. The Hyperboreans of mythology lived beyond (*hyper*) the North Wind (*Boreas*); beyond the ends of the earth; beyond the freezing rain and the death-dealing ice. There they lived in a land of joy and abundance. Cupitt writes: "Hyperborean faith represents an attempt to live a free and truthful Christian life, without nostalgia, illusion or the traditional insatiable hunger for power over others, in the world as it now is."

Now that is what I'm after; I want to believe in a way that is passionate, intelligent, and honest. I agree with his point that "in the twentieth century, and indeed in the foreseeable future, we need to find out how light we can travel."[3] I suspect that we can manage with a lot less than we imagine. It is said that during an uprising in India late in the last century, when British service families suddenly had to be evacuated, the road was strewn with such things as stuffed owls and Victorian bric-a-brac. I have no idea what the late-twentieth-century equivalent of a stuffed owl is, but no doubt our path will be just as littered with such "necessities." We will have to learn to travel light.

Of particular concern is the attitude to belief that insists that not one "stuffed owl" be lost. This sad and disturbing way of believing causes a deep and tragic split in one's mind, a split between what it knows to be the truth and the object of belief. When these two coincide, all is well; but when the "truth" begins to be at variance with belief, a pattern of self-deception and lying begins to emerge. Ask Christian believers what they would do if they had to choose between Jesus Christ and the Truth. There are easy ways to slip out from underneath this question, "Since Christ is the Truth, I don't see any conflict." But the way of believing that I espouse would always choose the Truth (even if one's perception of it turned out to be wrong) and allow the false object of faith to dissolve. I do not pretend that this is easy; but I can bear witness to the fact that when I have made the choice, a fresh and living "Christ" appears. There is an epiphany.

Philip Gosse (1810–1888), a contemporary of Charles Darwin, came to such a moment of choice. He was a marine biologist who also happened to have an unimaginative, literalist approach to the Bible. The fossils in the rocks told him that the world must have been created more than six thousand years ago. The Bible told him (or he *thought* it did) that God created the world in 4004 B.C. He had a choice: to believe the evidence of his own research, or to believe an unfounded, arbitrary authority. He chose the latter, and claimed that God deliberately put the fossils in the rocks to test our faith! It was a tragic decision, but the mind-set that asks us to make such choices is still very much alive. Fortunately, there are other ways to go. Such writers as Cupitt and Rahner, albeit in very different styles, point us in the right direction.

It may seem strange to place the Jesuit Karl Rahner's "orthodoxy" alongside Cupitt's "heresy," but I sense something of the same spirit in both writers even though they could be said to represent the extreme ends of the believers' spectrum. Rahner has, along with Cupitt, an uncompromising commitment to truth. In the Jesuit, however, there is an overriding appreciation of awe and mystery which is not as evident in the Anglican. Rahner never uses mystery to cover over the deep struggles of the believer. Yet Cupitt and Rahner, in spite of their differences, share the two characteristics I most admire in believers and unbelievers alike: honesty and reverence.

Karl Rahner, in *The Practice of Faith*, writes: "I would like to be a person who is free and can hope, who understands and shows by his actions that he himself is at the mercy of his freedom, a freedom which throughout his life is creating and making him finally what he should be . . . a person who is faithful, who loves, who is responsible." That is what I would like to be. Rahner is as aware as both Walker Percy and Don Cupitt of the pitfalls of belief. The word "God" is a fundamental problem, a necessary "evil" for those who have to use language. Rahner admits:

I know that this word is obscure, by definition the most obscure word there can be, the word which is genuinely impossible to include among the other words of human language as one more word. I know that what is meant by the word may be present in a person's life even if its name is never spoken by the person. (Anonymous theists do exist . . .) . . . I know that the word "God" has been used to do any number of terrible and stupid things. I know that it is very easy to keep on finding, in oneself and in others, stupid misunderstandings which do their mischief under the word "God."[4]

BEING AN ATHEIST FOR GOD'S SAKE

I am searching for a combination of Cupitt's Hyperborean faith and Rahner's way of believing, one which is free, hopeful, and honest. I've caught a glimpse of it in the attempts of the mystics to express the inexpressible: "pages that ought to be blank are crammed full of the very images and concepts which vanish where," Meister Eckhart tells us, "even God disappears" and Simone Weil reminds us that "there are two atheisms of which one is a purification of the notion of God."[5]

I am an "atheist" in this latter sense. That is why I find myself increasingly at home in that way of believing which flourished and still flourishes in the Egyptian desert. This book is for those who might care to explore further this *way* of believing. I will not be exploring the desert trdition historically; still less is it my intention to idealize it. The desert has its share of the mad and the intolerable. The tradition does, however, have certain characteristics that point to an alternative way of believing: characteristics of receptivity, silence, contemplation, clarity, and moral courage. I was fortunate in encountering this way of believing during a visit to the Egyptian Desert, which I made towards the end of a trip around the world.

TWO "ALIEN" WAYS OF BELIEVING

Before I arrived in Egypt, however, I collided with two ways of believing that I found suffocating and alienating. The first thrives on various forms of dogmatic vindictiveness; the second relies on the replication of certain experiences (described meticulously in prescribed and often repeated formulae). Both tend to be tyrannical with regard to believers (and often the tyranny is an inner one), and offensive to unbelievers.

For example, the first way of believing has a particular affection for the doctrine of eternal punishment. This apparently biblical theme receives prominence because it is thought to be a way of safeguarding the justice of God. I take the issue of moral choice very seriously, and believe that we suffer the consequences of our decisions. Our choices are critical, but I find no grounds for believing that the process of our making choices and living them through is irrevocably settled at death. God is just and life is sometimes "hell"; but to insist as many do, that a person is damned *everlastingly* if he or she fails to make a personal and verbal commitment to Jesus Christ is both absurd and morally repellent. What about all those who haven't made a decision for Jesus Christ because of the terrible example of those who have? Are we believers not implicated in their damnation? I wonder sometimes how many people need to be in hell in order to make some "Christians" feel safe? I did meet one kindhearted believer who was willing to allow that there would only have to be one person in Hell in order for God's justice to be preserved! I thought at the time that this would make the basis of a very touching medieval legend: the story of some holy man or woman who volunteered to "go to Hell" so that the rest of us could enjoy the delights of heaven! But my objection to this way of believing is not so much its doctrine of eternal punishment (so alien to the heart of Christianity) as its being closed in a private and individualistic world. There is little or no sense of the communal and collective aspects of believing; no feeling for the solidarity we human beings enjoy and endure with one another. In short, this way of believing distorts the Gospel. As J. Christiaan Beker points out:

. . . a Gospel based on God's redemptive act in the death and resurrection of Christ can tolerate neither favoritism for the so-called elect nor a cosmic vengeance and doom for the nonelect.[6]

Henry Scott Holland (a canon of St. Paul's Cathedral in London at the end of the last century who was deeply concerned about the poor and oppressed) wrote:

We are what our brothers are. We and they stand and fall together. If they are contemptible so are we. If we are struggling after higher things so are they. One fate; one flesh and blood; one story: one strife: one glory—this is the underlying secret of humanity.

It is this sense of solidarity that I find at the heart of the way I wish to follow.

The second way of believing insists that the authenticity of the believer's faith be demonstrated by the repetition of certain formulas, particularly this one: "Jesus Christ is my personal Lord and Savior." In one place I visited, *everyone* I met greeted me with this formula. Many of them I believed. Their faces radiated a love and openness that I found very compelling. With others, it seemed an empty phrase, uttered out of habit or the desire to belong and to say the right thing. Some said the phrase innocently, like a small child hurriedly reciting the Lord's Prayer or the alphabet. Perhaps a lot of our believing is like whistling in the dark? I still need the equivalent of the nightlight. Thus my weariness with this way of believing did not spring from a feeling of superiority; still less was it the result of a jaundiced intellectualism. I am not uncomfortable with passionate, experiential religion. What saddened me was the fact that "the experience of Jesus Christ" closed doors, settled questions, and (above all) knew the fate and destination of unbelievers. It was as if people had swallowed a book of rules rather than encountered something of the awesome reality we call God.

I had been away from home about six weeks when I began to wonder not only whether I was a Christian, but whether I wanted to be one. My faith was restored when I went into the Egyptian desert. There I rediscovered a way of believing that I found healing and sustaining. The strange thing about this *way* is that, while it isn't for everyone, the Gospel it proclaims is. It hopes for the salvation of everyone and of all things; and, while it allows for the terrible mystery and possibility of someone being lost and saying "No" to the movement of life and love in the heart, it resists making a judgment with regard to the end of those "whose faith is known to God alone." It believes and trusts in the working of the Holy Spirit in all human beings. Christians believe that there is an intimate movement

in God towards God. They believe that this movement takes place even if a person does not recognise it for what it is, and has been unable to see its historical manifestation in Jesus Christ, even in the descriptions of an explicitly Christian faith. Christians fear in their own case (and therefore in the case of others) that in the final balance of their lives they may freely say No to this deepest movement of their existence in an open or concealed unbelief or lack of hope. However, at the same time they hope for all others and so also for themselves that this movement may find its way through all the darkness and superficiality of life to its final "eternal" goal—Christians accept this ultimate threat to themselves from themselves . . . which can say No to God.[7]

For those in the desert, the issue of hope is of vital importance. Believers in this particular way trust in an ultimate triumph that has been hard won. Their hoping is characterized by the willingness to wait and to endure with a sense of both expectancy and suspense.

THE THREE GIFTS FROM THE MONASTERY OF ST. MACARIUS

The road from Cairo to Alexandria seems longer than it really is. The intense heat and the flat barren desert give the traveler the impression of being on a road to nowhere. The exit signs offer no comfort, since all that is promised is more of the same. On this particular morning, having lived out of suitcases for four months, I was not in the mood for an uninterrupted view of the desert. I wanted to get home. I wanted to be surrounded by the safe and the familiar.

I was on my way to see the Coptic Monastery of St. Macarius, the Egyptian. My visit was partly for the sake of pilgrimage, partly for professional reasons. I have always been attracted to the *Sayings of the Desert Fathers* and here I was, going to the desert region where most of the sayings originated. No one reading even a little about the history of Christian spirituality can avoid learning something of the desert tradition, the greatest and most formative tradition concerning prayer and the contemplative life. After the witness of the New Testament itself, that of the desert fathers and mothers has had the most profound and far-reaching influence on the spiritual development of both Eastern and Western forms of Christianity.

It had its center in the desert regions, particularly between Cairo and Alexandria, in the fourth century. The most famous and important center was Scetis, and it was to Scetis (now called Wadi-el-Natroon) I was traveling. Scetis was the home of Abba Macarius, one of the greatest of the desert fathers. There, it is said, he founded a monastery in A.D. 360.

The desert does strange things to the way one sees. It plays tricks with the imagination and, at the same time, intensifies and magnifies experiences. The hot sun and the apparent deadness of the desert clarify one's mind and reorder one's priorities. It is easy to see why codes of hospitality are strictly adhered to in this part of the world. Hospitality is a matter of mutual survival. It didn't take me long to realize what most mattered in all the world. Heat, dust, and loneliness made me appreciate our need for three simple things: food, shelter, and companionship.

It was with a sense of relief that I saw the monastery buildings appear on the horizon—although I didn't really trust that the vision was true until I came to the enormous gates of the monastery proper. Its spare, austere lines stood out in the bright sunlight and the buildings cast enormous, hospitable shadows. The monastery looked immaculate; its thick white walls and domed churches exuded both strength and safety. The sudden splashes of green delighted the eye. Flowers, shrubs, and even trees do grow. The desert is alive.

My host was Father Jeremiah. It's impossible to tell the age of a bearded Egyptian monk, but Jeremiah seemed very old indeed. The first thing he did was bring me tea and something to eat. Then he said with a deep laugh, "Father, we always treat guests as angels—just in case!"

I couldn't help but compare this greeting with the somewhat oppressive style of those Christians who want to be sure that I believe the right things in the right way before they will accept me. To Father Jeremiah I was, no doubt, at best a schismatic and at worst a heretic. If this was indeed the case, there was nothing in his manner to show either tentativeness or disapproval. After all, I just *might* be an angel! I experienced in Father Jeremiah a receptive, loving, and open intelligence. In his eye I saw something of what I had been looking for. Here was the embodiment of one of the most ancient ways of being a Christian. It didn't fit any of the labels that go with the forms of believing with which I was familiar. It was neither liberal nor conservative. This way was simply itself, and in Father Jeremiah I saw that the desert tradition was vibrantly alive.

A few years ago, the monastery had only a handful of elderly monks. The buildings were in a sorry state and some were in danger of collapse. Recently, there has been a great movement of renewal and rebuilding and the monastery has grown into a community of some one hundred monks. Old buildings have been restored, and archeological digs have discovered even older ones. Now the monastery gives the visitor a sense of openness, freedom, and above all, life.

The secret of the monastic life, at its best, is its apostolic simplicity: simplicity without naiveté. Always in Father Jeremiah's eyes were the twin qualities of compassion and wisdom. I could discern no feeling of spiritual superiority or the claim to special privileged knowledge in him or in any other of the monks I met. Being willing to explore the possibility of entertaining angels seemed to me to be both compassionate and perceptive, because it challenges the believer to live in a constant state of expectancy, openness, and vulnerability.

Being received as a possible angel was not the only sign of the refreshing openness of this way of believing. Another manifestation of it came as we were taking a tour through the monastery churches and chapels. We came to the tomb of John the Baptist and the prophet Elisha. Tradition has it that these two were buried side by side. The relics had made their way to Alexandria and had been received by St. Athanasius during the reign of Julian the Apostate. The relics were recovered during the rebuilding and excavations in 1976. After Father Jeremiah had proudly related this story, there was a pause. With humor in his eyes, he looked straight into mine and spoke directly to my skepticism: "Of course, it does not matter whether you believe any of this or not. All that matters here is fraternal love." His own reverence for the tradition was clear, but I felt no pressure from him to believe one way or the other. The way of believing I want to avoid often adopts a bullying attitude with regard to those who don't see things in the same way. Here, in the desert, there was no hint of spiritual coercion.

It was at this point that I began to see a little more clearly the *way of believing* that I was seeking. It is a *way* of hospitality that involves receiving others as lively images of God or as his possible messengers, regardless of whether they are believers or not. The loving receptivity towards others is not dependent on their sharing our beliefs or opinions.

At the end of my stay I was given three gifts, each of which was a concrete expression of the way of believing I had been seeking. They came as a complete surprise, as did the absence of a request for a donation. First, Father Jeremiah led me towards the refectory and stopped in front of a large trough filled with flowering shrubs. Without a word, he gave me a piece of jasmine, a carnation, a rose, and a sprig of mint. It was as if he were saying, "We human beings need things that will lift the spirit and enlarge the heart." This gesture was a direct response to our need to be brought "out of ourselves" from time to time and introduced to a wider reality. It reminded me of the Chinese proverb about wisdom: If you have two loaves, go and sell one and buy a lily.

The second gift was no less important than the flowers. I was very hungry and was taken into the refectory for a meal. Monastic hospitality is refreshingly realistic and speaks to human necessity. I need beauty in my life, but I also need food and shelter. There was no danger here of hospitality being so "spiritualized" that basic necessities were ignored. The soup, the rice, the cheese, the tomatoes, and the bread were solid enough.

The third gift was handed to me so naturally and spontaneously that it took me a while to appreciate its full significance. Father Jeremiah gave me three small phials of oil for the healing of the sick. The unspoken assumption was simply that we are all frail and suffer from all kinds of sickness of both body and soul. This is a brute fact and we need all the help we can get. It was as if Father Jeremiah had said: "There, brother, take these for your wounds and for the healing of others' hurts. We all need the saving and healing power of Christ."

What impressed me more than the gifts themselves was the way in which they were presented to me: *without words or explanations*. They spoke for themselves. Nor did they demand any particular response. Here was a way of believing that was first a way of being and action rather than words. There were no formulas to repeat, no dogmas to subscribe to. I was accepted simply as a fellow human being. Human beings can't do without formulas and dogma, but these must always be preceded by a way of being that expresses in action and receptivity the heart of what the formulas or dogmas are seeking to communicate. In the end, faith comes not from indoctrination from the outside, but from the Spirit of God bursting out from inside us.

The monks of the Monastery of St. Macarius treat the Christian life with the utmost seriousness, and yet they have a lightness of approach that is highly contagious. The Christian life is a battle and a struggle, but it is not without humor. We can laugh because the final victory has been won, and we can laugh because there are many ways of believing that truth.

The seriousness of the call to believe and the lightness and freedom with which we are invited to embrace it are best summed up in a story about St. Macarius. He was one of the most experienced and wise monks of the desert. One day one of the young men asked him: "Abba, tell us about being a monk." And the wisest of the monks replied: "Ah! I'm not a monk myself, but I have seen them." Father Jeremiah told me this story as I was leaving and then, with a laugh, made up his own version: "I am not *yet* a Christian, but I have seen them!" I have seen them too, particularly in the desert places. Seeing such Christians helps me to believe.

Father Jeremiah's version of the story would be incomprehensible to those whose way of believing involves formulas first and being and action second. He is a Christian, yet he is also becoming one. This way of believing which I encountered in the desert encouraged me to write this book. Father Jeremiah did not lay down the law. He invited me to look and this turned out to be an invitation to love. In the desert I found my soul awakened to new life.

I. THE INVITATION TO SEE

1. Children of the Desert

When Teresa of Avila described the soul as an interior castle which most people never explore, she was stating truth we needed Freud and Jung to demonstrate. In our fragmented society, in which we are alienated from our inner resources, we remain largely dismissive of the most ancient and neglected spring of wisdom in Western Culture, its mystical tradition.[1]

COLIN THOMPSON

I don't want you to go away with the impression that there's any—you know—any inconveniences involved in the religious life. I mean a lot of people don't take it up just because they think it's going to involve a certain amount of nasty application and perseverence—you know what I mean? . . . As soon as we get out of chapel here, I hope you'll accept from me a little volume I've always admired . . . "God Is My Hobby."[2]

J. D. SALINGER, *Franny and Zooey*

From time to time, the believer has to ask: "Am I who I say I am?" In my case, the question has a particular focus. "Am I a Christian?" or "Am I still a Christian?" I have my answer ready: "Yes, I am."

If I already have the answer, why pose the question in the first place? There are two reasons. One, a pattern of questioning is part of the *way* I believe. Questioning of this sort deepens and strengthens me in my belief. Probing doubt is the handmaid of faith. It is my way of entering the Interior Castle. Two, the questioning process (by which I don't mean mere intellectual puzzle solving) itself is a revelation to me of God's gracious way of dealing with us. That is why believers, from time to time, need a break with their old ways of believing. Believers as well as unbelievers are in need of conversion. But it's easy to see why this approach doesn't go down too well in our culture. Few would want to be free of either their idolatrous imaginings or their fixed opinions.

THE WORK OF THE HEART INVOLVES QUESTIONING AND WONDERING

My trip around the world set up a pattern of questioning and wondering. I met many different types of people, believers and unbelievers alike. I had occasions for soul-searching and reassessment. I was struck by the variety and complexity of human personalities and societies. Nothing can hold us together, I thought, unless it be something outside us or a commitment to waiting and silence.

All of this may sound simple-minded, but my distance from home forced me to ask basic questions: How am I to be in the world? How am I to be in the world with *all* these others? Whatever answer I came up with, the process would surely involve a lot of waiting and listening. I felt like a newborn baby. There was no choice but to begin again.

The poet Rainer Maria Rilke speaks of *Herz-Werk*. This "heart-work" is indispensable to those who wish to follow that "way of believing" associated with the desert. My particular *Herz-Werk* (which I trust is shared by many) involves posing this question: How can I be a believer in today's world in such a way that it involves my whole self—my passion, my intelligence, and my allegiance? My question always invites me to return to the desert.

The Roman Catholic theologian, Edward Schillebeeckx, has recently stated that it is no longer possible to believe simply on someone else's say so—that is, on naked authority.[3] This, he claims, has been true since the eighteenth century, the period known as the Enlightenment. But people are capable of believing what they will, and of believing "a hundred impossible things before breakfast." Nowhere is this more true than in the realm of religion where our almost infinite capacity for self-deception has all the room in the world to exercise its random craziness. I do not think for one moment that Father Schillebeeckx believes that the issue of authority is unimportant. What is of great concern today are the *grounds* for believing anything at all.

Those of us who follow the desert way of believing cannot believe something because someone in authority tells us it is so.

This is true with regard to the Bible and the Creeds as well as with hierarchial authority. I read the Bible and I recite the Creeds and I believe them; but I don't believe them because I am supposed to. I believe them because I find them to be true. My believing has to be grounded in experience, and has continually to be tested and authenticated by it. I have to admit that this doesn't get me very far. Having dispensed with external authority, I am left with the dubious witness of my own experience. I have become my own pope, but with no promise of infallibility. I have little to go on. How am I to judge and evaluate my experience? I'm not even sure that I know *how* to experience the world. How reliable am I? If I'm not careful, my version of the desert way quickly degenerates into a mere problem-solving device that helps me bypass the issue of my own profound unreliability.

There is, of course, a great deal that I can do to anesthetize myself with a "religious" solution. This solution often takes on one of two forms. The first is the pseudomystical one of the cults; these cheap ways to a commercialized Nirvana bypass the mind altogether. The second is the old-time authoritarian one of dogmatic or biblical fundamentalism. Either approach to believing is dangerously immature. Just as we are capable of believing impossible things or believing things on impossible grounds, so also we have the choice of remaining immature. Politicians, religious leaders, and teachers know of our longing to remain infantile. It takes a spiritually mature person to enter the Kingdom of God as a little child. We prefer to remain childish and have someone *tell* us what to believe. Our longing for authority runs very deep. One early Anglican writer complained: "Luther had a pope in his belly"; he meant that Luther repudiated one authority only to be made captive to another.[4]

THREE IMPERATIVES OF MATURE BELIEVING

What does mature religion look like?

I don't claim to *be* a mature believer, but I do insist that I *want* to be one. The task ahead is difficult because no one would choose to follow a hard path if an easier one were available. It seems to be a maxim of the spiritual life that no one undergoes spiritual or psychological growth and change *willingly*. We are either dragged into it kicking and screaming, or circumstances force us into the next scene of the human comedy. Ironically, the institutional Church is often an obstacle to spiritual growth. As we have seen, it has something of an investment in keeping its members in an infantile state.

Look! Weep! Live! These three great imperatives from the desert tradition open up for us a way of believing that is life-bearing. They shape and order this way of believing so that it breaks us open (walled up as we are in our fears and prejudices) and begins to "make us over." In this process we are born again and again and again. Trying to be obedient to these three imperatives rescues me from being mesmerized and rendered powerless by the sense of the unreliability of my own private judgment.

The first imperative is, *Look!* Looking means a contemplative willingness to see what is there in front of us without prematurely interpreting what we see. The desert tradition claims that if we look long and accurately enough, the tears will begin to flow. Thus the second imperative is, *Weep!* The fruit of honest contemplation is "the gift of tears"; and the sure sign that our attentiveness has been focused and honest and the tears cleansing is joy. Joy is the fruit of desert patience. Thus the third imperative, *Live!*

The pattern is simple. We look. We weep. We live. This pattern is repeated throughout the believer's life. It echoes and reverberates both in and out of the Christian tradition. For example, the philosopher A. N. Whitehead reflects this three-fold way when he insists that before we can know God as Friend, we have first to encounter him in the Void and as Enemy. If the word "God" is not to be debased, those who want to go on using it need to experience both emptiness and desolation. Without such experiences the word "God" becomes simply a way of talking about our highest aspirations, our likes and our dislikes.

The desert is known for its vast emptiness and its desolate vacancies. From the point of view of the believer, the purpose of emptiness and desolation is to prepare us for joy and ground us in hope. Unless joy and hope are the goal, the desert becomes a playground for masochists.

I owe a great deal of my way of believing not only to the ancient tradition of the desert, but also to the comparatively modern tradition of psychoanalysis. Both traditions invite me to *look*. Both bring me to the brink of a vast emptiness, which only God can fill. Both help to keep me in the fellowship of the believers. I realize that not everyone can take the time to visit a monastery deep in the Egyptian desert; still less can they afford the time and money that serious psychoanalysis involves. The "desert" and "psychoanalysis" are meant as metaphors for this way of believing. The mistake is to take these metaphors literally, as if actual hours on a psychoanalyst's couch or a long stay in a desert place would be the only ways to get into an exclusive spiritual club. The "desert" and "psychoanalysis" are metaphors of attentiveness, focus, receptivity and change.

What do we see if we take the time to look? We see disconnection, absurdity, and glory—certainly these are contradictory things. If we look hard enough, we will see a great deal of glory and promise. Unfortunately, our vision is often distorted by pain and suffering. But we need to look at pain and suffering if we are to see past them to the glory and the promise. There is real glory in a way of believing that tries to be honest about what it sees. This has, at least, the promise of maturity.

PSYCHOANALYSIS AND THE WAY OF THE DESERT

"Only connect," E. M. Forster proposed. "Only we can't," the psychoanalyst knows.[5]

In spite of the fact that Christian belief (particularly of the desert *way*) contradicts this gloomy conclusion of psychoanalysis with regard to human relations, they are, in fact, intimately related. The desert spawned them both. Psychoanalysis and the desert or contemplative way of believing are like twins who were separated at birth and who grew up thousands of miles apart in radically different cultures. Each knows the existence of the other, but neither recognizes their common parentage.

Spirituality rejoices in the interdependence of all things. In fact, spirituality (particularly with regard to the *way* of believing that is our focus here) may be defined as "the art of making connections"; connections not only between individuals, but also between communities and nations. Its raison d'être is for the celebration of unity in unimaginable diversity; of a transcendent meaning that holds all things together and gives us hope; of what the old theologians would have called the divine coinherence.

THE WAY OF IMAGES AND THE WAY OF REJECTION OF IMAGES

Traditionally, there are two ways in which interdependence is honored and celebrated. The first way binds the world together into a dense mesh of interconnections by means of images and ideas. The trouble with the way of images, however, is that it eventually becomes difficult to believe that the image is simply an image and not the thing itself. Thus there is a second way that complements the first. It is called the way of the rejection of images (the *via negativa*). This latter path, as we shall see, has a great deal to do with both the way of believing that we are exploring and the art of psychoanalysis.

The two approaches to the spiritual path belong together. It cannot be overemphasized that they are complementary: negation and affirmation are like the negative and positive poles of a fully charged battery. While one side says "Yes" to images, ideas, metaphors, the other side says "No" or is silent. This dialectic is vital for the transmission of life and energy. Without one or other of the poles there is death.

Medieval theology and philosophy had an apreciation of what was known as "the contradiction of opposites." Things came in complementary pairs: sun and the moon, night and day, up and down, man and woman. Today, Morton Kelsey has pointed out that there are

two quite different ways of leading people on the spiritual pilgrimage, which have often been seen as opposed to each other. The first is the sacramental method, in which we try to mediate the divine through images, pictures, symbols and rituals. Often this results in confusing the image with the reality and can lead to idolatry. . . .The second way is based on the idea that we can best find the divine through emptying ourselves of all images and contents. This point of view stresses the fact that all descriptions and pictures of the holy are inadequate. . . . This point of view gives few methods of handling direct confrontation with the evil within us and in the world around us . . . these two approaches cannot be separated from one another.

We cannot live without images and pictures, and yet they always fall short of the reality. Some would agree with the disciple who said to Ramakrishna: "Sir, we ought to teach the people that they are doing wrong in worshipping the images and pictures in the temple." Ramakrishna's response is stern:

That's the way with you . . . people: you want to teach and preach. You want to give millions when you are beggars yourselves. . . .Do you think God does not know that he is being worshipped in images and pictures? If a worshipper should make a mistake, do you not think that God will know his intent?

Religious controversy has often centered around the question of the meaning and status of images and pictures. If icons are inevitable, so are iconoclasts. There is a tendency for one to be emphasized at the expense of the other. The way of believing that is our concern here depends very heavily on balance, and on the *via negativa* being given its proper weight. This *via negativa* is sometimes called "apophatic" (which means against or away from the light) or contemplative. The word apophatic is used to describe the theological and spiritual approach of Eastern Christianity to Christian believing. One of the most famous exponents of this way in the West is St. John of the Cross, who wrote in *The Spiritual Canticle*,

Be thou never willingly satisfied with that which thou understandest of God, but rather with that which thou understandest not of him; and do thou never rest in loving and having delight in that which thou canst not understand and feel concerning him. . . .however much it seems to thee that thou findest and feelest and understandest him, thou must ever hold him hidden. . . .the less clearly they understand him, the nearer they are in approaching him.[8]

This way of not-knowing lies at the heart of the way of believing that helps me live as a believer. It is hard to imagine many who call themselves Christians in our culture being able to accept the advice of St. John of the Cross. Feeling, not understanding, is very much a part of popular North American religion. To suggest that there might be something beyond thought and feeling sounds very strange, and is very threatening. Religion in our culture has become something of a commodity. We want to possess as much "religion" as we can in order to enjoy the emotional satisfaction it brings. In *Franny and Zooey*, Franny is fascinated by the Jesus Prayer, which she has discovered through reading a classic of Russian Orthodox spirituality, *The Way of the Pilgrim*. Zooey attacks her for her attachment by saying (p. 148):

> ... there's no difference at all, that *I* can see, between the man who's greedy for material treasure—or even intellectual treasure—and the man who's greedy for spiritual treasure ... treasure's treasure. ...and it seems to me that ninety percent of all the world-hating saints in history were just as ac*quis*itive and unattractive, basically, as the rest of us are.

These are harsh words. Franny is well aware that she is as egotistical and self-seeking as anyone else.

Can we hope to get away from self-preoccupation altogether? We can try. The effort is worth it, because in seeking to pass through this narrow gate one begins to learn a little of what it is to love. It is hard, because it means looking and being temporarily blinded by what one sees. "There be in God, some say, a deep but dazzling darkness," wrote a seventeenth-century poet, echoing the earlier tradition of the Eastern Christians. This darkness forces us to talk about God only in terms of negatives, of what God is *not*. When we use positive terms, which we must on occasion, we must remember then that we are actually talking about an *idea* of God—just as when we see moonlight, we must remind ourselves that we are really seeing the sun's reflected rays.

We can only say that God is both unknowable and inexhaustible. The Christian believes that this unknowable and inexhaustible God has been revealed to us in Jesus Christ, and that it is after his image that we are made. *That* is a lot to swallow. To really believe we are made in his image means a revolution in self-understanding. "I" would have to be understood in terms not only of the life, death, and resurrection of Jesus; "I" would suddenly become unknowable and inexhaustible, and so would everyone else. It would mean giving up my patterns of knowing and feeling with regard to God and the world. The implications of this for self-understanding are momentous. Just as God is "hidden" from us, so too are we "hidden" from ourselves and from each other.

The apophatic approach affects not only the way we believe, but also the way we pray. According to the early spiritual writer Evagrius Ponticus, who lived in the late fourth century, "The spirit that possesses health is one which has no images of the things of this world at the time of prayer." In another place he says: "prayer is the rejection of concepts." Any attempts to trap God in an image, form, or figure is both futile and dangerous; dangerous because God becomes "God"—and terrible things have been and are done in the name of "God." Thus "happy is the spirit that attains to perfect formlessness at the time of prayer."[9] This is not prescription for gloom. Rather, the formlessness is for the sake of freedom and expansiveness; because the things that matter, like love and truth, shrivel and die when they are held captive too long in an image or idea.

THE IDOLATRY OF IDEAS

On the first Sunday in Lent, the Orthodox Church used to recite a set of anathemas or curses against those "who held that Plato's ideas had real existence." This strange way of proceeding springs from a deep insight. We have a tendency to make ideas into things, and so we're tempted to take our way of believing or our way of thinking and *imagine* that our way is the only right and sane one there is. We might add our own anathemas against those who claim that the "ideas" of Marx, Darwin, Freud, Jung, and Uncle Sam have real existence!

One can see why this apophatic tradition has not had an easy time of it within the Church itself. It fosters a spirituality of the desert; a spirituality that is difficult to pin down and control. Its adherents tend to be prophet-like in their attacks on and disdain for the conformism of established religion. Such people are important for the overall life of the Church, because without them the Church easily gets seduced by the values of the prevailing culture. As John Meyendorff points out: "the Church was saved from absorption into the Empire by the hermits of the desert, the stylites standing year after year on their pillars. . . ."10

The Church is always in need of such followers of different ways of believing, whether they be prophets, contemplatives, or people with a special vocation. For example, Simone Weil, the French writer and philosopher who died in London of malnutrition during World War II because she refused to eat more than her compatriots, was never baptized. She can never be numbered "officially" among the believers, yet she stood at the door of the Church reminding the institution of its true identity and destiny. I hope to be numbered with her. Yet the prophets and contemplatives need the institution, for without it they have nothing against which to rub. Each needs the other.

I have great love and reverence for the institution. In fact, the more I try to follow the *way* of believing that I've been describing, the more I appreciate the ordinary life of the Church. It is a question of balance. The more I follow the apophatic way, the more I need to be nourished by the images from the Bible and from the Liturgy.

These images point me in the direction I wish to go, but they are not the way itself. The way is a contemplative one, which simply means looking at someone or something without absorbing them into our little world of ideas and values. Contemplation means seeing what is there and refusing to hallucinate so that we see only what we want to see. We then wait to receive what chooses to reveal itself (as in the Greek word for truth, *aletheia*, which literally means to uncover. The truth then, is that which reveals or uncovers itself). It means being attentive to whatever and whoever is there as truly *other* than ourselves. This is what is suggested by the word *aesthetic*, which strictly means seeing things in such a way that the viewer is changed by what he or she sees. Perhaps that is why artists in totalitarian countries are often locked up. They help people see a new world through their art, and that is dangerous to the existing totalitarian political system.

Looking at things in this intense way is hazardous. What would it mean to be committed to a way of seeing that would challenge us to change? Contemplation (like art) requires of us a willingness to be transformed. So does the study of theology. John Updike points out the similarity between the artist and the contemplative theologian:

> . . . it is this surrender of self, this submersion of opinions and personality in the intensity of witnessing "life itself" with its weave of misapprehension, petty confusions, fitful and skewed communications, and passing but authentic revelations that strike us as momentous. . . .as heroic even, in the way great dogmatics are.[11]

This way of seeing (in which it is certainly true that seeing is believing), therefore, commits us to two attitudes. The first is openness to change and transformation; the second is detachment, so that we don't absorb or take over what we see into our little world. This is summed up in the maxim, "We either contemplate or we exploit." We either see things and persons with reverence and awe, and therefore treat them as genuinely other than ourselves; or we appropriate them, and manipulate them for our own purposes. This way of seeing and believing is a lifetime's work. It is a way of love. It is hard work but it is, in a sense, the only work that matters. I tremble before it. But I know of no other way.

It is not hard to see that the psychoanalyst (knowingly or unknowingly) stands in this apophatic, contemplative tradition. But it must be admitted that this way of seeing and believing is as uncongenial to many believers as it is unknown to many analysts. How does the psychoanalyst carry on this ancient tradition? Let us take another look at the two ways—the way of images and the way of the rejection of images. How are they reflected in the attitudes of the two great schools of analysis represented by the names Jung and Freud? Are there correspondences with Christian spiritual tradition?

Ignatian spirituality, for example, tends to be image-centered; and for people who need the treasures of the imagination unlocked and their symbolic life revived, the way of the affirmation of images is entirely appropriate. By analogy, Jungian analysis also emphasizes images and symbols. Perhaps this is why it is very popular among many religious people. For me however the Jungian approach—to which I owe much—is too "hot." I have an overactive imagination and a flourishing symbolic life. I *be-*

lieve everything! I need the *via negativa* to slow me down and help me to be still. In comparison with Jung, Freud seems "cold," and his stringent austerity refreshes me. Let us take a closer look at these "hot" and "cold" pathways of self-knowledge and discovery.

At a particular period in our lives, we may need to be encouraged to follow one way at the expense of the other—even though both ways are important and need each other. Each of us tends to put weight on one side to the detriment of the other, in order to compensate for a one-sided approach. I have what I've termed a "hot" imagination. I can believe, at least for a while, almost anything. I identify too quickly with what I see, read, and hear. I need to distance myself, to cool down. I need space and silence. So I compensate in an apophatic direction. But I love the life of the imagination. My trouble is that I find it hard to discriminate between that which is important and that which is merely interesting or fascinating. I am easily distracted or seduced by a new thought. Both my intellect and imagination need the chastening stillness of the desert.

AFFIRMATION AND REJECTION COMPLEMENT EACH OTHER

The pioneers of psychoanalysis in this century have continued the double way of affirmation and rejection, of the "hot" and the "cold," long known to the mystics. As one writer has put it: "As a discipline of the inner life, psychoanalysis is the secularized counterpart of training and the life of the mystical way."[12]

At the risk of sounding simplistic, one might say that Jung represents the affirmative (or kataphatic way), while Freud pushes us towards the *via negativa* or apophatic way. Much has been done, quite successfully, to use Jungian insights for the purpose of deepening Christian self-understanding. Believers who value Jung revel in the world of images, but in their weaker moments tend to believe in them rather in the way I believe the characters in a powerful movie. The useful images suddenly have a life of their own. They don't point to any reality beyond themselves. They *are* the reality. The *anima*, the *animus*, and the *shadow* are concrete realities stomping around in the psyche. As a means to self-understanding, I think these images are extremely useful; but if they are given "real existence," they can take on the power of Fate against which we poor humans are helpless. We become victims of forces beyond our control.

This, of course, is not argument against Jung as such. It merely points to our tendency and need to idolize our ideas. We long for explanations and rationalizations, and religion and therapy are often expert in explanations. The way of believing I wish to follow tries to resist the temptation for premature explanation. That is why I want to claim Freud as well as Jung as a possible ally in helping me to believe. In fact, it is my intuition that Freud, in the long run, will prove as great an ally to us, in spite of his so-called "atheism." Jung's "hot" imaginative way weaves an attractive web for self-interpretation, but it is easy to get overheated. Freud's "atheism" can provide a cooling response to Jung's "gnosticism."

FREUD AT HOME IN THE DESERT

Psychoanalysis needs to be seen in a much wider context than the one in which it is usually placed: clinical, therapeutic, and anti-religious. It might seem strange to place Freud among the mystics and contemplatives. No doubt Freud himself would be amused, but that's where I think this often mistaken genius belongs. It would, however, be a futile gesture to try to baptize Freud. All I wish to do at this stage is introduce him to his long-lost sibling, the desert or contemplative tradition. Freud needs to be reacquainted with part of his native land, the desert.

One writer who has done a great deal to demythologize Freud is Bruno Bettelheim. He demonstrates the fact that Freud's English translators have a great deal to answer for in their presentation of the Viennese psychoanalyst as a cold clinician who operated from a strictly medical model. Bettelheim comments: "The English renditions of Freud's writings distort much of the essential humanism that permeated the originals."[13] He insists that psychoanalysis is basically a humanizing process. Seen from the perspective of the believer, the evident willingness "to become acquainted with the lowest depths of the soul— to explore whatever personal hell we may suffer from" is not unlike the testimony of the desert fathers. The latter battled with demons in the great solitude of the wilderness. Both the psychoanalyst and the man or woman of the desert are committed to the same "demanding and potentially dangerous voyage of self-discovery"; a voyage aimed at becoming more fully human.

What a pity—scandal even—that "nearly all of Freud's many references to the soul and matters pertaining to the soul, have been excised in translation." Where Freud speaks of *die Seele* (soul), his translators into English have substituted "mind." *Seelischen* is translated as "mental." The result is that the warmth and immediacy of Freud's contribution to self-understanding is lost in a welter of scientific sounding neologisms. Freud is actually affirming "a spontaneous sympathy of our unconscious with that of others, a feeling of response of our soul to theirs." Psychoanalysis is "a cure through love," as Freud wrote to Jung in 1906. Maybe we do, after all, connect? "A cure through love" is what we all want, and this cure is promised us in the Gospel. The fathers and mothers of the desert were doctors and surgeons of love.

What is it, then, that makes us back away from the offer of a cure? Why do we resist the very thing we seek? Why should Freud deliberately be translated in such a way that warmth and feeling are drained away? Bettelheim goes so far to suggest that the mistranslations spring, in part, from a fear of self-knowledge on the part of the psychoanalytic establishment itself. The translator uses language that distances us from the immediacy of the issues under discussion so that we can more easily live under the illusion that we are analyzing other people's behavior apart from our own. Clinical-sounding translations keep the explosive subject matter at a safe distance. The persistence of the medical model further contributes to the distancing process. For example, *Mutterleib* (mother-womb) is translated as "uterus." Bettelheim bitingly comments about the world of difference between wanting to get back to the womb and wanting to re-enter the uterus! More important, *das Ich*, *das Es*, and *das Über-ich* are translated, as everyone knows, as "ego," "id," and "super-ego." French translators do better with *le moi*, *le ça* and *le sur-moi*. How different a sense we would have of Freud's work if we were to call the ego simply the "me."

This fear of self-knowledge is not confined to translators or psychoanalysts. As a believer, I can all too easily fall into the trap of trying to play a clever and exciting game with myself and others, particularly if I can be "helpful" and keep my distance at the same time. To be helpful *and* to feel superior seem sometimes to enter "the best of all possible worlds." I would much rather be isolated and "superior" than be committed to a way of quiet attentiveness. Psychoanalysts, counselors, clergy, truck-drivers, homemakers—none are exempt from our universal wish to remain unaware of our deepest selves. *Looking* at what is there is essential to right believing (right in the sense of "accurate"). The command at the heart of this way of believing is, "Look and look well!" At the same time the command is an invitation—an invitation to see. Both this way of believing and psychoanalysis lead to the void, the abyss, the empty space within ourselves. The believer dares identify this abyss as the dwelling place of God.

What can it possibly mean to receive such a revelation—the revelation of the "emptiness within"; the revelation that the desert is not simply the Sahara or the Kalahari, but the "inner" aspect of the human soul in all its relations with the world and with others? What does it mean to receive, undergo, endure, and, in the end, glory in such a revelation? What does it mean to continue believing when something is going on inside us that appears to be beyond our endurance? Indeed, it is not to be endured. Can we believe at such times? If so, *what* is to be believed beyond fantasies, projections, and lies? Are we prepared to journey "beyond the North Wind"?

These are serious questions, but they are in danger of becoming a little "cosmic" and inflated. They need a further question to keep them honest: Are we prepared to be both accurate and modest about our struggles? It can be humiliating to be honest about one's feelings. I would like to imagine myself engaged in an important battle, and not the puny ones in which I usually find myself. To tell the truth, I am not always "struggling with the tiger of despair on the edge of the abyss"! I often see wonder, hope, and possibility in an ordinary human life. If I am beginning to see them, then I have a legitimate hope that others are seeing them too. But what makes us turn away from wonder, hope, and possibility? To gain some understanding of the believer's resistance to new possibilities, we need to take a look at the neurotic element in religion.

2. The Christian Neurosis

> My mother always made it clear to me that my place in the world was
> unlikely to differ ever from her own. There was no reason why Mrs.
> Buffen or her daughter should care to speak to me. I had nothing to
> offer people like the Buffens, therefore why should they bother to
> acknowledge my existence? It was consistent with her view of affection
> or friendship as a system of rewards, blackmail, calculation and ag-
> grandizement in which people would only come off best or worst.
> Nothing ever strikes me with such despair and disbelief as the truly
> cold heart. It disarms utterly and never ceases to do so. I wish it were
> otherwise.[1]
>
> JOHN OSBORNE, *A Better Class of Person*

There is something frightening and immediate in this son's
unloving, but probably accurate description of his mother. For
the word "friendship" we can substitute the word "religion";
religion as a system of rewards, blackmail, calculation, and ag-
grandizement, in which people come off only best or worst.
Does this sound too harsh?

It is easy to document the "successes" of religion (if we take
the standards and statistics of popular evangelists). But how do
we document the casualties? How do we number those who have
been hurt and brutalized literally "beyond belief" by certain
ways of believing? Such things are hard to document; but there
is scarcely one of us who has not encountered many a wounded
believer who thinks that he or she is an unbeliever.

THREE NEUROTIC STRATEGIES

The believer is often bedevilled by a neurotic aim at perfection. Indeed, it is accepted in psychoanalytical circles that perfectionism inhibits human growth and saps our capacity for
delighting in life. And the great demand of religion is, of course,
"Be ye perfect!" Perfectionism uncovers those compulsions that
drive us to bring into being a tyrannical, idealized self. And if

the idealized self cannot make it, then so much the worse for others and the world.

In her pioneering work, *Neurosis and Human Growth*,[2] Karen Horney described this drive towards perfectionism brilliantly. In her view, we develop three basic strategies in order to cope with life. These strategies are movements towards, against, or away from others. First, we can move towards others in acts of friendship or compliance. Thus, in its neurotic form, perfectionism causes us to cling to the most powerful person in a group or the most powerful "God" in the pantheon of religions. Second, we can move against others by displaying our power in a hostile way. Third, we can move away from others by becoming emotionally withdrawn. We can, in short, cope with the world by strategies of seduction, aggressiveness, or withdrawal. These are the neurotic forms of three basic movements that are important to all of us: to give affection, to stand up for oneself, and to keep apart on certain occasions. These have their religious counterparts: the longing for intimacy, the desire to belong without being swallowed up, and the hope for a true identity in God.

PERFECTIONISM

When these natural drives are connected to a deep and unacknowledged anxiety, the roots of which lie in a neurotic desire for perfection, they become destructive; harmful to both oneself and to others. Here is a psychiatrist's account of one of his patient's (a believer or former believer) testimony to a prevailing perfectionist and brutalizing theology:

1. God is everywhere and is watching me every moment of my life. On the day of judgment he will ask me to give account of myself, even of my most hidden actions.
2. We must strive ceaselessly for perfection. That alone permits us to approach God, who is himself perfect.
3. We must forget ourselves, and sacrifice our own desires and needs to the desires and needs of others.
4. We must mistrust our instincts and our evil inclinations. The good Christian must always be alert, because Satan is about, ready to seduce us and draw us away from God.

The means appropriate for being able to follow such a course of life were as follows: prayer, abstinence, permanent self-sacrifice, daily struggles against evil thoughts, particularly sexual thoughts, and the quest for perfection in every action.

His confessor had often told him, "God is looking at you and judging you. Think of the suffering of Jesus Christ crucified. We must learn to die to ourselves."

"When I think of that period," he told me, "I still feel oppressed. That was really a kind of terrorist spirituality."[3]

This testimony, in varied forms, is not uncommon among Catholics, Protestants, and Jews. The *way* of believing represented by both the desert tradition and psychoanalysis does a great deal of anti-terrorist activity on behalf of the human soul.

Yet the command of religion is: "Be ye perfect." There is no getting around this. Religiously minded people are thus able to translate their neuroses into virtues. The neurotic desire to please becomes saintliness and forebearance; aggressiveness becomes heroism, the brave and steadfast adherence to received truth; aloofness becomes wisdom and self-sufficiency. If we are not careful, the three aspects of our basic anxiety or conflict are glorified and reconciled. Such is our capacity for self-deception. As Horney says, *"Self-idealization . . . is . . . a comprehensive neurotic solution."*[4]

Our longings can get us into serious trouble. Perfectionism can easily give way to neurotic ambition; the drive to win, to come out on top, to come off best. That which pushes us towards self-idealization also encourages us to demand and expect (not necessarily consciously) absolute fearlessness, mastery over life, or (worse still) saintliness. Jung tells a story about being visited by an uncommonly saintly man who, after a couple of days, begun to make Jung feel unworthy and uncomfortable. The saintly man seemed to be without a flaw. It was not until Jung met the man's unhappy wife that he realized the enormous cost to another of the man's "saintliness."

The saint who thinks he casts no shadow is very dangerous. That is why, traditionally, the two marks of the saint are joy and penitence: joy because one knows that one is not God, and yet with God all things are possible. The saint knows that perfection rests in divinity and not in the ability of the believer to negotiate reality so that one "comes off best." The saint knows that he or she is not God, and yet knows how easily one can forget this simple fact. The saint knows about darknesses and shadows that cloud judgment. A character in William Golding's novel *The Paper Men* exemplifies these neurosis-free qualities.

She had a kind of security—that kind which stems perhaps from getting on very well without some of our less attractive qualities, such as the need for revenge, more success than other people, protection from other people or indifference to them. . . .I remember ending our time together envying her bitterly. The things you could see that woman had no need of![5]

It often takes a great deal of hard work to come to such a place of security. Most of us muddle along and live off barely acknowledged delusions. The ordinary believer or unbeliever would probably think the suggestion that he or she entertains delusions of grandeur ludicrous. No one would claim to be God. Anyone who does is thought to be crazy. No one would claim to be master of the universe. And yet psychoanalysis claims that the tendency is there in all of us.

We do not put it in such crass terms, but the trend still has its effect on the deep recesses of the soul and comes out in behavior that is far more devious and manipulative than we would like to admit. Sometimes it leads to tragedy. John Mortimer relates the tragic end of his old college friend Henry Winter. Henry was a gentle pacifist during World War II, after which he became a caring and much-loved country doctor. One day he fell madly in love and, when the woman refused to run away with him, he shot her to death and then killed himself. John Mortimer writes: "I think about these things often, but I cannot explain them. I can only suggest that Henry Winter suffered terribly and unusually from having rejected the violence which was made available to us all at the age when we went to Oxford."[6]

Somehow, all the repressed material must come to light. Psychoanalysis is one of the ways in which that which is repressed comes to the surface and is integrated into a more honest and open life. I would claim that another way of integration is that of contemplative prayer.

VINDICTIVENESS IN RELIGION

Psychoanalysis, therefore, uncovers the neurotic elements in our way of being in the world. It is no comfort to reflect on the fact that neuroses are by no means confined to religious people! Perfectionism and ambition attack believers and unbelievers alike. But the most hidden, and therefore the most dangerous form of neurosis is that of revenge, the desire for vindictive triumph over others.

We sometimes feed our feelings of resentment by concentrating on the wounds we received in childhood. Lytton Strachey, the historian, poured much of his own accumulated poison into his bitingly witty and often sarcastic prose. Only continued literary success relieved his pain and freed him, for a while, from writhing with self-pity and lashing out at others. "In failure, he sank into hypersensitive awareness of his own insignificance and isolation, from which the only satisfactory outlet was hostility." Strachey longed for affection, "for the right to an answering smile," but his sense of terrible emptiness stirred up in him the contrary longing to make people squirm; "even from his silence they felt the radiating scintilla of his contempt—and returned it." One way to safeguard oneself from disappointment is to harp continually on the shortcomings of others. Ironically, Strachey stood for the virtues of tolerance, enlightenment and humanity. Yet

at the same time, the humanitarianism for which he stood was erected against a scathing contempt for the mass of humankind—the ugly, the boring, the stupid, the ambitious, the powerful and the ordinary. Towards these classes of persons he sometimes reacted with unselfconscious brutality . . . [7]

Strachey prided himself on being irreligious, yet he displayed to an exaggerated degree the common vices of religious people: high principles coupled with self-righteous vindictiveness.

As we have seen, many Christians nurse a deep affection for the doctrine of eternal punishment. They usually nurse it on behalf of others, although there are a few who believe with sadness that such is their fate and that nothing can save them.

The desire to shame, humiliate, and get the best of our neighbors runs very deep. Unconsciously, we like to hear bad news of others. We like the idea of frustrating, outwitting, and defeating others in personal relations. This desire can carry on even after the death of the other person. I remember a cartoon I once saw. It shows a cemetery in which one particular grave is festooned with flowers. The grave is being lovingly tended by an elderly woman, who smiles up at her companion and says: "O, I come here every day. He always hated flowers." A friend tells the story of two aunts who lived together in mutual hostility. At dinner, one aunt so needled the other that there was a scene. She so annoyed her sister that her sibling threw all the water in her glass in the offending sister's face. Dripping with water and indignation, she walked over to the piano and began to play and sing at the top of her voice: "Jesus loves me this I know, for the Bible tells me so!"

Most of us try to hide our vindictiveness as deep as we can, but it often wells up and finds expression in a variety of unlikely ways. These hidden drives need to be exposed if our religious commitment is to have any kind of maturity. Without such exposure, dreadful things can be done in the name of religion: cruelty is sanctified as moral rectitude; manipulation masquerades as love; vindictiveness poses as the desire for justice. Where does the vicious circle begin? And how is the terrible cycle of cause and effect to be broken?

The life of the late Maria Callas is an example of this tragic cycle. She was a brilliant opera singer, perhaps the most brilliant of this century. She was plagued by all three classic neuroses: perfectionism, ambition, and vindictiveness. As soon as she achieved fame and notoriety, she began to see her mother "through a distorting haze, as a shadowy, almost menacing figure." Right up until her death, Maria remained "frozen in her belligerence." Her striving for perfectionism was destructive. "The higher she climbed, the greater the reputation she had to maintain, the greater became the burden of the past and future that she had to carry. The past was no more, the future was yet to come, but Maria went on sacrificing the joy of the present to that unborn future and that dead past."[8]

Yet her story elicits from the reader not judgment, but compassion. In some sense we are all victims of victims. One of the saddest aspects of the human condition is our apparent inability to stop transmitting crippling neuroses from one generation to another. Those who receive self-hatred as their inheritance inevitably want to pass it on to others. The believer hopes and trusts that there is a way to break the debilitating circle of cause and effect. The perfection which he or she seeks is of a very different order from that of worldly success. It comes only as a gift and never as an achievement. It is far cry from self-idealization. "Be ye perfect! Be God-like!" The question is, which "God" would we choose to imitate? The one whose "perfection" is revealed in brokenness, availability, and self-giving love? God's perfection is very strange in the world's terms.

Robertson Davies, in his novel *The Rebel Angels*, writes of a kind of perfection to which we might all aspire. His way of understanding perfection speaks to our longing for wholeness and integrity. His clerical hero, Simon Darcourt, is musing over his various attempts to be and remain one of the believers.

Oh, the endless task! One begins with no knowledge except that what one is doing is probably wrong, and that the right path is heavy with mist. When I was a hopeful youth I set myself to the Imitation of Christ, and like a fool I supposed that I must try to be like Christ in every possible detail, adjure people to do the right when I didn't really know what the right was, and get myself spurned and scourged as frequently as possible. Crucifixion was not a modern method of social betterment, but at least I could push for psychological crucifixion, and I did, and hung on my cross until it begin to dawn on me that I was a social nuisance and not a bit like Christ—even the tedious detraqué Christ of my immature imagination . . . Gradually it came to me that the Imitation of Christ might not be a road-company performance of Christ's Passion, with me as a pitifully badly cast actor in the principle role. Perhaps what was imitable about Christ was his firm acceptance of his destiny, and his adherence to it even when it lead to a shameful death. It was the wholeness of Christ that had illuminated so many millions of lives, and it was my job to seek and make manifest the wholeness of Simon Darcourt.[9]

THE PSYCHOANALYST AS MIDWIFE

Who can possibly lead us through the crippling maze of self-deceit? How can we tell the difference between a neurotic desire for perfection, and a genuine longing for wholeness? The two traditions of psychoanalysis and the desert can help us; but there are no shortcuts and no easy answers. Freud hoped for the development of a whole new profession dedicated to this art of inner healing. He wrote: "I want to entrust [psychoanalysis] to a profession which does not exist, a profession of secular ministers of souls, who don't have to be physicians and must not be priests." In spite of the fact that Freud has a low opinion of priests, his way of describing the work of analysis is definitely "priestly." He often wrote of the analyst as "midwife," a word commonly found in the literature describing the "cure of souls."

The goal of psychoanalysis, like that of spiritual formation, is to aid in the integration of the emotional with the intellectual life, to uncover and examine the various neuroses that strangle the hope and possibility of freedom in human action. It involves a marriage of mind and heart, which in turn leads to fullness of soul. The midwife (psychoanalyst, friend, and even priest) encourages us to allow things to take their course; and when things come to term, they assist at our birth. Pregnancy and delivery are apt images for the way of believing we are exploring; apt because the process of birth combines the ideas of struggle and conflict with that of hope. As we have seen, part of the struggle is with seductive images (some positive as well as negative), which attempt to tell us who and what we are. We are to be "atheists" with regard to the "Gods" of this world and skeptics with regard to our perception, not least to the way we see ourselves.

Freud, the midwife, wanted to help rescue people from their patterns of self-diminishment. His radicalism, to quote Erich Fromm, lay not in the area of sexuality, but in

his insistence on the central role of repression and the fundamental significance of the unconscious sector of our mental [life]. This theory was radical because it attacked the last fortress of man's belief in his omnipotence and omniscience, the believe in his conscious thought as an ultimate datum of human experience. . . .Freud deprived man of his pride in his rationality . . . most of our unconscious thought is a sham, a mere rationalization of thought and desires, which we prefer not to be aware of.

Erich Fromm goes on to deplore the degeneration of psychoanalysis into game-playing. Freud's radical art has been tamed. What was once a revolutionary theory is now simply one of adjustment. Happiness (or at least relief from distress) is what is offered. To become more human, more free, and more independent takes a more radical surgery than the one that tries to make people happy or adjust to circumstances. Happiness and adjustment are, perhaps, worthy goals, but they fall short of Freud's hope for psychoanalysis. He discovered that his patients "did not want to be free men but successful bourgeois and did not want to pay the radical price that the change from the predominance of having over that of being would have required."[11]

This charge of game-playing can also be laid at the feet of Christianity. Much in Christianity has been tamed and reduced to liberal or conservative theologies of adjustment. Does the average believer want to pay the radical price of becoming more human and more free? The highest in religion is concerned with *being* rather than *having*, but how many of us aspire to the highest?

Where psychoanalysis talks of neuroses, the Christian tradition, with its roots in Plato, talks of the appetites or the passions. Christianity can easily be misunderstood as a system of beliefs that suppresses both feeling and passion. A passion is, in this context, an unintegrated drive, an unconscious compulsion. The will has little or no power over it. "Passion" in this sense refers to the danger we are in when we refuse to allow things to come to consciousness, when we repress what we see, when we avert our gaze and turn our eyes away.

WE ARE VICTIMS OF APPETITE

The issue raised by both psychoanalysis and the desert tradition is that we do not yet know how to experience the world. In Platonic terms we are the victims of appetite, including and

especially our appetite for ideas; our desire to comprehend or—
better—devour reality. Jacob Needleman poses an illuminating
question: "Is it possible to see ourselves without prematurely
explaining ourselves . . . just to see without program or position, what we are as individuals and as a civilization?"[12] For our
purposes, we can paraphrase Needleman: Is it possible to look,
simply look, without prematurely interpreting what we see? Could
we do this without subjecting ourselves to immediate self-defi-
nition and self-imaging?

William Golding writes in much the same vein. He laments
the fact that none of us is capable of breathing so much as a
lungful of "psychically unpolluted air." We cannot see ourselves
without prematurely explaining ourselves. We do not know how
to look and to look well. Golding ascribes our problem to "the
glum intellect," which constructs "bolts and bars, fetters, locks
and chains" on our inner life. The result is that phantoms,
images distorted by psychic pollution, condition and define our
world. In a flash of hyperbole, he claims that Marx, Darwin,
and Freud are "the three most crashing bores of the Western
world."[13]

Why? Because the simplistic popularization of their ideas has
put our culture into a mental straightjacket by advancing a
consistent strategy of reductionism. Golding suggests that the
mindless violence of our age is a revolt against the culture's
reductionist tendencies. For him, the typical American Thanksgiving Day Parade is emblematic of the twentieth century. The
gas-filled figures of Mickey Mouse, Uncle Sam, and Yogi Bear
are like the ideologies with which we are enthralled. Imagine
the scene. These idiotic, grotesque figures, grinning, bobbing,
and swaying in the breeze, dominate the ant-like figures below
to whom they are tethered. One of the great moments in the
parade is when one of the inflated figures begins to lose gas,
sagging and arching in pseudo-menace over the streets below.

Little by little the procession with its totemistic figures has become my
metaphor for the processional life, the hurrah of X the hero, the lowest
common denominator of belief. Down the main street of our communal awareness they come. They dwarf the human beings, dwarf the
buildings. Here comes plastic Marx, bearded and bellied with "workers
of the world unite" across his vest, Darwin is inscribed with "natural

selection," Freud stares with Jahvistic belligerence from behind his own enormous member. Whether we are in the procession and holding one of the ropes that support our idols, whether we are among the crowd on the sidewalk, or whether we work in the offices that line the street we all know to one degree or another—that these simplistic representations of real people are what goes on and what counts. They, inept, misleading, farcical, are what condition our communal awareness. . . .At one time or another in my life I have walked in the procession, held a rope and felt the upward tug of the gas filled balloon.[13]

The way of the desert and the way of psychoanalysis are two methods by which we can be weaned away from dependence on inflated ideologies that inform and nurture our neuroses. Both methods involve attentiveness, a very disciplined way of seeing. The religious traditions have certain words for this special way of looking. In Buddhism it is simply called "emptiness"; Meister Eckhart writes of *Abgescheidenheit* (indifference). Hinduism speaks of detachment; the Sufis of sobriety. The early Christians speak of the desert of *apatheia*,[14] which might be freely translated as a way of looking at the world without craziness. In every case, this detached way of looking is related to compassion. It is not an escapist strategy. Rather, it is a way of relating in love to the world and its inhabitants.

INVOLVEMENT AND DETACHMENT: THE APPROACH TO MYSTERY

Thus we find two ways in the ancient religious traditions that have been taken up unwittingly by psychoanalysis in its treatment of human neuroses. The first is the way of deep immersion and involvement in human experience; the second is that of radical separation from it. As Jacob Needleman points out, "The greatest saints and sages of the world have exhibited this breathtaking contradiction in their own being—an extrordinary passionate involvement in the whole life of man together with a luminous detachment from it." The message of the traditions is simply, "Be silent, wait and watch." The message of psychoanalysis is the same.

Both psychoanalysis and these contemplative traditions call into question our very experience or rather our interpretation or explanation of experience. It is never quite what we imagine it to be. Why, Needleman asks, do we distrust the experience of the mentally ill? Because we judge that these experiences have been filtered through the person's desires and/or fears. But doesn't desire or fear rule the rest of us? How do we know what we have experienced? Are not all our experiences distorted? We receive our knowledge of the world, others, and ourselves only from the monstrous and distorted shadows cast upon the back of Plato's case. Life is like scratching an itch (and let us not forget that there are intellectual itches). Experience, then, "is the satisfaction or dissatisfaction of our appetites . . . and the desire for truth becomes the desire to master reality rather than experience it."[15]

The problem with many popular therapies is that they feed our appetites rather than give us a way of experiencing the world. They promise far more than they can deliver. It is hard (when you're hurting and unhappy) to distinguish between genuine growth and the development of a mere coping mechanism. Maybe the shallow therapies are right? Helping needy and unhappy people cope isn't such a bad thing. Better the adherence to a "vital lie" than to a painful truth; better to take lots of aspirin rather than find out the cause of the pain. Perhaps it is best not to dig too deeply? Psychoanalysis is a long, hard road. The radical therapy of the Gospel involves drastic surgery. Perhaps it is only for those who are not wise in the world's terms, or for believers who stumble into it by "accident."

As a person deeply committed to the healing and transforming ministry, I find it extremely difficult to allow others to be instruments of healing and transformation to me. This, in part, is why I do what I do; precisely to keep everyone at a safe distance. Psychoanalysis is not the only "impossible profession." As we have seen, much of what is claimed for psychoanalysis was known to the great mystics under such names as *apatheia*, indifference, emptiness, or detachment. Freud's most original and radical discovery, the phenomenon of transference, was not unknown to the desert fathers, to St. Ignatius Loyola, and to Mahatma Gandhi. But where Freud saw despair (or, at best, routine unhappiness), the mystics saw hope. What Freud called transference was a cleansing operation that made way for hope and love. It was the second way of "atheism": the purifying of the concepts of God. The process of purification frees us from the tyranny of the neurotic and prepares us for an encounter with the numinous. Morton Kelsey wisely points out that Jung was far more concerned with helping people approach the numinous than with concentrating on their neuroses. Real therapy lies in this approach to mystery. Jung believed that insofar as one is in touch with the truly numinous, the more likely one is to be released from the curse of pathology.[16]

How can we describe this *way* of looking? It involves a kind of dual vision. We need to be able to see, at one and the same time, the glory to which we are called and the distance we have fallen from that glory. It is the task of the artist to help us develop that "double vision." The greatest of them are able to help us see the glory in life without sentimentalizing or trivializing it. They also enable us to see the suffering and horror of life without pushing us into despair.

Music can foster this double vision in some people. Andrew Porter, writing about the music of Kurt Weil and the latter's opera, *Rise and Fall of the City of Mahagonny*, confesses that the music has healing power and arouses intense contradictory feelings: "horror, compassion, delight, and mirth are mingled; and the end is not despair but a joyful proclamation of belief in mankind's essential goodness, shining through the clear-sighted and critical contemplation of society's selfishness, wickedness and greed."[17]

The concern of both psychoanalysis and the desert tradition is precisely "clear-sighted vision and critical contemplation" of what life has to offer. This *way* of believing is a way of looking at the world, oneself, and others critically and compassionately. It makes no easy promises. It insists on an apparently bleak reality because it takes time to develop double vision. We have to take time to look at the side of things that we have taken a great deal of trouble to avoid.

Once acknowledged, the phenomenon of transference deals a terrible blow to our sense of well-being. Personal relations become

a messy jangle of misapprehensions, at best an uneasy truce between powerful solitary fantasy systems. Even (or especially) romantic love is fundamentally solitary, and has at its core a profound impersonality. The concept of transference at once destroys faith in personal relations and explains why they are tragic: we cannot know each other. We must grope around for each other through a dense thicket of absent others. We cannot see each other plain. A horrible kind of predestination hovers over each new attachment we form. "Only connect," E. M. Forster proposed, "Only we can't," the psychoanalyst knows.[18]

Do psychoanalysts know? I do not believe that they have the last word, but I do believe that they are on the right track. The psychoanalyst is on to something very important; there are striking similarities between this way and the way of believing we hope to follow.

THE COMMON PATH

These ways have at least eight patterns in common. All have to do with attentiveness, with the invitation to see. They are

1. The need for detachment.
2. The belief that nothing is accidental.
3. The fact that we are not as free as we think we are.
4. The conviction that remembering is an important part of the process of growth.
5. The belief that while we have to do much of what we do alone, companionship is essential.
6. The necessity of contemplative commitment.
7. An appreciation for our "fallenness."
8. The mystery of having to let go of the things and people we love the most.

DETACHMENT

A good analyst, like a wise father or mother of the desert, is committed to a path of detachment. The professional insists on it for the sake of clarity and objectivity; the *abba* or *amma* of the desert for the sake of love and freedom. Learning to love is learning to renounce the other for the sake of the other. We struggle daily with people who understand love only in terms of possession. To bring them and us through the thick wood of transference to the reununciation of love for the sake of love is one way of describing the task. The poet Madeleine L'Engle puts it this way:

> To learn to love
> is to be stripped of all love
> until you are wholly without love
> because
> until you have gone
> naked and afraid
> into this cold dark place
> where all love is taken from you
> you will not know
> that you are wholly within love.[19]

This is a poem about transference and the pain that battle with it involves. Learning to be truly indifferent to one's beloved is an arduous task, and struggling to love God in this way is a lifetime's work. It would mean nothing but struggle and discouragement, were it not for the fact that believers have the faith that God loves them "indifferently" through and through. We are concerned, then, with nothing less than a pattern of conversion by which a person is "forced by extraordinary circumstances to transcend the self-centered demands of the ego, who comes to see another person as real and full and who can finally see that person without the distortions of fantasy or ulterior motive; who can, that is, love someone else."[20]

NOTHING IS ACCIDENTAL

In both psychoanalysis and the desert way, there are no accidents; or rather, "there is nothing arbitrary or haphazard or accidental or meaningless in anything we do."[21] There is, however, a drastic difference in the way the two traditions interpret this fact. The psychoanalyst tends to see this as evidence of psychic determinism; the desert Christian as a sign that God is *always* trying to reach out to us. The believer wants to go further—much further than Freud, who claimed that the most that could be expected of psychoanalysis was the transformation of "hysterical misery into common unhappiness" (p. 27). The believer claims that the difficult process of accepting and working through our neuroses brings both joy and peace.

THE LIMITS OF FREEDOM

We are not as free as we think we are. Freud has shown what the desert fathers knew centuries earlier: that man/woman is not even master/mistress in his/her own house. As Janet Malcolm graphically puts it: "It was as if a lonely terrorist working in his cellar on a modest explosive device to blow up the local brewery had unaccountably found his way to the hydrogen bomb and blown up half the world. The fallout from this bomb has yet to settle." (p. 23)

Dealing with such fallout is no easy matter. The way of both psychoanalysis and the desert tradition is one of interiority, which includes a willingness to explore the cellars and dungeons of the psyche. This inward journey is traveled by only a few people, although they are by no means an elite.

How do we cope with the dislocation, tragedy, and conflict we encounter when we begin to realize that we are not as free as we think we are? Shallow therapists offer band-aid cures and propagate "vital lies"; but then, so do some religious people. Slaveries are easily disguised as freedoms, since our preference tends to be for enslavement.

The Good News is that in Christ we no longer have to lie. That *is* good news. In fact it's the best there is. Unfortunately, too much of both religion and therapy has to do with passing on mere information. The notion is that, once our ignorance of something has been lifted, all will be well. Recovery and new life is bound up with "understanding" something or other. Freud's biting response to this view was to liken it to the distribution of menu cards to those suffering from a severe famine (p. 27). A mere description of mystery or the numinous doesn't feed the soul any more than the words "filet mignon" satisfy hunger.

Many a priest, minister, or counselor seems to be playing the game of a distributor of menu cards. A psychiatrist told me of a patient who was suffering from *anorexia nervosa*. She weighed fifty-seven pounds and brought to each session a bag of doughnuts, which she begged him in vain to eat. The patient couldn't eat, but was obsessed with food. This, for me, is a powerful image of many of us—starved psychically and spiritually as we attempt to force others to eat. We are not as free as we think we are.

THE PAIN OF REMEMBERING

Remembering is an important part of the process of growth. We often get caught on the treadmill of repeated acts. Every confessor knows the agony of people who are tormented by a "besetting sin." The treadmill of repetition can only be stopped by a process of remembering, which is often painful. From the point of view of the believer, memory plays another important role in the work of healing. We are not only urged to remember our own past, but to enter contemplatively into a corporate memory that guards healing stories of salvation.

The medieval writers called such an entry into the corporate memory "meditation." It was a matter of hard chewing and digestion. The Latin word to describe this was *ruminare*, to ruminate, to chew the cud. As the old collect has it with regard to the Bible: we are to "read, mark, learn and inwardly digest" the saving stories. Another significant word associated with meditation was *parturire*, to bring to birth something new. Thus we are to struggle with our own memories and the corporate memory in order, by the grace of God, to give birth to ourselves. Our own history has, in some way, wounded us. Our neuroses spring from the hurts we received as children. Salvation history (which, for the believer, is rehearsed in the Bible and the Liturgy) provides the antidote for those hidden early hurts that continue to wield great influence over us in adult life. "By his stripes we are healed." From the point of view of the believer, this means that my history and salvation history are inextricably bound together in the love of God.

OUR COMPANIONS: THE ANGELS OF GOD

While we do much of what we have to do on our own, companionship is essential if we are not to lose our way. Sometimes we need the sustenance of a peculiar relationship: peculiar in the sense that it is "out of the ordinary" or even abnormal (at least by our own standards). It may even be the guidance we receive from a casual encounter with a stranger on a plane, the chance meeting with someone who brings the discomfort of "revelation." Sometimes we are given a relationship with someone for only a brief time. It is short-lived, but it has a particular purpose. For example, an old man strikes up a conversation with a little boy at the corner store and, through a few chance meetings with an open and loving child, the revelation comes. The light in the child's eyes reveals the dried-up and shriveled character of the old man's dull routine. Scrooge, in Dickens's *A Christmas Carol*, is a good example. In Scrooge's case the revelation came in the form of memory, with its unnerving knack of bringing into our minds unbidden and painful thoughts. The revelation can come at any time, in any place, and through any medium. The trouble is that it often comes and goes in a split second. The opportunity for conversion is brief, and our lives are littered with missed opportunities.

The two traditions we are considering provide a disciplined way to train ourselves to notice these frequent but short-lived opportunities. They provide us with the chance to take a long, hard look at what is there. Psychoanalysis requires us to enter into a very different kind of human relationship. Janet Malcolm points to the fact that a relationship with a psychoanalyst is radically unlike any other human relationship. In a purposeful way, it renounces the niceties and decencies of ordinary human intercourse. It is abnormal, contradictory, and demanding (p. 37).

Such abnormality and oddness is also present in a relationship that looks to the desert tradition. There, too, purposeful renunciation springs from a commitment to a contemplative availability to another, which always allows for a third to be present in and between them. The believer allows for the possibility of God; not only allows for it, but hopes and trusts in it. The desert tradition insists on detachment, indifference, or *apatheia* for the sake of honoring the sustaining presence of the transcendent, the not-known, and the not-yet of true human interaction. God is present and, in the silence, is acknowledged to be so.

From time to time, everyone needs someone to play the role of "analyst" or "desert father or mother." It is not a role that many of us are fit for on a long-term basis, but there are moments when we can play that part for someone else. Each of us needs someone to behave towards us in such a way that our neuroses are not allowed to take over and dominate the relationship. We do not always appreciate such people, but they serve, at particular moments of revelation, to move us from the neurotic to the numinous. Here is how Janet Malcolm describes the analyst's behavior towards his or her patient:

[It] is as neutral, mild, colorless, self-effacing, uninterfering, and undemanding as he is able to make it, and as it is toward no one else in his life—with the paradoxical (and now absolutely predictable) result that the patient reacts with stronger, more vivid and intense personal feelings to this bland shadowy figure than he does to the more clearly delineated and provocative figures in his life outside analysis. On this paradox—on the patients' quickness to overfill the emotional vacuum created by the analyst's reticence—the analysis is poised, and it may as easily founder as take off. If the patient sees the analyst as a cold, callous person of limited intelligence and unbounded tactlessness, he may decide to quit the analysis. (p. 38)

There is a great deal here that would describe casual encounters and short-lived relationships. I have often missed a "revelation" because I could not see the creative possibilities of a relationship with someone who appeared neutral, mild, colorless, and uninterfering, and yet who was willing, for that moment, to be there for me. The monk in the desert treated me as an angel "just in case." He was willing to entertain the possibility of a revelation. We need such "angels," and the desert is full of them.

Here are three examples of angels and their unexpected visitations. The late Alexander Schmemann, a distinguished Orthodox priest and teacher, once told a group of students why he believed in the existence of angels. When he was a young man living in Paris, he was traveling on the metro one day with his fiancée. They were very much in love and bound up in each other. The train stopped and an elderly and very ugly woman got on. She was dressed in the uniform of the Salvation Army and she came and sat near them. The young lovers began to whisper to each other in Russian, exclaiming to each other about the grossness and ugliness of the old woman. The train came to a stop. The old woman got up and, as she passed the two young people, she said to them in perfect Russian: "I wasn't always ugly!" That, insisted Father Schmemann, was an angel of God. She brought the shock of revelation, the shock that was needed for him to *see* that what was there was much, much more than an ugly old woman. Next time he would be able to look at an unattractive person in a self-effacing, uninterfering way.

It takes practice to spot angelic presences. But practice alone is not enough, unless one can practice being taken by surprise. The second example is taken from J. D. Salinger's *Franny and Zooey*. He writes of the figure of "the Fat Lady," who represents the unattractive, the unlovely, the rejected in all of us. She is the despised one, and we are to do everything we do *for* her. Franny's friend was told to shine his shoes before appearing before a studio audience:

I was furious. The studio audience were all morons, the announcer was a moron, the sponsors were morons, and I just damn well wasn't going to shine my shoes for them. . . . I said they couldn't see them *any*way, where we sat. He said to shine them anyway. He said to shine them for the Fat Lady. I didn't know what the hell he was talking about . . . but I shined my shoes for the Fat Lady every time I went on the air again.

Franny too had been told about the Fat Lady, and both she and her friend had formed a clear picture of her in their minds. She sat on a porch all day, swatting flies, with her radio going full blast, and she had cancer. Franny's friend goes on:

I'll tell you a terrible secret—Are you listening to me? *There isn't anyone out there who isn't . . . [the] Fat Lady . . .* There isn't anyone *any*where that isn't . . . [the] Fat Lady. Don't you know that? Don't you know that goddam secret yet? And don't you know—*listen* to me now—*don't you know who the Fat Lady really is?* . . . Ah, buddy. Ah, buddy. It's Christ Himself. Christ Himself, buddy.[22]

A friend of mine met "the Fat Lady" at the wake held after the death of Dorothy Day, the indefatigable champion of the poor. He writes:

A friend and I drove to Manhattan on a dismal and damp cold December day. Dorothy was laid out in Maryhouse. It smelled awful. But the house was quiet for a change. In a small darkened and almost empty room, Dorothy was lying in a cheap casket . . . in second-hand clothes with one fresh rose on her breast. She held her rosary. A fat lady was sitting in the corner. She was either crazy or drunk—maybe both. She was talking out loud and not making any sense. And she was smoking a cigar.

There is no doubt in my mind that it was the Fat Lady mourning the death of a great-hearted believer.

The third example comes from a young woman's experience of the poor and hungry in rural Mexico. When Bobbie Gerber was a student, she went to Mexico as a volunteer. She visited a family whose twins, a boy and girl, both had dysentery.

I went to the little boy. His face was thin and wrinkled, his eyes wide. His abdomen was distended and he looked like an old man. His arms and legs were only a little thicker than my thumbs . . . The light weight of his body was ghostly. I wished I could nurse him at my own breast, and felt sadder than I've ever felt before or since in my whole life . . . His name, like that of many Mexican boys, was Jésus. . . .[Later] the missionaries who'd hosted the students in Mexico mentioned in a letter that the little boy twin had died. I went out and bought a crucifix and hung it in my room . . . Under it I taped a lettered sign that read, "Jesus died for your sins in Cuatemoc, Chihuahua, on August 18 . . . of infantile dysentery and malnutrition". . . .My sense of the presence of Christ in the world today is still inextricably entwined with the memory of that weightless, withered body and those suffering, innocent eyes.[23]

Bobbie Gerber saw Christ in the suffering and death of a little Mexican boy. Alexander Schmemann met the Fat Lady on the Paris subway, but in order to see her as an angel of God or as Christ himself he had to accept the shock of revelation. He had to be open to the holy.

"Holiness" is another name for this self-effacing, uninterfering stance towards another human being. Psychoanalysis seems to lack an ongoing tradition of hope to sustain this neutral and colorless waiting with another person. This, in part, is due to its own built-in arrogance, which assumes that it and it alone is exploring genuinely new frontiers. On the one hand, psychoanalysis claims too much for itself; on the other, it is not sure of its ground. It suffers from being cut off from its roots in the great religious traditions, which, like it, are committed to *looking*, to simple attention, to the path of self-knowledge.

Psychoanalysis often seems uneducated and provincial in its outlook, well nigh incapable of following its own logic. For example, "implicit in the idea of transference is the assumption of some true, or truer, state of things that is being obscured."[24] What, one wonders, is this true state of affairs? What is "reality" and who is to judge? These are questions of increasing importance as analysis has shifted from being a symptom-curing therapy to a character-changing one (p. 40). As we begin to face issues of character, we find ourselves running into the numinous, the realm of mystery, the dimension of the moral and spiritual.

What are we to make of the apparently universal longing for an omnipotent parent? This craving can be triggered by almost any authority figure—doctors, politicians, pop stars, priests, analysts. The acknowledgment of this longing makes a believer nervous. It raises severe doubts. It seems to hit at the very heart of faith. I ask myself: "Isn't my belief in God simply a projection of my craving for an omnipotent parent?" I feel threatened and naked when I ask myself this question. Isn't "God" that which provides me with a neurotic solution for my basic anxiety?

It is easy for doctors, politicians, pop stars, priests, and analysts to play the parent to my child. This is where the second kind of atheism is very important for the desert believer. A process of contemplative purification is essential if there is to be any healing work done in the soul. Strict psychoanalysis provides us with a model of "indifference and detachment" that can help free the soul of its dependence on an omnipotent parent.

But does not the thought of all this make us feel inferior and inadequate? That is why there is a strong tendency in me to belittle psychoanalysis and make fun of its practitioners. Underneath lurks my fear of self-knowledge and of the ice-cold promise of self-confrontation. And so I fight against that for which I long. I cannot face what I have to do on my own. I need help. And help comes. God doesn't send me a comforting authority figure, the omnipotent Parent. He sends me the Fat Lady.

THE WAY OF ATTENTIVENESS

Contemplative commitment is a necessity. The command is "Be attentive!" In the *Divine Comedy*, Beatrice uncompromisingly ordered Dante to look and to look well. I too need someone who will relentlessly draw my attention to those parts of my life that remain hidden even from myself, and yet which hold me in their power. The psychoanalyst does this for some people;

the holy man or woman for others. Most of the time we rely on our being able to notice and then receive the innumerable "angelic visitations" that come to us in the course of a day. This is how one analyst describes his work:

all I could do was every now and then direct the patient's attention to what she was doing in her attempts to keep that stuff from spewing out—something she preferred not to watch. . . .The right way is just to point out to the patient how he keeps himself from thinking certain things, so that he becomes self-conscious and the evasion doesn't work so automatically. That's all. That's the analyst's scalpel. He can't open up his patient's mind and start tinkering. The only thing he can do is tell the patient, "Look there," and most of the time the patient doesn't look. But sometimes he does, and then his automatic behavior becomes less automatic. (p. 73)

Most of us, however, find the command "Look!" hard to obey. This way of naked attention for the sake of love seems impossible to maintain. We prefer to love others by interfering with them. We enjoy tinkering with others in the name of love. We enjoy, above all, being demonstrably useful. All in all, we need rescuing. We need a Savior, but we need one who will save us from our craving him. This is the painful paradox of this way of believing. Our longings must be purified in the fire. Our neuroses must be given up.

This is why I long for a stronger and more mutually respectful alliance between psychoanalysis and this way of believing. Each has a great deal to learn from the other. The desert tradition could teach psychoanalysis about its own unconscious but deeply religious base. Psychoanalysis could help believers face the fact that much of what passes for religion is bogus and/or neurotic. Believers claim to be born again. Analysis provides us with a second chance to grow up. My vision is of a way of believing that would bring new birth *and* help me grow up. As we have seen, the churches tend to breed, nurture, and encourage infantilism. A number of us believers are caught between what we have been taught and what our own hearts tell us. This makes us infantile. The learning and the loving is in the waiting in the desert. As one analyst wrote: "If only we can wait, the patient arrives at understanding creatively and with immense joy, and I now enjoy this joy more than I used to enjoy the sense of having been clever" (p. 73).

THE APPRECIATION OF WEAKNESS

In the light of all that has gone before, we need to appreciate anew our "fallenness." Psychoanalysis documents "the Fall" in uncompromising terms. Analysts talk of a basic fault or even a maimed inner core. There is no doubt that we need help! We need a savior.

Freud and Jung have done a great deal to document this need. Jung explored the modern consciousness and found it to be without historical roots. It was stranded. It was solitary. It felt guilty. Believers and unbelievers alike are plagued with the fear of discontinuity, the sense that things do not hang together. We are haunted by a sense that there is something for which we should atone, but we aren't sure what it is. Of course, in our "happy" extroverted culture there are many who would claim that all this talk is the result of morbid introspection; sour grapes on the part of the discontented; an evil spirit gnawing away at the guts of faith.

In the face of our "happy" culture, psychoanalysis simply points to this "fallenness" and remains steadfastly "unhelpful": unhelpful in that it refuses to lie to us in the face of the evidence. For the believer of the desert way, psychoanalysis is an austere preparation for good news. God knows how we long for some news once we have begun to face this "basic fault" in ourselves and have seen its consequences. The paradox of psychoanalysis is that "the less the analyst tries to help the patient, the more likely it is that he will do so" (p. 139).

Konrad Lorenz pointed out that if you walk in front of a little chick at a certain time in the chick's life, it will follow you. There is a particular time when it gets "set." Psychoanalysts claim that we too get "set" at a certain time in our lives. Aaron Green, Janet Malcolm's analyst in *The Impossible Profession*, claims that the Oedipal period—roughly three and a half to six years—is like Lorenz standing in front of the chick. It is the most formative, significant, molding experience of human life, and is the source of all subsequent adult behaviors" (p. 158).

Even if there is some disagreement among different schools

of psychoanalysis, the consensus is that at some point the pattern of our behavior is set. Is there any good news in this? Believers bet their lives that there is. It means that we are not in control. We are not master in our own house. The analyst would go so far as to say that I am determined in all my actions. I have no real freedom. I cannot change my fate. I am predestined, and my only "freedom" is to learn to accept that fact. Doesn't this sound very much like a common strand in Christian believing; albeit an apparently unattractive and repressive one? St. Augustine and John Calvin knew something of which psychoanalysis speaks, and at their best were able to speak eloquently of the miracle of grace.

Suffice it to say here that while we may well be "fixed" into certain patterns, within those patterns there is an almost infinite variety of possibility. The structure of a sonnet is fixed. Its form is inflexible, but within its tight boundaries unimaginable variety is possible.

LOVE MEANS LETTING GO

We inevitably must let go of the things and the people we love most. Everything comes to an end. In psychoanalytical terms, the relationship with the analyst has to come to an end. It is like "a sojourn in the desert, a final stoical acceptance of the uncertainties of adulthood and the inevitability of death" (p. 155). There is death in the desert. The analyst gives us the accuracy and insight, but little or no good news. There isn't much hope, but then hope isn't the analyst's stock in trade. We should not expect the analyst to do our believing for us. Accuracy and insight are valuable gifts he or she can offer us.

As a believer, I place all that psychoanalysis has to teach me in the context of the desert tradition—the place of imageless, contemplative silence; the place where men and women are prepared for actions that will change the world. In the desert we might even dare to hope for happiness and not simply opt for "routine unhappiness." But before we can do this, death must be stalked in the wilderness. Just as there is something bigger than our neuroses, there is a power stronger than death. There is hope "beyond the North Wind." And the Fat Lady is everywhere.

3. Death in the Desert

Some people believe . . . that life could be redeemed, but it couldn't
be and that was what was so terrible. He had loved only a few people
and loved them so badly and selfishly. He had made a muddle of
everything. Was it only in the presence of death that one could see so
clearly what love ought to be like? If only the knowledge that they
had now, this absolute "nothing else matters," could somehow go
backwards and purify the little selfish loves and straighten out the
muddles but it could not.[1]

IRIS MURDOCH, *Bruno's Dream*

Is it only in the presence of death that we can see so clearly
what love ought to be like? The answer of the believer is "Yes."
It is for the sake of learning how to love and for no other reason
that the believer is committed to looking death straight in the
eye. Facing death gives our loving force, clarity, and focus. But
how awful to discover what love ought to be like only at the end
of one's life, when it is too late.

The believer, however, is at odds, even here, with the despairing interpretation of the novelist's hero: that life cannot be
redeemed, and our loving selfishly and badly counts for nothing.
Who, then, can be saved? The believer affirms that even our
despair has to be given up and seen as the ego-grasping device
that it really is. Despair about ourselves and our world is, perhaps, the ego's last and, therefore, greatest attachment. It is
hard to let go. True love requires detachment, and the contemplation of our death helps us to discover what true love is. The
"unbeliever," John Mortimer, can talk of "the courage to return
to the essentials of childhood, a state of carefree individuality
that can only be completely recaptured at the moment of death."[2]

SILENCE, THE PRELUDE TO DEATH

A desert father was asked for a word of wisdom by one of his
disciples. "Go to the cemetery and curse the dead," said the old
man. The disciple went off and stood among the graves and

shouted: "You cowardly, sinful brood! The strench of your sins is an offence to heaven. I curse you with all the power at my command. May you never see the light!" The young man went back to his master and told him that he had completed the task. "Did the dead say anything to you?" the old man asked. "Not a word!" answered the disciple. "Now go to the cemetery and praise the dead." The young man ran off, stood among the graves, and began a great eulogy: "You are greater than the apostles. Your good deeds rise up to heaven like the incense. You inspire those you have left behind to great deeds. Such is your power, you glorious saints!" The young man hurried back to his master's cell. "Well," said the old man, "how was it this time? Did the dead have anything to say?" The disciple answered, "They were as silent as before." After a period of silence, the old man said, "That is how you have to be—like the dead; beyond cursing and praise, unaffected by the opinions of others."

Silence and a feeling of deadness seem to go together. To be utterly silent can feel like death. And silence is important to both the desert tradition and to psychoanalysis. As we have seen, the psychoanalyst's role is sometimes to sit with the patient and remain completely silent and apparently unhelpful. Stephen A. Kurtz, looking at this from the psychoanalyst's point of view, writes:

In renouncing speech . . . we yield up something fundamentally human—a central means for declaring and expressing our existence. It is a kind of annihilation. Viewed this way, silence is equated with death. To discover that our lives are "rooted in silence that is not death but life" one must first keep quiet. And keeping quiet entails anxiety.

Kurtz goes on the quote Theodore Reik's 1926 lecture on "The Psychological Meaning of Silence":

At the deepest level the anxiety of silence is death anxiety. Thus if speech and silence seem to us to be verbal expression of life and death drives, it becomes clear to us that silence came before speech, that speech arose from silence as life from death. In the beginning was the word, but before this was the great silence. If we here are only "on leave from death" then all speech is only a fleeting interruption of the eternal silence.

Reik's interpretation is inadequate in the light of the desert tradition, although he is accurate in describing the first feelings that come to us when we are silent. The good analyst, like the wise teacher of the desert, knows that silence leads to life and acceptance. For the mature teacher, silence is "nothing less than the expression of his particular way of being."

It is, perhaps, in the use and understanding of silence that the psychoanalytic and the desert traditions are most alike. Silence is important in all the great religious paths. It involves a kind of breakdown, an annihilation for the sake of reorganizing the way we perceive ourselves and the world. When this happens the quality of the silence changes; it becomes the bond that holds two lovers together. "Many shared silences . . . are concentrated moments of communion." They are periods of deep mutual appreciation, which Kurtz defines as "the ability to love without blurring one's boundaries."

Silence, in the end, can become a healing and comforting experience. And if silence is necessary in order for us to be with each other without manipulation and control, this will be all the more true when we are with each other in God. Prayer becomes primarily an encounter with death and a waiting in silence. Indeed, prayer is, from this point of view, a daily willingness to place ourselves on the threshold of death and wait there. Prayer becomes an anticipation of and a participation in our death so that new life may be revealed in us. Prayer is the time when "we move from the agitated periphery of our lives— and which we identify with our lives *tout court*—to a silent interior space."

According to the desert tradition, this empty space is actually indescribably full. The process of detachment from this "agitated periphery" (with which we identify our whole being) can be extremely painful. It is a kind of dying, because it means giving up the manipulative concepts we have about ourselves and (worse, if you are a believer) our "God." A kind of "atheism" sets in with regard to the infantile "God" of our immature imagination. In the silence we feel deserted. God is lost to us, and we are lost to ourselves. In fact, "we" are dead. Kurtz puts it this way: "The loss of the old God—however nagging and infantilizing he may have been—can be experienced as desertion.

Knowing no other way, we took these attentions for love, and when we come to recognize them for what they are, we are left pained, rageful, and then alone."[3] It is out of this deadening silence that we are reborn.

THE SECRET OF HERMES

This way of believing may seem rather gloomy and heavy. Where is the lightness? Where is the humor and joy? It is true that detachment is the key to freedom, but it does have its lighter side. The humor is not, however, escapist; rather, it is a device to help us take ourselves less seriously. If we are not careful, the desert way can become yet one more "project of the ego." Humor helps to keep us on the right track.

The way of believing we have been pursuing is not without its funny side. And since the going sometimes gets rough, it is good to remind ourselves of the existence of angels and laughter. One playful warning before we proceed. The god Hermes is said to be the patron of both psychoanalysis and of the tradition committed to contemplative attention. Hermes is the god who goes between the dead and the living. He is the messenger who carries news between that which is hidden and that which is manifest. He is a psycho-pomp; that is, he is the one who conducts the dead to the underworld. Frank Kermode writes:

The God Hermes is the patron of thieves, merchants, and travelers: of heralds and what heralds pronounce, their *kerygma.* . . .Hermes is cunning, and occasionally violent: a trickster, a robber. So it is not surprising that he is also the patron of interpreters.[4]

The late Urban Holmes described the priest as a follower of Hermes. Those who wish to follow the desert way are also among his retinue. One who is loyal to Hermes subverts our basic assumptions, does not carry his or her own message, travels a dangerous road, and is rarely rewarded by those to whom he or she brings news.[5] Because Hermes travels between the dead and the living, he invites us to look death in the face. One should not expect to be thanked for encouraging one's fellow pilgrims to think about death. Great artists, as followers of

Hermes, often administer the shock of revelation when they present us with a picture of life's terrible fragility and wonder.

Walker Percy likens the serious novelist to the canary that coal miners used to take down the mines to test the air. "When the canary gets unhappy, utters plaintive cries, and collapses, it may be time for the miners to surface and think things over."[6] Some people, for example Søren Kierkegaard, Simone Weil, Mahatma Gandhi are like these canaries. They put themselves at considerable risk—even to the point of death. Not everyone is called to follow this way, no more than is everyone expected to be psychoanalyzed. But it is good to know that this path exists. It may offer comfort in a time of unexpected extremity. I suspect that, for most of us, the austere and creative "indifference" of the twin ways of the desert and of psychoanalysis is something of which we catch only a brief glimpse from time to time. We drift in and out of this way of believing.

GO AND SIT IN YOUR CELL!

One of the best-known sayings of the desert fathers is this: "In Scetis, a brother went to see Abba Moses and begged him for a word. And the old man said: go and sit in your cell, and your cell will teach you everything."[7]

Sitting in one's cell is like resting in one's grave. It can feel like death. It is learning to do nothing and, indeed, to be nothing: to be, like Abraham, one who is as good as dead. It was then, remember, that God called him out of his deadness to make him into a great people. The desert truly stretches, breaks unto death, and remakes the soul. It challenges us with one basic command: "Go and sit in your cell and your cell will teach you everything."

"Sitting in one's cell" is similar to the Buddhist doctrine of *anatta*, "not-self." This "death of the self" comes when we realize that the impression that we possess persisting and permanent souls or selves is an illusion.

What does such a "dying" accomplish? For one thing, it pushes the believer more and more deeply into the desert. It invites the believer to sit loosely to his or her "self." In fact, it challenges the believer to *dis*believe in the self as an abiding entity. The point is that we do not have to believe a dogma (in this case, the dogma of the "self") to be literally true in order for it to be useful and effective. All that is required is that we accept it as a working hypothesis. That is to say, the doctrine that the self is an illusion need not discourage us from using it as an instrument of spiritual growth and insight.

This way of thinking makes many believers and unbelievers, particularly in the West, angry and confused. Something either is true, or it isn't. To one degree or another, we all suffer from a fundamentalist mindset. It is hard for us to see that truth operates on many levels and comes to us in many forms. The way of believing with which we are concerned insists that we let go of our desire to have a conceptual control of things. We have to die to our ideas. The psychoanalyst and the desert hermit both tell us: "You don't have to *believe* what I am saying. Simply act *as if* what I say is true. Try the way of indifference, detachment, not-self, just for a while." We have to face the fact that what we are dealing with in the various religious traditions are simply spiritual techniques masquerading as ultimate truths. "Sitting in one's cell" is a technique for wearing down our sense of self, which is based on our attachments to things and ideas. "Dying" seems to be the best word to describe this process.

This dying process accomplishes two things. First, it undermines our dependence on material things; second, it renders our strategies of self-deception less and less efficient. "Not-self" lays bare another way of being a self. It is important to see this as a technique rather than a dogma because, if taken literally, we might indulge in a destructive cycle of self-rejection and self-hate. This way of believing leads us to a place of disturbing openness with regard to our self-understanding. Life becomes a genuine journey of naked faith.

Our "dying," then, has to do with the stripping away of illusions.

The goal of psychoanalysis is to free the patient from the slavery of impersonal behavior so that he may become capable of personal deeds. A deed is a voluntary act by which the doer discloses himself to others; behavior is involuntary and discloses, not a unique self, but either those natural deeds common to all men, or those diagnosable complexes which the patient shares with other sufferers of the same kind. Thanks to psychoanalysis, it is now a matter of public knowledge that, frequently, when we imagine we are acting as ourselves, we are really only exhibiting behavior, and it is one of the analyst's tasks to unmask this illusion in his patients.[8]

The goal of this way of believing is to place this unmasking of illusions, this process of "dying," in the context of hope; so that we may not only disclose ourselves to others, but also lay ourselves bare to God's disclosure of himself to us.

Both psychoanalysis and the desert tradition point us in the direction of the straight and narrow gate that leads to life. We are invited to live, but we must die in order to do so! We enter that gate stark naked. I wonder if any of us are capable of that? Do we not rather slip in and out of illusions? Occasionally, the fog lifts. We catch a glimpse of what we hope are "things as they really are," and then the fog creeps over us again. I do not find this a gloomy prospect at all. The fog keeps us humble and compassionate, the flashes of light keep us hopeful and exhilarated. Doesn't this way of believing sound contradictory and impossible? This tradition of believing inspires both fear and hope at the same time. The mystics would answer: "Yes. For us it is impossible but with God all things are possible." "For now we see in a mirror, darkly; but then face to face: now I know in part; but then shall I know even as also I have been known" (1 Cor. 13:12).

Seeing in a mirror, darkly; living with the tentativeness of our knowledge; accepting the illusory quality of our sense of self; these are, of course, only minor examples of the little "deaths" we all have to undergo. There is also the question of our *actual* dying. We are all terminal cases; and this knowledge always lurks in the murky bottom of consciousness. When we have been able to look at the death of our petty aims and ideas, and face the termination of our own narrow view of ourselves, the desert then makes us look at the question of our own physical dying and death.

Historically, ours is one of the more heroic (if naive) of death-defying cultures. We try to cheat death on every front. Economically and technologically, we have amassed great wealth and expertise to silence the voice of death that speaks softly inside the skull. Medically, we can cheat death by plugging ourselves into life-support systems that will enable us to live forever—albeit as vegetables. This image of a *living* death is far more terrifying, to me, than death itself.

DEATH AS A FRIEND

In the desert tradition, death is a companion, a friend. St. Francis of Assisi called death "sister." He was a believer of extraordinary power, at home with the desert way of believing. Death, far from being the terror we encounter at the *end* of our earthly existence, is the companion and friend who walks with us now. Sister Death is with us always. Her shadow marks and influences every moment.

To live our life from the point of view of our death is not necessarily a capitulation to despair, to withdrawal, to passivity. Rather, it can become the basis for our being and doing in the world. The more we refuse to *look* at our own death, the more we repress and deny new possibilities for living. We are all going to die, and our life is a movement to that sure end. Believers find that meditation on this simple fact has a wonderful way of clearing the mind! It enables them to live every single moment with new appreciation and delight. When I say to myself, "This moment may be my last," I am able to see the world with new eyes.

The desert way of believing relieves us of having to lie about anything, especially about suffering and death. Real hope cannot be based on sham or sentimentality. I don't know why it is, but there are some things that cannot be learned apart from suffering.

Sometimes we suffer not individually, but collectively. The German chancellor, Bismark, once observed that God looked after idiots, drunks, and the United States of America. In the 1920s Andre Gide said that America did not deserve to have a soul because she had not yet been plunged into the crucible of suffering. This accusation is no longer true, and the United States has no particular claim to divine protection. In fact, there is no place in the modern world that does not know suffering in one form or another. As we have seen, much of the suffering lies so deep that it can only come out in the form of neuroses and anxieties. While there are plenty of hungry and homeless people in the West, there is one way in which the affluent and poor both suffer: from an underlying and constant anxiety about the future.

The threat of annihilation hangs over everyone. Acknowledged or not, the possibility of nuclear war affects us all. Such a threat seems to have two opposite effects on us. On the one hand, we have the survivalists: defensive, paramilitary, and quasi-religious. Some people have fled "to the hills" and have dug themselves in as a protection against what they see as the inevitable collapse of civilization. On the other hand, some people are beginning to realize that there is only one world and if we are to survive in it we will have to develop strategies to enhance mutuality and cooperation. We really are bound up with one another. This is a statement of fact. We live and we die together.

While the desert way of believing is always ready for the appearance of an angel, it also seeks to identify elements in human life that keep us apart and are the bearers of deadliness. Death comes in many guises and has to be unmasked before it can become for us sister or friend. Tielhard de Chardin describes death for the believer as the final moment of ex*cent*ration; the moment when we are truly con*cent*rated on God.

The desert way and the way of psychoanalysis often "feel like death" because both are concerned with our not being the center of our own attention. To realize that I am not the center of everything (even of my struggle and self-pity) makes me panic. If I give up that centrality, surely I shall be no more? When I cling to my being at the center, a deadliness sets in from which there is no promise of resurrection.

Something of this "deadliness" hovers over the hopes and aspirations of us Westerners. It is becoming harder and harder to dream of a stable and prosperous future. Like spoiled children, we look for short-term solutions to meet our immediate infantile needs. The voice within, demanding satisfaction, is relentless. It has to be. To be quiet, even for a second, would be to entertain the possibility that we are not, after all, at the center. The hero of Saul Bellow's *Henderson the Rain King* is tormented by such a voice. It repeats over and over again, "I want, I want, I want. . . ." Henderson doesn't know what he really wants, and only two activities will silence the voice within: quick and easy sexual intimacy and playing his violin. They quieten, for a while, the awful chorus of "I want, I want, I want. . . ."

This voice within is the enemy of our peace. If we sit still and really listen to it, the fact of our own death will come to us with clarity and freshness. Attention to the voice will force us to experience our fragility, futility, and creatureliness. We will be confronted with the emptiness, terror, and formlessness that lies deep in the heart. This is the desert experience of the saints and mystics, and it is also known to psychoanalysis. Such phrases as "the cloud of unknowing" and "the dark night of the soul" are different ways to try to talk about this experience of emptiness. To the believer, this vast inner emptiness is nothing less than the dwelling place of God.

The realization that there is a vast emptiness within comes to us as shock. From a psychological and spiritual point of view, we have a twofold task: one, to be open to the shock of revelation when it comes; and two, to keep the shock alive in us after we have said "Yes" to it. The Angel of Death taps us on the shoulder from time to time to shock us out of our tiny and prejudiced view of things. We need such visitations to shatter our parochial perspective.

STOPPING THE WORLD

In Carlos Castaneda's book *Journey to Ixtlan*, there is a useful and illuminating model for spiritual and psychological growth that involves the constant presence of Sister Death as our traveling companion. Don Juan, the shaman and *brujo* who is Castaneda's spiritual master, sets down a pattern for receiving the salutary shock of a revelation. There are four steps:

(1) "Stopping the world" is a way of breaking open a person's consciousness and releasing it from its stifling provincialism. (2) This leads to seeing the world in a new way. (3) The willingness to *look* involves a confrontation with death in a positive as well as in a negative way. (4) This confrontation with death leads to renewal and presents us with fresh opportunities to accept both greater freedom and responsibility.

When we surrender to the vast emptiness within, we experience dislocation. As Castaneda insists, "the world of every day life is not real, or out there, as we believe it is. For a sorcerer (*brujo*), reality, or the world we all know is only a description."[10]

This is a very important psychological and spiritual point. Most of us find it well nigh impossible to tell the difference between reality and what we *think* reality is. For example, few find it easy to distinguish between their *idea* of God and the reality of God. I get into trouble when I cannot tell the difference between the perceptions I have of my loved ones and the mystery which they really are.

"Stopping the world," therefore, is an inescapable first step. It is the means by which we break out, or are broken out of, a way of thinking and believing that confuses our descriptions of things, people, and events for the realities themselves. This breaking out not only widens our vision, it changes it. "Stopping the world" may be caused by a terrible cataclysmic experience of conversion or calamity; you learn that you have a cancer; your child runs away from home; there has been a mindless and gratuitous act of violence in your neighborhood; your friend loses her job and cannot support her children. Any experience that shatters our existence and shows up the terrible fragility of things is capable of stopping the world.

One of our children was severely injured in an automobile accident a few years ago. Everything seemed to be broken. Would she live? If she lived, would she be permanently brain-damaged? Suddenly a beautiful and vivacious little girl was lying in the road like a limp rag doll. It was as if our world had not only stopped, but had been ravaged by an obscene beast. I thought of those fragile Japanese screens covered with rice paper. They look firm, but one little push and your thumb breaks through. This screen became my metaphor of the fragile frame that gives our lives the illusion of permanence and stability. Sometimes it is pierced through and we discover that there is nothing behind it. My family found not only the "emptiness" behind the screen, but also the intimacy, love, and care from those around us who had, at one time or another, seen the same abyss.

Our daughter eventually recovered. The hole in the screen repaired itself and the world went on. In spite of the pain—or perhaps because of it—our family has never been quite so "on its toes" and alive since then. We saw the world and each other with a new intensity and clarity and we loved each other with a reverence and hilarity I long to recapture. Prayer seems to be one of the appointed means of remembering the experience so that its effects live on.

"Stopping the world" is an exhilarating experience. Just for a moment, we have no choice but to see all our dogmatic and philosophical baggage thrown overboard as we stand ship-wrecked on an unknown island. There we are, naked, stripped of the fig leaves of our prejudices and presuppositions. The believer's world is full of images of this "dying." It is strange how many believers are caught off guard, since some form of "dying in order to live" is at the heart of all the great religions. Yet the really creative and free souls I have encountered all have been shipwrecked at one time or another. They have had their world taken from them, and lived to tell the tale.

"Stopping the world" is another way of talking about the process of "dying to self," which, as we have seen, is central to all the great religious traditions. An old name for it is *mortification*, which certainly sounds forbidding! It suggests, perhaps, strange and masochistic practices that denigrate the body: lice-infested hair shirts, ice-cold water, and premature death. It is easy for us to make fun of the ascetical practices of the past; but our ancestors were trying, in their own way, to live life with both integrity and passion. Our own "ascetical practices," no doubt, will seem amusing to those who come after us: diets, jogging, therapies, and the dedicated if frantic pursuit of power and security. All these require a certain amount of mortifying disciplines.

It is important, however, to understand that the process of mortification, of dying to self (or better, self-simplification), can easily degenerate into a game the ego often plays to keep itself at the center of our attention: the game of self-rejection. To call it a game is not to deny its seriousness and power. The basis of true self-surrender is a proper self-love. Without a regard for the nature and dignity of the self, how can there be a genuine self-offering? Believers begin with the assumption that they have a self to surrender, even if their sense of it is minimal.

The new life promised in the spiritual traditions requires only this minimal sense of self in order to set its healing power to work. Donald Nicholl writes of a man lying desperately ill in hospital. He was frightened, confused, and in despair. His world had stopped.

Nothing of his true self seemed to remain except a tiny particle the size of a grain of mustard seed. Outside that particle all was chaos and darkness. Suddenly he heard a voice from the nearby corridor: "I'm that bloody lonely I could cry." It was the voice of an old miner who was in hospital for the first time in his life . . . Hearing the terror in the old man's voice the desperately ill man . . . from the pit of his own terror, said to himself: "I'll go out and sit by him if it's the last thing I do." And he did. And from that moment his own terror began to lift. . . .In the voice of the old man he had heard the voice of God calling him to wholeness and holiness. You can begin anytime, anywhere, even if you are only a tiny grain of mustard seed lying in a pit of terror.[11]

Our terror reaches out to the terror in others. This reaching out to one another from the inner places of deadness and deadliness is the beginning of new life in us. God comes to us under the guise of Fat Ladies and old men.

The believer is concerned with life. Why, then, all this talk of death and pits of terror? We all have a desire to *be*—indeed, the believer is convinced that this is what God wants for us. The messge is unambiguous: If you want to live life to the full, you must surrender life. What a paradox! The self, which is concerned above all else for its own security and future, soon ceases to be a real self at all. Those who seek to preserve their own lives have already lost them. To move in the direction of self-surrender, however modestly, can be terrifying. It *sounds* deadly. Don Juan says,

. . . you must erase everything around you until nothing can be taken for granted, until nothing is any longer for sure, or real. Your problem now is that you're too real. Your endeavors are too real; your moods are too real. Don't take things for granted. You must begin to erase yourself.[12]

Our world suddenly stops and our old sense of who we are begins to fade. There is a moment of panic; but we wait, and a new way of knowing ourselves and the world begins to appear. This way of knowing does not give us control ana power over things. It is not "useful" knowledge for the purpose of power and manipulation. We are introduced to a way of *un*knowing that is liberating, if frightening at first.

DEATH, OUR COMPANION AND COUNSELOR

Don Juan's sense of self is bound up with his sense of the universe. He is not mesmerized by his own little history, but his heart beats with the rhythm of creation. Like St. Francis, he walks with Sister Death. Don Juan says:

Death is our eternal companion . . . It is always to our left, at an arm's length . . . It has always been watching you. It always will until the day it takes you. . . . How can anyone feel so important when we know that death is stalking us . . . The thing to do when you're impatient . . . is to turn to your left and ask advice from your death. An immense amount of pettiness is dropped if your death makes a gesture to you, or if you catch a glimpse of it, or if you just have the feeling that your companion is there watching you. (pp. 33–34)

There is a startling parallel to this in the life of the seventeenth-century philosopher Blaise Pascal. He was convinced that over his left shoulder there lurked a threatening yet salutary presence. For him it was the threat of the abyss, the possibility of annihilation. When it came to the question of his own soul, Pascal was awed and terrified by the emptiness he encountered in himself and in the vast expanse of infinite space. The story goes that at the end of his life, when he was very ill, he would sometimes be overcome with the sensation that the abyss was about to swallow him up, that he would fall into a great emptiness. It appeared, from time to time, without warning, at his left side. The sensation was so real that he had to cling to a chair to stop himself falling in.

For the believer, this terrible inner absence, while never ceasing to have something awesome about it, is gradually perceived as a gift. Slowly, in the life of faith, the thing that we dread becomes both companion and friend. Prayer, for the believer, is one of the ways in which this companionship is fostered and deepened. The descriptions of the life of the believer are dominated by metaphors of death and resurrection. Our daily life is characterized by a continual process of dying and rising. Death, then, is our constant companion—according to Don Juan, it

is the only advisor we have. Whenever you feel, as you always do, that everything is going wrong and you're about to be annihilated, turn to your death and ask if it is so. Your death will tell you that you're wrong; that nothing really matters outside its touch. Your death will tell you, "I haven't touched you yet." (p. 34)

As we live into the truth of this, our dread is transformed into delight. Sister Death challenges us to live life as fully and as creatively as we can. The willingness to live with the knowledge of our inevitable death enables us to face, more and more, both the freedom and responsibility that life offers. This willingness to walk with Sister Death is the first sign of the believer's maturity.

Death allows no room for sham or pretense. What would be the point? As Don Juan reminds Castaneda: "In a world where death is the hunter . . . there is no time for regrets or doubts. There is only time for decisions" (p. 40). We should note how the metaphor shifts and changes with regard to our death. She is our sister and companion. Death is our counselor, advisor, and friend. Death is also a hunter. We are both hunters and hunted. The dread remains as the sense of companionship grows.

How are we to commend this way of believing? Who would wish to meet death in the desert or travel to beyond the North Wind? This way of believing has "a take it or leave it" quality about it. It commends itself simply and directly to those who find it to be true. It makes no attempt to look alluring or attractive. That is why this way of believing, in spite of the fact that it is fundamental to all the great religious traditions, has had so few adherents. Perhaps the times are such that many more people will find themselves on this path because the ordinary pablum of popular religion simply will not do anymore. Do not the times demand men and women who will be able, by God's grace, to stand on their own two feet and not whine or despair when the familiar structures that provide the secure framework of everyday existence begin to collapse? More and more people must recover this way of believing if we are to be able to stand the coming realities.

Thomas Merton once spoke of his friend, a Tibetan lama who had to leave Tibet or be killed by the Chinese communists. He sent a message to a fellow monk, an abbot, asking, "What shall we do?" The abbot sent back the austere message: "From here on, brother, everybody stands on his own feet." Merton comments on this:

The time for relying on structures has disappeared. They are good and they should help us and we should do the best we can with them. But they may be taken away, and if everything is taken away, what do you do next?

The Zen people have a saying . . . "Where do you go from the top of a thirty foot pole?" . . . Which is where we all now sit.[13]

To "stopping the world" and "dying to self," we can add one more phrase: We sit on the top of a thirty-foot pole. To sit there and ask ourselves the question "What do we do now?" is one way of stopping the world. The funny thing is that we are able to make ourselves at home even at the top of a thirty-foot pole and pretend that we are not really up there. In the same way, we pretend that we are not really going to die, that there is no companion standing just over our left shoulder.

THE HUNT IN THE DESERT

A powerful incident in *Journey to Ixtlan* brought Carlos Castaneda face to face with his own death. Here the hunter was confronted by the fact that he too was being hunted. The incident started off easily enough. Don Juan insisted that he stalk, catch, kill, skin, roast and eat a rabbit. This was no ordeal for Castaneda, since he had been a hunter for many years and was used to killing animals for sport and for food. The task was to accomplish all this before twilight.

Castaneda started off with enthusiasm. The exercise was going to be easy, and he had no difficulty in catching a male rabbit in a trap. But things began to fall apart when Don Juan gave the command, "Now kill it." Castaneda put his hand into the trap and grasped the rabbit by the ears. Then the terror suddenly seized him. He dropped the rabbit back in the trap and refused to kill it. Don Juan turned his ferocious eyes on Castaneda, and with all the force of his authority repeated the command, "Kill it!" It was the rabbit's time to die. This was the moment. Still Castaneda refused. This time Don Juan yelled at him. The rabbit had to die. Castaneda goes on:

A series of confusing thoughts and feelings overtook me, as if the feelings had been out there waiting for me. I felt with agonizing clarity the rabbit's tragedy, to have fallen into my trap. In a matter of seconds my mind swept across the most crucial moments of my life, the many times I had been the rabbit myself.

I looked at it, and it looked at me. The rabbit had backed up against the side of the cage . . . We exchanged a somber glance, and that glance, which I fancied to be of silent despair, cemented a complete identification on my part.

"The hell with it," I said loudly. "I won't kill anything. That rabbit goes free."

Castaneda panicked. He tried to grab the rabbit by the ears to set the creature free. By this time the rabbit was so terrified that it moved out of his reach. Castaneda became desperate, and in frustration tried to break the trap. He kicked as hard as he could. At all costs that rabbit was to run free again. The cage would not break. So with a supreme effort he brought his right foot down on the corner of the cage with tremendous force. The wood broke, and he grabbed the rabbit with relief. But it remained motionless in his hand. It was dead. Don Juan stared at Castaneda. The *brujo* put his hand on his pupil's head and whispered in his ear. He had not completed his task. The rabbit had still to be skinned, roasted, and eaten. Castaneda felt sick to his stomach.

He very patiently talked to me as if he were talking to a child. He said that the powers that guided men or animals had led that particular rabbit to me, in the same way they will lead me to my own death. He said the rabbit's death had been a gift for me in exactly the same way my own death will be a gift for something or someone else.

I was dizzy. The simple events of that day had crushed me. I tried to think that it was only a rabbit; I could not, however, shake off the uncanny identification I had with it.

Don Juan said that I needed to eat some of its meat, if only a morsel, in order to validate my finding.

"I can't do that," I protested meekly.

"We are dregs in the hands of those forces," he snapped at me. "So stop your self-importance and use this gift properly."

I picked up the rabbit. It was warm.

Don Juan leaned over and whispered in my ear, "Your trap was his last battle on earth. I told you, he had no more time to roam in this marvelous desert."[14]

Several points can be made about this telling incident, not least that the confrontation with death took place in the desert. The turning point was Castaneda's terrifying identification with the rabbit. He was the rabbit. The rabbit's tragedy was his own, and yet the rabbit's death was a gift not to be wasted, just as his death would be a gift to someone else. Acceptance of this gift depended on Castaneda's ability to set aside the sense of his own importance. The receiving of such gifts requires some kind of dying to self. As we have seen, the feeling of dread does not disappear when such gifts are accepted.

The mystery of this kind of gift is found at the heart of the Gospel. Our death is a gift from God. The New Testament puts it this way: "You have died and your life is his with Christ in God" (Col. 3:3). That is, I am already dead—the "I" I cling to so desperately. My sense of who I am is often illusory and it is the illusion to which I cling. Who I really am is largely hidden from me.

I, of course, only half believe this. I want to hold something in reserve. I am, in this respect, only an occasional believer. It is not that I am cavalier or casual in my believing. Rather, I can only bear a little of it at a time. The Good News to which I cling is based on the conviction that I might not know who I am, but God does; and this enables me to live in hope. I find it hard to "relax and be myself" because I do not always know who I am. I sometimes envy the person whose identity has hard and clear edges.

I am convinced, however, that something positive begins to happen within me when I do look death, *my* death, straight in the eye. When I say "Yes" to it, however haltingly, something new and fresh stirs in my soul. To paraphrase Karl Rahner:

Death puts my whole existence into question without being able to answer the question. I have to surrender to the uncertainty of death, and this surrender can be simply an act of despair in the ultimate futility of being. On the other hand, my act of surrender can prepare me for the possibility that the answer may come from a totally unexpected quarter. It is, then, not a surrender to despair, but to the Unknown. Finally, my surrender can be an act of faith that a radical rescue is at hand. I am caught in all three responses; and to be thus caught is, in some sense, to be a participant in a great passion (the believer in me would call it *the* Passion). I want to be a believer with both passion and intelligence and my longing always brings me into a desert place—a place of emptiness and death. And it is there that I begin to learn how to love.

A character in Iris Murdoch's *The Nice and Good* is trapped in a cave that is filling up with water at high tide.

He thought, if I ever get out of here I will be no-man's judge. Nothing is worth doing except to kill the little rat, not to judge, not to be superior, not to exercise power, not to seek, seek, seek. To love and to reconcile and to forgive, only this matters. All power is sin and all law is frailty. Love is the only justice. Forgiveness, reconciliation, not law.[15]

I want to kill the little rat and learn to love, to reconcile, and forgive. The man in the cave may not have had the purest of motives, but a process of healing was begun in him. He began to live from a new place in himself. I want to do that too. But before I can begin, a process of purification is necessary. I would dearly love to avoid the desert stage. But I get into a terrible mess when I try to bypass it. I fail to notice angels who might bring me a saving word. The desert is the place of the encounter with death. It is also the place where we know ourselves to be truly free. We do not go into the desert in order to wall up our heart. We go there in order to give it away, to God and to the world.[16]

> . . . the garden is the only place there is,
> but you will not find it

Until you have looked for it everywhere
and found nowhere that is not a desert.[17]

To find the garden, to give one's heart away, to be free, one must enter the desert, stop the world, face death. Now the tears begin to flow. Yet these, it is promised, are also capable of being transformed into gifts.

II. ENTERING THE EMPTINESS

4. The Gift of Tears

Crying is a natural phenomenon and the withholding of tears appears
to be dangerous to health.[1]

NEW YORK TIMES

He who is aware of his sins is greater than one who can raise the
dead. Whoever can weep over himself for one hour is greater than
the one who is able to teach the whole world; whoever recognizes the
depth of his own frailty is greater than the one who sees visions of
angels.[2]

ISAAC OF NINIVE

The desert tradition claims a great deal for the power of
tears. Tears are agents of resurrection and transformation; they
can raise the dead. Such tears are surely a gift.

It may be difficult for us to grasp the association between
weeping and the bursting forth of new life. Something positive
is released when tears flow. The common expression "to have a
good cry" comes close to what is meant by the "gift of tears";
at least it is a way of beginning to understand their liberating
and cathartic effect.

The "gift of tears," however, is concerned with something
much more radical, threatening, and life-bearing than the occasional and necessary release from tension that "having a good
cry" affords. The tears of which the desert bears witness are
not tears of rage, self-pity, or frustration. They are a gift, and
their fruit is always joy.

TEARS AND OUR FRAGILITY

The therapeutic value of tears is well documented; but are
there not human situations out of reach of their healing effect?
What of extreme human misery? Surely it cannot be conveni-
ently washed away by tears? Sooner or later, believers and unbelievers alike have to face the issues of misfortune, pain, and
death; and these issues lie at the heart of religion. The various
religious traditions respond to the issue of pain, for example,

in different ways. Pain is an illusion; pain is punishment; pain is reformative. There is no doubt that suffering is a problem for the believer. Some of us are tempted to side-step the issue by making our religion one which is presided over by a kind of Sanctified Computer, which automatically answers difficult questions. This is to surrender our ability and obligation to think.

The tradition of "the gift of tears" offers no help with regard to the meaning of pain and misfortune. It gives no answers. Instead, it calls us to an attentive obedience and points to a way through the desert into what might be called "the pain of God." Tears flow when the real source of our life is uncovered, when the mask of pretense is dropped, when our strategies of self-deception are abandoned. Trials and humiliations are necessary only insofar as they are the means by which our true life is uncovered.

To come to this place where one is truly alive, one must hit rock-bottom. There must be a breakthrough to the place of deepest helplessness. "Then at last," writes André Louf, "a beginning can be made."

Tears come when we learn to live more and more out of our deepest longings, our needs, our troubles. These must all surface and be given their rightful place. For in them we find our real human life in all its depths. And when one begins with these unacceptable feelings and desires, which have to be submitted for examination, we must look closely at, and learn to live with, this amazing degree of weakness of ours.[3]

Learning to live with this amazing degree of weakness is an essential element of the way of believing that we are exploring. It means learning to live gracefully with our own extreme psychic frailty. Perhaps this is the point where the believer and the unbeliever are forced to part company: not over a piece of dogma, but over the experience of grace. The believer knows that grace enters into our experience precisely at the point where we are wounded, where our longings are deepest and most inarticulate.[4] The believer is brought to the end of his or her rope, placed *in extremis*, forced to wait in weakness. The believer weeps. This way of believing is shocking. It cuts more deeply, and there is a great deal more to it than just having a good cry.

THE SHOCK OF CHRISTIANITY PIERCES THE HEART

Christianity is a shocking religion, although many of its adherents have managed to protect themselves from its terrible impact. Tears, an awareness of one's psychic fragility, and a deep sense of peace and joy are not the most obvious marks of believers today. Yet the shock of Christianity remains: the shock of its materialism and its particularity; the shock of its calling us to a messy and untidy intimacy. It claims that the flesh matters. It insists that history (the particularity of time and place) matters. Above all it claims that, in the end, nothing else but love matters.

Much of the discipline of the desert is concerned with keeping the shock and promise of love alive. Without the occasional abrasive brush with the unexpected, human life soon becomes a mere matter of routine; and, before we know where we are, a casual indifference and even brutality takes over and we begin to die inside. The shock breaks open the deadly "everydayness" that ensnares us and brings something awesome and terrifying to our reluctant attention: the believer's name for that "something" is God. God ceases to be a subject for philosophical debate, still less the object of our part-time and casual allegiance. This God is no hobby. God is felt in places too deep for words; in depths beyond ideas and concepts.[5] God is felt in pain, sorrow, and contradiction. This, in itself, comes as a shock, since we tend to make religion only of our better moments. Our worst moments tend to be repressed and denied. When that happens, we begin to lie to ourselves; and when we lie, the very fabric of life begins to fall apart.

One of the ways in which the shock of Christ is kept alive is by means of what the desert tradition of the East calls *penthos*. In the West it is called compunction, and has to do with a kind of "puncturing" of the heart. *Penthos* (compunction) is the word for that which pierces us to the heart, cuts us to the quick, raises us from the "dead." Penthos administers the shock that is necessary for us to be who we really are. From a psychological point of view, tears show up the idealistic, perfectionist, and neurotic self for what it really is: a false and fraudulent self—

an imposter. *Penthos* frees the soul from the lying and the pretense that tend to dominate us when we are frightened, anxious, or insecure. It is also known as the gift of tears. In the East, the sacrament of confession is sometimes called "the Mystery of the Second Baptism." The truly penitent is "baptized" again in his or her own tears, which represent the tears of truth and insight breaking in and flooding the soul with new life.

Talk of tears, penitence, and confession is hard to take nowadays. Such things are considered by some to be both unfashionable and unhealthy. In fact, they are neither. The gift of tears is concerned with living in and with the truth and with the new life that the truth always brings. The tears are like the breaking of waters of the womb before the birth of a child.

Tears are cleansing. They wash away the grime of our misperceptions (both willful and involuntary) and help us to see with a clear eye. But we receive more than clarity with this gift. The will is also liberated for action. Seeing without the possibility of transformation would be hell. The two (clarity of vision and freedom of action) are brought together in the well-known dictum, "Purity of heart is to will one thing." When we can see purely we can also act freely. "Purity of heart" begins to happen when a person is willing to be pierced through with the arrows of compunction.

In the desert tradition, therefore, the gift of tears has something to do with both life and joy for the sake of the restructuring of our identity, for the re-ordering of our self-understanding. The gift ushers in a radical and sometimes painful transformation. The tears lead to greater self-knowledge. They help clarify choices, and in this way restore in us the life of the will. The desert believer would go on to claim that tears also contribute to the building up of the Kingdom of God, which is a kingdom of both knowledge and love. This, of course, is flowery language about something that requires courage, discipline, and faith. The believer is one who finds something of genuine substance under the sometimes exotic and exaggerated language of religion.

OUR STRUGGLE FOR AIR: LEARNING BY SUFFERING

As we saw in the last chapter, "stopping the world" is an important first step in breaking down our resistance to the truth. So it is in the tradition of "the gift of tears." Our first job, as we have seen, is to wake up! Indeed, it is a commonplace of all the great religions to see this as the first step. The goal for many of them is "enlightenment," and initiates have to ache for the light with every fiber of their beings.

The story is told of a young pupil who yearned for enlightenment and went to a wise man for advice and counsel. The guru, without a word, led the disciple to the river and held the young man's head under the water. When the pupil began to struggle for air, the old man held his head under with all the strength he could muster. At last the younger man, with a tremendous surge of energy, broke away from the old man's grip and came up out of the water with an enormous and hungry gasp. The old man looked at him and said: "Don't come to me to ask about enlightenment until you want it as much as you wanted that lungful of air." Enlightenment is not a mere intellectual affair. It is a matter of life and death.

Christian believers have tended to be nervous about and suspicious of the waking-up process because it is thought that Christianity has nothing to do with enlightenment, but only with salvation. The distinction is an unfortunate one. Enlightenment, without some truly saving aspect to it, is little more than an intellectual exercise. Salvation without the inner transforming power of self-knowledge is little short of magic.

To some, englightenment sounds too much like a self-centered process of inner transformation without any reference to outside help. Yet this is not a necessary inference. There is no way to avoid the fact that religion (including the Christian religion) is about knowledge of some kind. All religions lay claim to the truth, even to *the* Truth. They want to share their particular *gnosis*, or knowledge, with others. The issue is what kind of *gnosis*. The danger with *gnosis* (that is, any specialized and esoteric form of knowledge) is that it easily degenerates into technique, into a religious or pseudo-scientific technology by which we are "saved." It becomes a form of idolatry. Those who are unwilling to stop the world, or who wish to remain in a stupor of half-sleep, often get hold of sacred ideas and think that they are techniques for getting what they want. Religion then becomes just another project of the ego. I can read a little of St. John of the Cross or a paperback on Zen Buddhism and then suck what I have read into my own little storehouse of information in order to serve my own ends: to feel safe, to feel superior, to feel enlightened, even to feel saved.[6]

In this tradition, then, believing is closely related to being and to our refusal to be. Tears flow when we begin to realize just how deep that terrible refusal goes. Believing is never simply a matter of assent to a doctrine. In fact, it is not primarily that. Harry Williams, who knows first hand what it means to be a theologian/believer and the victim of a nervous breakdown (and hence the grateful recipient of the grace of psychoanalysis) puts the issue of believing and being this way:

A doctrine, to be fully appropriated, had to be knit to my personal identity. I saw that I could not truly say "I believe" unless it was another way of saying "I am." And the "I" here was the total me, which included the unconscious self as well as the conscious.

It is not insignificant that it took a breakdown and fourteen years of psychoanalysis to bring Williams to that conclusion. To bring believing and being together can be a painful and tearful process.

It is no wonder that many religious people are deeply angry and resentful. To be sure, their true feelings are often covered by a veneer of "oughts," "shoulds," and "good manners." Resentment is a natural response to unrealistic and unreasonable demands made on people, as if they were finished and complete entities. Harry Williams comments: "Why do people imagine that in order to have God you must also have all this kind of nonsense? It is because . . . religion is to a large extent what people do with their lunacy: their phobias, their will to power, their sexual frustrations."[7]

It is no use knowing certain apparently unacceptable things about ourselves (those neurotic tendencies that we examined earlier) unless there is a way of being able to bear this knowledge. Sometimes we can know too much for our own good. Knowledge without love can lead to despair. We suddenly see something about ourselves, and the sight of it is unbearable. For example, a friend dies unexpectedly, and we see, with an awful clarity, a series of lost opportunities. They haunt us like Marley's ghost, showing up the Scrooge within us for what he really is. Such a vision is often too much for us. It is intolerable for two reasons. The first is that we are not ready for it. The stripping away of a mask can be a terrible thing. The second reason is that no matter how much truth we have seen about ourselves, it is never the whole truth. A despairing view of ourselves, while it contains an element of truth, is at bottom a cruel lie.

From the believer's point of view, all our knowing has to be set in the context of grace and hope. Our knowledge is never full and final, and we may thank God for that. Sometimes the gift of tears will help us acknowledge the simple and graceful fact that all our knowing is partial and incomplete. A psychiatrist wrote to Harry Williams: "There is a young clergyman preaching at the church I go to in London who knows much more than he can take. Sooner or later he will break down."[8] He will have to learn (as the common expression goes) the hard way. It's an ancient principle: learning by suffering.

Knowing more than we can take: Isn't that the source of a lot of the pain, anger, and frustration in the hearts of many of us today—believers and unbelievers? Ironically, we add to our pain and confusion precisely by our good intentions. We want to love God. We want to love the Good. But we want this without the necessary foundation of self-knowledge. We demand a great deal of ourselves without realizing how deeply resistant we are to our developing "a pure and clean heart." We lack both psychological knowledge and simple compassion. As Jacob Needleman points out, it is useless to command people to love and know God or themselves. If love and knowledge are commanded, they can only be drawn out of us in the context of a method of how human beings grow and develop. In other words, such things cannot be commanded without a sound grasp of a religious psychology. Needleman comments: "How much of the religious hypocrisy and unnecessary suffering of this world [is] rooted in the failure to see this point."[9]

TEARS AND SELF-SIMPLIFICATION: THE BIRTH OF THE SOUL

It is necessary to cultivate a simpler (not necessarily easier) way of living with ourselves based on an honest attentiveness to what is there, and on a sound knowledge of what makes us tick. The process of self-simplification can make us very uncomfortable. The practice of simple attention will eventually bring us to the verge of tears. What do we do at those moments of anxiety, hurt, or confrontation, when tears are near the surface? We seek to neutralize this form of radical self-questioning by backing off and explaining it away. Maybe it was something we ate. We're over-tired. Another way of escape is by means of the device of an emotional outburst. Get them before they get you! Perhaps the most favored ploy of all is the escape into frenetic activity: busyness is a sure, if temporary, cure for the inevitable pain that comes to us when we're attentive.

Simple attentiveness puts an enormous question mark beside everything, and this question mark makes us anxious and brings us close to tears. Needleman rightly says that the task of the believer is to contain the energy of the Question within oneself. The holding in of the energy in simple attention gives birth to something new. The soul comes into being. The desert fathers would say this tearful containing of the energy that this radical questioning occasions is the agent of resurrection. The trouble is that this new resurrection of life does not happen inside us with any kind of consistency. In fact, we simply do not "happen" all the time. Tears flow at those moments when we do, Needleman writes:

—in short, the soul is not a fixed entity . . . it is a movement that begins whenever man experiences the psychological pain of contradiction . . . But almost always, almost without any exceptions whatsoever, this new energy is immediately dispersed and comes to nothing. A hundred, a thousand times a day, perhaps, the "soul is aborted." (p. 170)

Is it conceivable that the psychological pain of contradiction, when acknowledged, can be the source of new life in us? This is the claim of the two traditions that help me go on believing with all the passion and intelligence I can muster. But I need help. We need to help each other. Without help I get trapped inside myself, and the pain of contradiction is translated as despair because I don't know how to interpret what is happening to me.

I find it hard to contain within myself the frequent explosions in my psyche. Yet, when I am attentive to them, I catch a glimpse of what believers call "new life in Christ." Krishnamurti once observed that there is a wholeness "that comes about from precisely observing, without altering, the fragmentation of our nature" (p. 51). My struggle "to pull myself together," to harmonize the bits and pieces I call "me," is doomed to failure. Strangely, I have to try simply in order to demonstrate to my unbelieving psyche that I cannot, after all, do it by my own will. Tears of frustration, anger, and rage give way to tears of relief, acceptance, and joy. Many unbelievers have been surprised by belief when they have been brought to the end of their rope.

When do we feel most alive? Isn't it during either vivid or painful moments? When I encounter death, disappointment, or profound contradiction, I also experience a surging sense of "presence." I am able to say "I am" in a new way. I begin to *be*. I back off, usually very quickly. When I am in this middle state between being able to say "I am" in a new way and yet wanting to run away from it, I am pulled in two directions. On the one side is what one might call a "higher" self; on the other the so-called "lower." A psychoanalyst might describe this as a conflict between my idealized or neurotic self and my real self. However we may describe this state of in-betweenness, "it is always experienced at first as painful and unpleasant" (p. 172).

When do tears come for the attentive believer? They begin to flow at the moment when we see the contradiction between what we hope for and what we actually are; when we see the deep gulf between the Love that calls us and our response to it. Father Sylvan (Jacob Needleman's intriguing correspondent) writes: "You will not find Christ by going to 'Christ,' but only through seeing, clearly and with precision, how you crucify Him. Only then will *you* appear" (p. 207).

This is hard both to understand and accept, but Father Sylvan describes a deep fissure in the heart of the believer. The sense of dislocation is common to all those who believe and who are willing to wait and to look. It is the pain I experience in that middle state where I am neither a believer nor an unbeliever. There's a sort of no-man's-land in me with which I am unfamiliar, and yet which is very much my own. It is the place familiar to all of us where we know ourselves and yet are strangers to ourselves. It is here that we experience what Needleman calls "a sort of suffering" (p. 65).

What, then, is this "sort of suffering"? It surely is not suffering for its own sake, as if pain in itself were the God-given means for the formation of character. That would be a barely disguised form of sadomasochism. No. This "sort of suffering" comes when we are caught between the "now" and the "not yet" of our identity. This experience of being stretched out goes a long way to provide us with an understanding of the gift of tears. But this gift is much more than the experience of being strung out between past, present, and future. Tears are the result of waiting in the desert and being pierced to the heart and cut to the quick, with the result that we are left with a deep sense of joy.

Flannery O'Connor, without mentioning the gift of tears specifically, describes its effects on a Mr. Head in her short story "The Artificial Nigger." In this case, the gift comes as an action of mercy that overcomes Mr. Head in a deep experience of horror and agony. He realized that this agony was all that he had to offer to his Maker,

and he suddenly burned with shame that he had so little to take with him. He stood appalled, judging himself with the thoroughness of God, while the action of mercy covered his pride like a flame and consumed it. He never thought of himself as a great sinner before but he saw now his true depravity had been hidden from him lest it cause him to despair. He realized he was forgiven for sins from the beginning of time, when he conceived in his heart the sin of Adam, until the present . . . He saw that no sin was too monstrous for him to claim as his own, and since God loved in proportion as He forgave, he felt already that instant to enter Paradise.[10]

Imagine what it would be like to judge yourself with the thoroughness of God and then to discover that you are known, accepted, and forgiven! Flannery O'Connor, in story form, describes the double action of the gift of tears. I am able to see in such a way that I not only judge myself with the judgment of God, but I am given the grace to love myself with the love of God. My tears, then, are the tears of joy as well as of sorrow.

TEARS: THE SIGN OF JOY AND THE HUNGER OF BEING HUMAN

C. S. Lewis, in *Surprised by Joy*, bears witness to the sort of suffering that is so joyful that it hurts. He knew the gift of tears firsthand. It came to him as a shock, and he somehow wanted to keep the shock alive in him. Lewis tells of an incident in his childhood where he caught a glimpse of joy while reading Beatrix Potter's *Squirrel Nutkin*:

. . . it administered the shock. It was trouble. It troubled me with what I can only describe as the Idea of Autumn. It sounds fantastic to say that one can be enamoured of a season, but that is something like what happened; and the experience was one of intense desire. And one went back to the book, not to gratify the desire (that was impossible—how can one *possess* Autumn?) but to reawaken it. And in this experience . . . there was the . . . sense of surprise, and the . . . sense of incalculable importance. It was something quite different from ordinary life, and even from ordinary pleasure.

Lewis defines joy in a strange way in the light of this experience. It is "an unsatisfied desire which is itself more desirable than any other satisfaction. I call it joy." What I find disturbing is my fear of this joy, my terror at the thought of being possessed by real desire. That is why I would often prefer to make do with second best. Surely my desire would consume me?[11]

Joy is "an unsatisfied desire"; "a particular kind of unhappiness or grief" about which there is no hint of sickness or masochism. It is the joyful agony of learning to love without possession, manipulation, and control. I can possess an autumn day or a beautiful view of fruit trees in blossom no more than I can possess my wife or my children. Learning to love without possession and finding that one is loved without conditions is what it is to receive the gift of tears and to be surprised by joy. This comes as a shock, and believers want to keep this shock alive. They want to allow the shock of Christ (who is the sign and bearer of this way of loving) to penetrate into the deepest self.

Rowan Williams, in *The Truce of God*, writes of the threat of nuclear war and of the believer's obligation to be a peacemaker. He deals with our longings and desires and shows that inner transformation contributes to the peace of the world. My willingness to struggle with myself contributes to the well-being of the commonwealth. The desire for security and the anxiety over safety at all costs makes war more and more a possibility and springs from our "impure hearts" and double minds. Williams writes:

The "impure heart" is a heart which never wants anything enough to be intolerant of substitutes. Beneath its readiness to make do with less than reality is the fear of real desire. For real desire means the candid acknowledgment that I am incomplete and need something in order to be real myself. Impure desire, on the other hand, assumes that *I* am solid and important: I take things to myself as my fancies suggest, as much as I want of this or that, so as to keep myself solid and steady. I *consume* things—to stop myself being consumed by real desire, which shows me my lack of solidity, my need to find and nourish my identity in and with others.

Joy is related to our deepest desires, where we are at our weakest and most vulnerable. It means that we have to learn to live with the fact that we are not entirely at home with ourselves, and that finding our way home is the most important thing we have to do. Rowan Williams continues:

Pure desire is desire that longs to grow endlessly in knowledge of and rootedness in reality and truth. Impure desire desires to stop *having* to desire, to stop needing; it asks for a state where, finally, the ego can relax into self-sufficiency and does not have to go stuffing bits and pieces of the world into itself in order to survive. Real desire can live with an unlimited horizon—which religious people call God—while unreal desire stumbles from moment to moment trying to gratify an immediate hunger, without accepting that "hunger" is part of being human and so cannot be dealt with or understood by an endless succession of leakplugging operations.[12]

The hard lesson to learn about joy is that we have to choose over and over again not to grasp at the world (the people and the things in it) and try to make them our own. Joy is not to be had in possession; and of all the choices that we have to make, there is none harder than having to give up something good for the sake of something better. Giving up a present good for the promise of a greater requires faith and a willingness to risk. It is suffering of a sort. All the way along we are faced with the choice of living with the shock or of suppressing it.

It is as if God has placed time-bombs inside us, programmed to go off at certain intervals in order to make a gaping hole in us so that we can continue to be open to life. He is always creating new space in us by means of these explosions. We are continually being given the space to choose either "heaven" or "hell," to act in such a way that we are either more and more curved in on ourselves or more and more turned towards God. As W. H. Auden puts it: "Man chooses either life or death, but he chooses; everything he does, from going to the toilet to mathematical speculation, is an act of religious worship, either of God or himself."[13]

TEARS: FOR THE MENDING OF CREATION

Suffering and joy are bound together in our struggle to choose life and not death. The gift of tears comes to our rescue when we despair of ever seeing clearly, when we want to give up the struggle to achieve "purity of heart" and be capable of a truly free act. As we have seen, all our desiring and striving eventually brings us to the end of our rope. Only to struggle to no avail would bring us to despair. We cannot do what is demanded of us without help. The last word for believers is not their own failed efforts, but the free, spontaneous, and explosive love of God forever making new space in them. This affirming love allows the fearful self to let go of its usual and habitual defensiveness. The Christian tradition calls this explosion of love the Kingdom or the Reign of God. The Kingdom of God is concerned with the restoration of lost harmonies, with the healing of fractured integrities, with the creation of new spaces within the soul. One way of understanding the Kingdom of God is to think of it as a code word for "mending the creation" and for enlarging the space in which it can flourish.[14]

In order to work on the mending of creation, the Kingdom of God breaks open communities and societies as well as individuals. The community also lives under the judgment and mercy of God. *Penthos* or compunction is the way believers accept both the judgment and the mercy simultaneously. The gift of tears is a sign of the mending of creation. We and the world are on the mend when we wake up to our deep desire and longing for God. We wake up to the fact that God reigns. We catch a glimpse of our thoughtlessness and banality. The Kingdom breaks down the protective walls we have built against reality and show us that if we and the world are to be mended then all things, by virtue of their very existence, are to be attended to. Tears, whether they be drops of water flowing down the cheeks or a silent inner response to a painful confrontation, are inevitable.

As we have seen, from the point of view of the desert tradition, this mending of the world involves a commitment to self-knowledge so that we can see ourselves, others, and our world as accurately as possible. For the early believers this meant intense inner struggle. In order for me to have an accurate sense of who I am, I must also have a sense of limits and order in my life. Life without borders, with no reason *why* I should do one thing rather than another is, in the end, destructive. A proper sense of limitation is also a sign of the healing power of the Kingdom. To be truly free we have to be accountable, to be able to answer for ourselves and our actions. A world that has no place for us to lay our burden of guilt (the real not the neurotic kind), and which allows no possibility of our expressing gratitude and joy, is a deeply broken one. It is a world over which one would spontaneously weep.

"Blessed are those who weep" (Matt. 5:4). Happy are they who have been given the gift of tears. Real unhappiness is for those with dry eyes and a cold heart; and "*Metanoia*, or repentance, is that moment when the truth about ourselves and God strikes us, pierces the heart, and makes new life possible."[15] *Penthos* is the "moment of truth" that tells us not only who we are, but who God is. In a famous scene from T. S. Eliot's *The*

Cocktail Party, Celia's conversion begins with a painful insight (the believer would call it a sense of sin):

> "It's not the feeling of anything I've ever *done*,
> Which I might get away from, or of anything in me
> I could get rid of—but of emptiness, of failure
> Towards someone, or something, outside of myself;
> And I feel I must . . . *atone*—is that the word?"[16]

"Atone" is the word, if the world is to be mended. Weeping is an essential beginning to this atoning work because, without tears, the ego might run off in a frenzy of atoning zeal and harm itself and others in the process. Attempts to do some atoning on our own can do great damage by fostering attitudes of self-righteous rigorism. The gift of tears will have nothing to do with either abject fear or compulsive behavior. But it does bring with it discomfort and pain; not least the pain of our trying to avoid any direct experience of reality.

Penthos (from the same root as *pathos*, suffering) is often translated as mourning. Its direct opposite is *accidie*, a lazy sullenness that often masquerades as sorrow, but actually dries up the source of tears. The fruit of true *penthos*, as we have seen, is joy and gratitude. The fruit of *accidie* is self-centered morbidity. It hardens the heart, and this hardness must be softened by tears. Evagrius Ponticus, one of the early desert believers, wrote: "First pray for the gift of tears, to soften by compunction the inherent hardness of your soul."[17]

TEARS SOFTEN THE SOUL, CLEAR THE MIND, AND OPEN THE HEART

Weeping, then, has a triple function. It softens the hardened and dried-out soul, making it receptive and alive. It clears the mind. It opens the heart. Tears soften, clarify, and open. We weep all the more when we see what and who we are in the light of what we are called to be. We are not mourning, according to St. John Chrysostom, "for a wife or a child but for a soul and not for another's soul but our own." Why do we weep? To catch a glimpse of the divine loveliness, and in that light to catch sight of our own. Who would not weep, writes St. Ephrem, that

such a lovely image of his goodness should be lost? . . . God is distressed because of the image which has been lost to him. A soul is far dearer to him than the rest of his creation. Through sin it becomes dead, and you, sinner, think nothing of this! You should grieve for the sake of the God who grieves for you. Your soul is dead through vice; shed tears and raise it up again![18]

The key phrase here is, "You should grieve for the sake of the God who grieves for you." This says something startling about the kind of God to whom the believer owes allegiance: a God who grieves, who weeps, who suffers. This presupposes an intimacy between God and the soul. This theme has been taken up by Jürgen Moltmann in *The Trinity and the Kingdom*. He suggests that we reflect not only on our experience of God, but also on God's experience of us.[19] According to this long tradition, of which Moltmann is a contemporary exponent, God "experiences" suffering and sorrow. God too is in mourning. When the believer begins to see just how much he or she is loved (so loved, in fact, that God is willing to weep and to "die" for it), the tears flow.

For the desert believers, these tears are capable of raising the penitent from his deadness and deadliness. They are tears of a kind of baptism, and, therefore, agents of resurrection. Tears act as a medicine that restores the disfigured soul to its true likeness. St. Ephrem writes:

Over a dead body you weep, but over a soul dead and separated from God you do not weep! Tears falling on a corpse cannot restore it, but if they fall on a soul they will bring it back to life . . . Give God weeping, and increase the tears in your eyes; through your tears and his goodness the soul which has been dead will be restored. Behold, Mercy waits for your eyes to shed tears, to purify and renew the image of the disfigured soul.[20]

This may be very different language from that of psychoanalysis, but it is not far from its heart. Both traditions are concerned with the transformation of the soul. Indeed, one could argue that psychoanalysis more closely embodies the desert tradition than does current church practice. Ironically, the development of the practice of "going to confession" by using a formalized rite has contributed to the dying out of genuine compunction. Tears cannot be forced. They must spring up naturally from a person who has been brought to a heart-piercing place of new insight.

When it comes to tears, we are all in the same boat. There is no special place for the clever or even the holy and the good. Weeping is for everyone. This is hard for the modern consciousness to understand and accept. Nevertheless, the word from the tradition is consistently and uncomprisingly: "Weep! Truly there is no other way than this."[21]

It is hard to imagine, in these days of self-serving and self-congratulatory politics, a national leader calling the people to repentance. Imagine a president or prime minister saying to the nation, "Weep! There is no other way." I can imagine this happening in a comedy or in a movie concerned with the deliberate manipulation of religion for political ends, but it's hard to see it in real life.

Weeping is for everyone. We live in a democracy of tears. They put us in a place of openness and make us realize that there is no place of safety, no place to hide. The battle for the human heart goes on right up to the end—and the tears keep us open, free, and alive.

A story is told of a holy man who was dying. Satan appeared before him and, looking abject, said, "At last, you have beaten me." The old man, near death but still alert, replied, "Not yet!"[22] He had a quality of quiet and poised presence that accompanies the gift of tears. It is no wonder that we resist the offer of the gift. To accept it means being radically attentive. Our temptation is to drift. Before we know it, we have slipped into either thoughtless pleasure-seeking or self-centered melancholy. The latter is the most likely because the human heart gravitates towards those points that threaten its sense of well-being and self-esteem. There is a telling incident in Robertson Davies's *The Rebel Angels* that humorously illustrates this slide towards disappointment. A university professor has just heard that his students call him "Fatso":

Had I been deceiving myself? Did my students speak of me as Fatso?

But then, if the Fairy Carabosse had appeared at my christening with her spiteful gift of adiposity, there had been other and better-natured fairies who had made me intelligent and energetic. But because human nature inclines towards dissatisfaction, it was the fat that rankled.[23]

Our happiness revolves again and again around the issue of satisfying our desires. We are unhappy when our desires are not met and when, in consequence, we try to make do with less and less. We long, as we have seen, for a place where the ego can relax into self-sufficiency. The striving to get to such a place is one of the causes for a person's sense of hopelessness. Hell is the self-suffering itself, forever. Tears are the means by which we have the chance to *see* things differently and be rescued from whatever little hell we may have chosen for ourselves.

I must confess that I am tempted to try to make the gift of tears sound more cheerful! The line between this kind of weeping and downright melancholy is very fine. A lot of believers go in for an enforced kind of jolliness because they have been told that this is a sure sign of genuine faith. I am caught, therefore, between the scylla of melancholy and the charybdis of jolliness. Is it possible to find a way through? Is it possible to be, as the tradition demands, single-minded in such a way that we do not come across as rigorous or moralistic? Have we not come full circle and entered even more deeply into the believer's neurosis by clobbering ourselves with a slightly more subtle form of perfectionism?

Some writers in the tradition went to extremes by suggesting that smiling as well as laughter, was to be avoided. The question sometimes arose: Did Jesus ever laugh? Some thought that such a thing was impossible. Others saw humor and laughter as part of the divine life. All agree, however, that the final test to see whether the gift is genuine or not is joy. I find it difficult to imagine joy without smiling and laughter.

DISCERNING THE GIFT OF TEARS

There are other ways of probing the gift's authenticity. We can ask: "Does our weeping bring us closer to others and the whole created order? Do we have a deeper sense of the solidarity of all things in God? Are we able to weep with those who weep?" Evagrius wrote: "A monk is one who considers himself one with all because he seems constantly to see himself in everyone."[24] When we make such an identification with our fellow human beings, how could we stop the tears? What inspires *penthos* is the love we have for one another. Compunction is the means by which we begin to love our neighbor. It is related to the Kingdom, which is God's plan for healing creation. All things are held in being by the mercy and love of God; and the gift of tears helps us to see just that.

What saves it from becoming a burden too grievous to be borne is that it deflects us from being attached to our own ends, goals, and schemes and leads us into the heart of God. There we can see that the pursuit of our own perfection is as ludicrous as it is impossible. In the heart of God is our heart's desire, and nothing less than God will satisfy us. The desert believers are a great source of encouragement in this regard. There is humor and gentleness in the desert as well as rigor and discipline. These believers know that they have not made it as perfected beings. More important, they know that they don't have to make it.

The important point is that our weeping is caused by the love of God. The mercy of God is its motivating power. Tears help me see my neighbors as they really are. They wash away the grime of my possessiveness and projections that obscures my vision. Tears give love a chance to happen. Like love, tears are reciprocal. They are not only a gift presented to us; they are also a gift we can bring to God. St. Gregory of Nazianzen says: "Let everyone bring tears."[25] Even the poorest and the least gifted of us can at least bring tears; they have the power of resurrection.

Tears, then, are a gift from God that we can return to the Giver. If we keep this in mind, we will find it more difficult to make the flow of tears the occasion of self-indulgence or, worse, the means by which we inflict ourselves with self-hatred. "Do not . . . make a passion out of the remedy for passions" (p. 54). These tears bring proper self-love, in that they wash the penitent's face so much that it shines "with glory before God and his holy angels. A face bathed with tears has an undying beauty"

(p. 55). As flowery as this language is, it attempts to put into words experiences known to many people today. In any age, it is difficult to put into words experiences that transform us and make us new.

TEARS ARE FOR THE BUILDING OF THE KINGDOM

Ours is the shared glory of the Kingdom. Tears are for the making of a People. The hardness of the human heart (which tears are to soften) affects the lives of nations and the destinies of communities. It is often the tragic spiral of outward political events that brings us to our senses so that we see the way things are. It is a pity that it often takes tragedy to bring us to the realization that our lives are held together by an extremely fragile web. It often takes an event totally beyond our control to soften the hardness of the human heart.

Why do we need the occasional thunderbolt? It seems that we are incurably forgetful and need a jolt from time to time to wake us up. A *memento mori* has a wonderful way of clearing the mind! It opens up the path to self-knowledge. Even sin can turn to our good because it is the knowledge of the sin that releases the tears. Some years ago I framed this prayer by our front door in New York City:

> Christ look upon us in this city
> And keep our sympathy and pity
> Fresh and our faces heavenward
> Lest we grow hard.

Tears kept our sympathy and pity fresh for the sake of the city, for the sake of *the* City of which we are all citizens.

I am not sure that I have the courage that it takes to make a good citizen and to look at what God chooses to reveal to me about myself. On the occasions when I have looked, grace has come not only to help me bear what I see, but also to give me the courage to rejoice. The saints are those who have been allowed to see into themselves and have not refused to look (p. 61). I want to look away; and when I do that I miss not only the tears, but the joy as well. Sin often begins as a kind of forgetfulness, an absent-mindedness that allows us not to be truly present to ourselves—to be "not at home" so that we can, without compunction, steel our hearts against others and undermine the foundations of the City.

As we have seen, the battle with the ego goes on until the moment of death. That is why the desert believers tell us to keep that final moment always in mind. Tears and an abiding sense of our terminal state go together. Without tears our mania for self-justification and self-satisfaction knows no bounds. A shock is necessary to bring us out of the prison-house of our own willfulness.

This desert way of believing is a far cry from the kind of believing in which many of us were nurtured. The desert stands as a haven between the sterilities of a liberalized, watered-down way of believing and the tyranny of passionate fundamentalism. The tradition of "the gift of tears" provides another *way* of believing. It gives the believer's commitment the gravity it deserves and the joy that is its mainspring. On the one hand, it rejects the bland, passionless believing described by Evagrius: "Christianity is no longer anything but good manners, politeness. There is nothing stable, nothing weighty and lasting!" (p. 98). On the other, it undermines the kind of passionate believing that makes us into bigots.

While there are insurmountable differences between us and the wild-eyed early ascetics, they have much to teach us. They were concerned with the passions in their disordered and unruly state. Later, the Ignatian tradition spoke of inordinate affections. What they were after (and what I believe what psychoanalysis is also after) was fullness of life within the will and love of God. This meant a chastening of the intellect as well as an ordering of the desires.

If I am to be a true theologian, then the gift of tears will be an essential part of my armory as a believer. In one sense, all believers are called to be theologians; to be signs of who God is and what he does in the world. I do not want to be like an Egyptologist who has never been to Egypt. Compunction places the keenest-minded professor in the desert regions. The intellectual life, uninformed by the gift of tears, becomes self-indulgence. Evagrius, an intellectual himself, says: "Cranes fly in the form of a letter, but do not know the alphabet" (p. 114). It is one thing to *talk about* God. It is quite another to *know* him. We would prefer to know *about* things; and when we know a lot about things, the intellect is often taken in by its own cleverness.

COMING HOME TO OURSELVES

What are we meant to be about? The desert way of believing claims that we are most truly ourselves when we are most at home with ourselves. The tradition puts it in the form of a maxim: "God can command only what is for our good and in accord with our true nature" (p. 121). In psychological terms we may say that since God commands only our good, we may trust the inner processes of our own development. In fact we are released from the burdensome worry about progress as such. God wills our good. This means that everything that happens to us, including our sinning, can be turned to our good. It also means that, while we are rescued from the pursuit of goals and performance, we can legitimately talk about stages of insight and vision. The reason is that while our identity is in safe keeping (in the hands of God), who we are is not completely clear to us. Our true nature is, in part, hidden from us. We have not yet come into full being. We move by degrees.

In fact, the gift of tears comes relatively late in a person's walk with God. St. Gregory Nazianzen said that tears are the fifth baptism. The first is that of Moses—a matter of simple water. The second is that of John the Baptist, which is greater than that of Moses because it is one of repentance. The third is baptism of the Spirit. The fourth is baptism by blood in martyrdom, "which is the most perfect because Christ himself received it. . . .Finally there is that of tears, more painful than martyrdom because it consists nightly of bathing one's bed and covers with tears . . . " (pp. 123–124).

Perhaps we no longer know how to weep in this way. In our post-Freudian, post-Jungian world, who can learn this ancient practice—and who would want to? There is one point of entry for us if we would care to look: our concern for the poor and the oppressed, our fellow citizens. James of Saroug shouts at us from the tradition:

You have no tears? Buy tears from the poor. You have no sadness? Call the poor man to moan with you. If your heart is hard and has neither sadness nor tears, with alms invite the needy to weep with you . . . Provide yourself with the water of tears, and may the poor come to help you put out the fire in which you are perishing . . . You can make your own baptism flow from yourself, and you will be purified. All the waves of the immense ocean would not wash you as would these streams which the heart sends to the eyes. (pp. 130–131)

St. Simeon, the New Theologian, sees the true baptism of the Spirit as the baptism of tears—the great *photismos*—the illumination by which a person becomes all light. Tears are part of the process by which the believer is made anew in Jesus Christ through the gift of the Spirit. Tears are an antidote to the passions (by which is meant that shifting, unfree, unintegrated part of ourselves). And in this tradition, sadness is considered to be one of the enslaving passions. To know that one is a sinner and, at the same time, to know that one is standing in the grace and love of God is what the gift of tears is all about.

True *penthos*, therefore, guards against despair and discouragement. St. John Chrysostom writes in one of his letters: "Even in the case of our own faults, for which we will be held accountable, it is not necessary or prudent—it is even very harmful—to afflict ourselves excessively . . . Let no sinner despair, let no man trust in his virtue . . . " (p. 163). It is not a matter of repressing our emotions and feelings so much as one of winning them back. We ache for their restoration, not their destruction. This is at the heart of what we might call "the believer's secret," which is the exchange of our living death for God's dying life. This is one of the many ways in which the apparent contradiction of the Christian life is expressed. There is *per crucem ad lucem* and *per angusta ad augusta*: through the cross to the light and through the narrows to the heights. The end of it all is joy. It was precisely for this that we were created. St. Irenaeus said that God made us in "order that he might have someone in whom to place his great gifts."[26] Joy, always joy, is the mark of the believer. As St. Francis de Sales said, "A sad saint is a sorry saint."

THE DRAGON'S SKIN

In sum, we need waking up. Christianity administers the shock we need in order to find out who we are and who God is. This shock of Christ is a like a knock on the head. It makes us see double. We see, at one and the same time, the depravity and the glory of human life. We see, at one and the same time, that which delights us and that which makes us weep. We see, as all of a piece, mercy and judgment, love and justice. And this vision invites us to share in "a sort of suffering." This suffering is the struggle with our own identity. It is the antidote to sadness and despair because the gift of tears is an affirmation of the reign of God for the mending of creation. Tears keep us soft and supple in the loving hands of God for the healing of the nations. Irenaeus wrote:

Offer him a heart which is soft and pliable. Keep the form in which the creator shaped you. Keep a good disposition, lest being hardened you lose the imprints of his fingers ... To make is proper to God's kindness, and to be made is proper to human nature ... If then you hand over to him what is yours, that is, faith and subjection, you will receive his craftsmanship and you will be a perfect work of God.[27]

C. S. Lewis put the theme of the gift of tears in story form in *The Voyage of The Dawn Treader*. Eustace is an obnoxious little boy whose selfish and thoughtless behavior so hardened him that he was eventually turned into a dragon.

He had turned into a dragon while he was asleep. Sleeping on a dragon's hoard with greedy dragonish thoughts in his heart, he had become a dragon himself ... In spite of the pain, his first feeling was one of relief. There was nothing to be afraid of anymore. He was a terror himself now and nothing in the world but a knight (and not all of those) would dare attack him. [But then] he realised he was a monster cut off from the whole human race. An appalling loneliness came over him. He began to see the others had not really been fiends at all. He began to wonder if he himself had been such a nice person as he had always supposed ... When he thought of this the poor dragon that had been Eustace lifted up his voice and wept.

Eventually there had to be some skin-shedding. Eustace was able to get three layers of skin off by himself, but there was more to come. This was the work of the Lion, with his great and terrible claw. Eustace says,

The very first tear he made was so deep that I thought it had gone right into my heart. And when he began pulling the skin off, it hurt worse than anything I've ever felt. . . .there it was lying on the grass; only ever so much thicker and darker, and more knobbly than the others had been. And there was I as smooth and soft as a peeled switch and smaller than I had been. Then he caught hold of me—I didn't like that much for I was very tender underneath now that I had no skin on—and threw me in the water. It smarted like anything but only for a moment. After that it became perfectly delicious and as soon as I started swimming and splashing I found that all the pain had gone . . . [28]

5. The Fiftieth Gate

Then I saw a new heaven and a new earth, for the first heaven and the first earth had vanished, and there was no longer any sea. I saw the holy city, new Jerusalem, coming down out of heaven from God, made ready like a bride adorned for her husband. I heard a loud voice proclaiming from the throne: "Now at last God has his dwelling among men! He will dwell among them and they shall be his people, and God himself will be with them. He will wipe every tear from their eyes; there shall be an end to death, and to mourning and to crying and pain; for the old order has passed away!

REVELATION 21:1–4

We have taken a hard look at some of the obstacles to our joy and delight. Isn't it time, now, to rest? Haven't we been through enough? Well, the story isn't over yet. Sometimes I wish things were different. In fact, our wishing can often get the better of us and we begin to hallucinate in the desert. We start seeing what we *want* to see. Sometimes the reverse is true. If we wait long enough, the desert will make us see things that we would prefer *not* to see.

PURSUING QUESTIONS TO THE BITTER END

The more we question and probe the more we need to be rooted in a community. A Hasidic story shows the importance of home and place if we are to remain human and open. There was once a gifted disciple of the famous Rebbe Barukh of Medzebozh. His intellectual questioning led him far away from the community. In fact, he was following a dangerous path that could only lead to darkness and destruction. His mind was undisciplined. He read voraciously and indiscriminately. He began to delve into matters that were too much for his soul to bear. He found out secrets that were unbearable to him because he was not yet ready to hear them. He felt himself to be on the edge of the abyss and was even tempted to take his own life. At first his master, Rebbe Barukh, did nothing about his erring disciple. It made him sad, but the old man thought to himself: "He's young and inexperienced. He has to have the chance to make his own mistakes. When he comes back I'll give him a good talking to and bring him back to his people and to God." But the young man did not return. Terrible rumors began to reach the ears of the master. The young man had stopped praying; he had even stopped studying. Worst of all, he would have nothing to do with the Hasidic community. In fact, he no longer lived among Jews. By this time the Rebbe was very unhappy, but still he did nothing. The young man would surely turn up in desperation and then he would talk to his disciple severely about his foolishness and compel him to return to his people.

The disciple never came, and finally the Rebbe decided that it was time for him to act. One morning he went off in search of the young man. The master had to travel far away to another town and there confront his former pupil. The young man looked at the master in astonishment. Before he could open his mouth, the Rebbe motioned him to sit down and be silent.

"You are surprised to see me here, in your room? You shouldn't be. I can read your thoughts, I know your innermost secrets. You are alone and trying to deepen your loneliness. You have already passed through, one after the other, the fifty gates of knowledge and doubt—and I know how you did it. You began with one question; you explored it in depth to discover the first answer, which allowed you to open the first gate; you crossed and found yourself confronted by a new question. You worked on its solution and found the second gate. And the third. And the fourth and the tenth; one leads to the other, one is a key to the other. And now you stand before the fiftieth gate.

Look: it is open. And you are frightened aren't you? The open gate fills you with fear, because if you pass through it, you will face a question to which there is no answer—no human answer. And if you try you will fall. Into the abyss. And you will be lost. Forever. You didn't know that. Only I did. But now you also know.

"What am I to do?" cried the disciple, terrified. "What can I do? Go back? To the beginning? Back to the first gate?"—"Impossible," said the Master. "Man can never go back; it is too late. What is done cannot be undone."

There was a long silence. Suddenly the young disciple began to tremble violently. "Please, Rebbe," he cried, "help me. Protect me. What

is there left for me to do? Where can I go from here?"—"Look in
front of you. Look beyond that gate. What keeps man from running,
dashing over its threshold? What keeps man from falling? Faith. Yes,
son: beyond the fiftieth gate there is not only the abyss but also faith—
and they are next to one another . . . " And the Rebbe brought his
disciple back to his people—and to himself.[1]

This is a very moving story, but it is not without its complications. It could be interpreted as an anti-intellectual parable,
the moral being: Stay close to home and don't read books. The
Rebbe's authority is absolute and seems to override the young
man's integrity. Katzantzakis's St. Francis asks one of the bright
young men seeking to join the order: "Will your intellect be
able to bear our certainty?" There does come a point where the
intellect ceases to work, but most of us have never come near to
that stage! For the Rebbe's disciple there is no turning back. He
has reached the fiftieth gate where there are, as it were, two
abysses: one is self-destruction; the other the believer recognizes
as the abyss of faith.

This abyss of faith is discussed in Iris Murdoch's novel *Henry
and Cato*. A young priest is talking to an older one about the
fact that believing is not unlike "falling in love."

I've told you. You fell in love. That's a start, but it's only a start. Falling
in love is egoism, it's being obsessed by images and being consoled by
them, images of the beloved, images of oneself. It's the greatest pain
and the greatest paradox of all, that personal love has to break at some
point, the ego has to break, something absolutely natural and seemingly good, seemingly perhaps the only good, has to be given up. After
that there's darkness and silence and space. And God is there. Remember St. John of the Cross. Where the images end you fall into the abyss,
but it is the abyss of faith. When you have nothing left you have nothing
left but hope . . . The point is, one will never get to the bottom of it,
never, never, never. And that never, never, never, is what you must take
for your hope and your shield and your most glorious promise. Everything we concoct about God is an illusion.[2]

If we are willing to pursue our line of questioning to the
bitter end, we eventually come to the fiftieth gate. Here we
realize that not only is everything we concoct about God an
illusion, but everything we concoct about ourselves and our

world is also an illusion. We have reached the abyss. We have come to the point where we need to help each other.

The question, then, is not one of anti-intellectualism (which is the last thing that needs to be encouraged in our culture), but of the means by which we come home to ourselves and to each other. We need companions who will struggle with us (and sometimes against us) for the sake of value and meaning. The disciple had the Rebbe to bring him back to his people and to himself. St. Francis had Brother Leo waiting for him when he emerged, crazed and excited, from his cave. The young priest had the older one to help him grow through the doubts and disappointments of first love. -

Companionship, if it is direct and honest, will lead us in the direction of the fiftieth gate. It is there, and only there, that love worthy of the name is born. It is only at the edge of the abyss that the parody that passes for love is unmasked. Power plays, manipulation, and unhealthy dependence often masquerade as love. Love that is energized by anxiety and insecurity is hardly love at all. For some of us, it's the best that we can do. The only thing that releases us from the bondage of our anxiety-dominated false loves is the experience (however faint and short-lived) of unsolicited, unconditional, disinterested love. I catch glimpses of this in my family and my friends. As a believer, I am slowly coming to realize that God loves us like that. He delights in us. He enjoys us. When such a truth begins to take hold of a believer, the world is changed. A contribution is made towards the peace of the world. A blow is struck for justice. Why? Because the freer I am to *be* in the world, the freer I am to contribute to its welfare and its flourishing.

NO ESCAPE FROM LOVE

In Nikos Katzantzakis's *St. Francis*, Brother Leo, one of the earthiest of the Franciscans, describes with both humor and terror his leader's exit from a cave after three days of solitude. Francis had seen visions of such terrifying clarity that he appeared to be out of his mind. Katzantzakis puts these words into the mouth of Brother Leo.

The three days came to an end . . . I felt delighted but . . . I was trembling at the thought of seeing Francis. To talk three days with the Almighty was to expose yourself to immense danger. God might hurl you into a terrible chasm where He was able to survive but a man was not . . . Francis suddenly emerged from the cave. He was radiant—a gleaming cinder. "Well, Brother Leo, are you ready . . . Have you donned your warlike armor? . . . He seemed delirious. His eyes were inflamed . . . I was terrified. Could he have taken leave of his senses? He understood and laughed, but his fire did not subside. "People have enumerated many terms of praise for the Lord up to now . . . but I shall enumerate still more. Listen to what I shall call Him: the Bottomless Abyss, the Insatiable, the Merciless, the Indefatigable, the Unsatisfied. He who never once has said to poor, unfortunate mankind, 'Enough.' Coming still closer he placed his lips next to my ear and cried in a thunderous voice, 'Not Enough!' . . . If you ask, Brother Leo, what God commands without respite, I can tell you, for I learned it these past three days and nights in the cave. Listen! Not Enough! Not Enough! I can't go further, whines man. You can, the Lord replies. I shall break in two, man whines again. Break! the Lord replies." Francis's voice had begun to crack. I became angry . . . "What more does he expect from you?" I asked. "Didn't you restore St. Damiano's?" "Not Enough!" "Well what more does he expect?' "I asked Him, Brother Leo . . . He answered, 'Go to My Church, the Portiuncula. I shall tell you there.' So, Brother Leo, let's go down and see what He wants. Cross yourself, tighten the rope around your waist. We're dealing with God and from Him there is no escape."[3]

To see God as the Bottomless Abyss, the Insatiable, the Unsatisfied, is surely enough to unhinge the mind. We would do almost anything *not* to see God in this way.

The fact is that, as a friend of mine puts it,[4] we still have a fractured, broken, and sinful heart. This organ of perception is notoriously unreliable. We will believe almost anything to relieve the stress under which we live—not least the strain of serving a Bottomless Abyss! We long to be free; but often the kind of freedom we want is to be free of responsibility, creativity, and maturity. We want to go back, to regress; we want to turn away from the kind of freedom that may be summoning us into a "darkness" in which our true liberty can be found. How, then, do we know whether we are truly free or simply escaping into a deadening childishness? The fact is that we never know in an absolute sense. And it is this "not-knowing" that we need to explore now. "Not-knowing" is part of what it means to serve an unfathomable mystery.

We are approaching the "fiftieth gate," beyond which there is nothing to hold on to. We are entering the realm of Faith—which is not assent to a set of propositions, but walking into the Unknown. We need to understand that even St. Francis did not think he could go it alone. The believer is committed to being with others. Believing means not only coming home to oneself, but coming home to others as well. Many of us find belonging to a community of like-minded people sustaining and comforting. The believer, however, understands that the relationship is not to a group of the like-minded, but to the whole human race: the ugly along with the beautiful, the failures as well as the successful, the brilliant along with the moronic. This realization, far from being sustaining and comforting, is at first threatening and repellent.

I find this all very disturbing, and am often puzzled why others are able to view it with equanimity. On the one hand, I know (by faith) that I am God's delight; and, on the other, I still don't know how to love. I am learning very slowly what others appear to know spontaneously. I am disturbed, but not depressed. I am disturbed because I don't see how I can begin to live up to what I believe. Sometimes I feel like a mole scratching away in the dark. What is it that I'm supposed to *do*? How should I order my life? The further I "progress," the further there is to go. The goal towards which I tend seems to recede every step I take. Maybe I'm on the wrong track entirely? Maybe I still haven't understood. All my questions have the habit of turning themselves inside out. I find myself being questioned in my questioning and being probed in my probing. I grow impatient. I want simple answers. I find myself in the company of the believers who have cried through the ages, "How long, O Lord? How long?" God, whoever he is, appears to be at best ineffective and at worst indifferent. As I get older, I want my faith to be simple, straightforward, childlike. But my childishness continues to get in the way. I come to another impasse. I ask yet again the fundamental questions of the believer: Who is God? What is he up to?

The response I get threatens my very identity: *Who is it who wants to know?* I get agitated and angry and would like to go back. I wish that I'd never started this project. Why? Because behind the question "Who is God?" is the question "Who am I?" I have been led into a trap by my own questioning and am confronted with a "me" I hardly know. Now I have to give up the luxury of apparent detachment, because my own life may be at stake.

ANGER AND DOUBT AS SIGNS OF STRUGGLING FAITH

Whoever God is, he catches us off-guard; and even in our disbelief we are somehow engaged in a struggle with him. In Samuel Beckett's *Endgame*, a character utters a pious blasphemy something like this: "God! He doesn't exist—the bastard!" The struggle here is not only with "God," but also with that elusive entity, "me." And the statement comes back: "Alan! He doesn't exist—the bastard!"

Raging at God is not unknown to the believer. Indeed, contending with God, even in anger, is part of what it means to pray. The Hasidic tradition bears witness to that struggle we call prayer. A rabbi, looking at the affliction of his people, taunts God with these words:

Why do You leave Your people in exile? Why is it to last so long? Only because we did not—and do not—observe Your Law? But tell me, tell me, who compelled You to give it to us? Did we ask for it, did we want it? It was You who made us receive it . . . Furthermore, Master of the Universe, tell me: didn't You know then that we would not comply with all Your laws? Still you chose us—then why are you angry?[5]

The believer understands that God reveals himself in our very questioning. Doubt is part of the arsenal of faith. It keeps it fresh and honest. In our daring to argue and in our struggle to understand, the blood begins to flow through a tired and worn-out faith. But it is important not to try to do all this alone. We have seen that part of this desert way of believing is an invitation to "a sort of suffering," and we need companionship if we aren't to get lost. The quest for love inevitably brings us face to face with our own bankcruptcy. All our efforts to go it alone comes to nothing. We need each other.

Stevie Smith, in one of her poems, describes a scene where a man is discovered drowned on the beach and it is the dead man who chants the terrible refrain, "I wasn't waving but drowning." I wasn't waving but drowning might well be the chorus of millions of our fellow human beings, who live lives of quiet desperation. I am a believer, and that means that I enjoy and endure the fellowship of other believers in the body we call the Church. There others enjoy and endure me. Here I am back with Walker Percy's assholes and relieved and glad to be with them. I need a home. The Church is a sign that I am truly coming home to myself when I am in the company of others.

THE INVITATION TO CHANGE

If the world is to change, then, first I have to change. The way I change (often kicking and screaming) is by coming to the fiftieth gate, where the abyss of faith is located. I believe in a new way: not by suppressing the questions and the doubts (I cannot go back), but by living more and more deeply into the questions and the doubts. I come to faith in a God who is paradoxically revealed in the very struggle to name him. The closer I get to the fiftieth gate, the more *I* am questioned in my questioning, the more *I* am probed in my probing. I begin to wonder how it all fits together, especially when I don't fit together too well myself. I feel naked and exposed and frightened. I identify much more with Brother Leo than with St. Francis. I wait outside the cave and see crazed people stagger out into the daylight, all but destroyed by the Bottomless Abyss, the Insatiable, the Merciless, the Indefatigable, the Unsatisfied, and I tremble. I cannot believe in the God of TV evangelism, who is either domesticated or vindictive. Yet I hesitate to follow Francis into his cave to find himself before the flaming Love of God "as terrible as an army with banners." I look for a way of escape. Who knows where such a God might spew me out?

My fear and anger are very useful, provided I am able to resist that first panicked impulse to run. If I stand still in whatever cave I've been pushed into, my anger and fear can be a means to my understanding more clearly and with precision what is going on, not only within me but in the world. The desert tradition permits me to be angry with God. The Jews, the pioneer believers of this tradition who were formed into a people in the desert, know how to be angry with God—and with good cause. One rabbi said this to a person struggling in anger with his suffering:

I know there are questions that have no answers; there is a suffering that has no name; there is injustice in God's creation—and there are reasons enough for man to explode with rage. I know there are reasons for you to be angry. Good. Let us be angry. Together.[6]

Doesn't God reveal himself in the areas of our greatest weakness—in our questioning, our probing, our suffering, and our anger? I believe he does. This is why the questions are important. They stretch and enlarge the heart so that it is capable of receiving a deeper revelation. They expand our horizons. It would be strange if we didn't find this enlarging and expanding process deeply disturbing.

The simple truth is that reality reveals its secrets to us in proportion to the level of our willingness to ask questions. We receive "answers" to fit the kind of "questions" we pose. If our questions are narrowly and unimaginatively conceived, the answers will be too.

Graham Greene has created a modern hero of the desert way of believing in his character of Monsignor Quixote. Father Quixote is a naive, old, and unsuccessful priest who, through a series of absurd accidents, is honored by the pope and made a monsignor. His bishop is furious and sends the old priest away on a leave of absence. Father Quixote takes a friend along as his companion. This man is a communist, the ex-mayor of the little community where they both live. They are very fond of each other—the believer and the unbeliever. As they set off on their journey in the priest's old car (aptly named Rocinante), he muses on the fact that "sharing a sense of doubt can bring men together perhaps even more than sharing a faith. The believer will fight another believer over a shade of difference; the doubter fights only with himself."

One day, during his siesta, Father Quixote has a dream. It is of the crucifixion. All the familiar figures are there—the Roman soldiers, the crowd, the Mother of Jesus. But Jesus doesn't die. He appeals to a legion of angels and they save him.

So there was no final agony, no heavy stone which had to be rolled away . . . Father Quixote stood there watching on Golgotha as Christ stepped down from the cross triumphant and acclaimed. The Roman soldiers . . . knelt in His honor, and the people of Jerusalem poured up the hill to worship Him. The disciples clustered happily around. His mother smiled through her tears of joy. There was no ambiguity, no room for doubt and no room for faith at all . . . The whole world knew with certainty that Christ was the Son of God.

It was only a dream, of course it was only a dream, but nonetheless Father Quixote had felt on waking the chill of despair felt by a man who realizes that he has taken up a profession which is of use to no one, who must continue to live in a kind of Saharan desert without doubt or faith, where everyone is certain that the same belief is true. He had found himself whispering, "God save me from such a belief."[7]

In a world where there is no room for doubt, ambiguity, or questioning, there is no room for genuine faith.

A younger and more gloomy Graham Greene addressed a group of believers shortly after World War II. He asked his audience to consider what they thought was particularly distinctive about Christians. Could it be that they are morally superior? To make such an assertion would be to invite ridicule. There is a continuity of a way of believing of the Graham Greene of 1948 and the Graham Greene of today. Thirty years ago *he* was the young Father Quixote, struggling with doubt and yet insisting that doubt was the fertile ground of his faith. In 1948 he wrote, "The Apostle Thomas should be the patron saint of the people in my country, for we must see the marks of the nails and put our hands in the wounds before we can understand."[8]

The distinctive marks of the believer, then, will include the willingness to bear the marks of doubt. But these marks are to be found on God himself, at least according to the believers in the tradition we are exploring. Graham Greene (and he is not alone) would have us believe that our doubts and ambiguities are sanctified, since God took us on in Jesus Christ so that our despair and failure are part of God's life as shown forth on the

Cross. To come to such a realization brings us well over the threshold of the fiftieth gate.

THE DIFFERENCE BETWEEN BELIEVERS AND UNBELIEVERS

How, then, are we to distinguish between the believers and the unbelievers—or, to use old-fashioned terminology, between the Christians and the pagans? Graham Greene, from his vantage point beyond the Fiftieth Gate, writes: "Perhaps, truthfully, we can count on nothing more than the divided mind, the uneasy conscience, and the sense of personal failure."[9]

At first sight, these sound remarkably unpromising! These distinguishing characteristics of the believer are, however, the very things that make life worth living and enable us to face tomorrow with hope. How is this so? The divided mind, once acknowledged, is unlikely to persecute others. The persecuting personality is marked by clarity and precision. There is no room for indecision. There is no room for guilt. There is no room for doubt. Such are the distinguishing marks of a totalitarian state or totalitarian church. The divided mind, the uneasy conscience, and the sense of personal failure, bring us in their own way to the fiftieth gate, to the place of faith; and it is at that point that they lose their crippling power and become vehicles of hope.

It cannot be claimed that believers are better than unbelievers, or that the coming of Christ (for example) has made the world a better place to live in. Believers may claim modestly that because there are those who believe there is a glimmer of hope in the world; but they can claim little else. The Anglo-Saxon Chronicles, describing the terrible situation in England during the reign of Stephen baldly stated the "men said openly that Christ and His saints slept."[10] In Shusako Endo's novel *The Samurai*, a samurai in seventeenth-century Japan says these words to the emaciated Christ nailed to a massive crucifix:

I . . . I have no desire to worship you . . . I don't even understand why [these Spaniards] respect you. They say you died bearing the sins of mankind, but I can't see that our lives have become any easier as a result. I know the wretched lives the peasants lead . . . Nothing has changed because you died.[11]

There have been many times in human history (not least in our own day) where men and women might have said as much. Believers can own up to their crimes. They *know* that they are guilty—and this, when accepted in sorrow and faith, involves the possibility of hope. Why? Because they have no need to find someone else guilty in their stead. The terrible cycle of blaming others, of finding a scapegoat, of persecuting the marginal, is brought to a halt everytime believers repent and accept their guilt.

An uneasy conscience and a sense of guilt are two of the distinguishing marks of a believer. Wherever human beings have a conscience sensitive to moral failure there is the possibility of change, because the believer knows that he or she has been an accomplice to all the crimes committed by human beings against their own kind and against the world in which they live. We, the believers, acknowledge our guilt—whether it be due to cowardice, inertia, indifference, or ignorance. Believers experience a radical solidarity with the guilty, and this sense of solidarity prevents them from treating others as disposable or as insignificant. Guilt for the atrocities of the world makes us all one. Father Zossima in *The Brothers Karamazov* identifies with all and loves all.

Hate not atheists, the teachers of evil, materialists, even the most wicked of them, let alone the good ones among them . . . Remember them in your prayers thus: "Save, O Lord, all who have no one to pray for them, and save those, too, who do not want to pray to thee."[12]

THE THREE MARKS OF THE BELIEVER

Graham Greene offers us three distinguishing marks of the believer. First, the believer has an uneasy conscience, and so is incapable of committing atrocities (however minor) with equanimity. Second, the believer identifies with all human beings—the good the bad and the indifferent—and thus is an unlikely candidate for totalitarian seduction. Finally, the believer has a certain capacity for disloyalty—disloyalty to existing arrangements, to the principalities and powers. The believer is not good at the usual excuses. The phrase "I was only obeying orders" would stick in the throat of the believer. The Nazi war criminal, Adolf Eichmann, has become the exemplar of this unimaginative obeyer of orders from above. He was pronounced perfectly sane; and, as Thomas Merton has pointed out, "It is the sane ones, the well-adapted ones, who can without qualms and without nausea aim the missiles and press the buttons that will initiate the great festival of destruction that they, *the sane ones*, have prepared."[13]

Believers reject this kind of "sanity" and choose the kind of craziness that is committed to expanding existing horizons, crossing frontiers, and stepping over boundaries. They don't believe in abstractions, which are the spiritual weapons of governments. They are suspicious when their "responsibility towards the State" is invoked. Their loving is local, particular. To quote William Blake, they know that those who invoke the general good are often "scoundrels, hypocrites, and flatterers." The believer is a sort of subversive in the world, one of God's spies trying to make room for hope.

Graham Greene once wrote the outline of a story (which he never completed) called "The Last Pope." It was set in a world ruled by one party with ruthless efficiency. Catholicism has been stamped out completely. Only one believer is left: an old man in a shabby raincoat, carrying a battered suitcase. No one on the street knows him, no one recognizes him. He is the last pope, kept alive by the all-powerful dictator. He even receives a small pension. He is a useful symbol of how dead the Church is under the dictator's régime.

In the end the World Dictator got tired of the game. He wanted to put an end to it in his own lifetime . . . he did not wish to surrender his place in history as the man who, with his own finger on the trigger of the revolver, had put an end to the Christian myth . . . The Dictator, after offering the Pope a cigarette, which he refused, and a glass of wine, which he accepted, told him he was going to die on the spot— the last Christian, the last man in the world who still believed . . . Then he shot him in the left side of the chest and leaned over the body to give the coup de grace. At that instant, in the second between the pressure on the trigger and the skull cracking, a thought crossed the

Dictator's mind: "Is it just possible that what this man believed is true?" Another Christian had been born.[14]

To some this may appear to be a story of despair, but to the desert believers it is a story of hope. While men and women hesitate because of an uneasy conscience, there is hope; and belief is a possibility. Nevertheless, many believers treat "God" as a mascot, hobby, or household god. If our questions about God are narrowly based, then the kind of God we believe in will fit the shape of our questions. If we believe, without question, that God is all powerful and really rules the universe, we are likely to suppress questions about this all-powerful God's responsibility for suffering, injustice, and evil. If we are willing to ask shocking questions about, for example, the pain of God, then a wider view of who God may be begins to emerge. We need to let our uneasy conscience, our radical identification with others, and our sense of failure speak to us of God.

A popular view is that such questioning betrays a lack of faith. For the way of believing I am advocating, such questioning is a prerequisite. Yet human beings seem to long for definitive dogmatic statements, as if such statements were explanations: like the little girl who saw a monk floating in the air and asked her mother how it was he could do such a thing. "It's levitation, dear," said the mother. "Oh, I see," said the little girl. The child actually *saw* nothing, but was the victim of a typical adult ploy that tries to pass off descriptions as explanations.[15]

THE LIMITLESS HORIZON

If we look to God for tidy explanations, we shall soon find that the "God" who is revealed to us is as shallow as our questions. The fiftieth gate is a symbol of the limitless horizon that the believer calls God. Much of our talk about God is like using a laser to cut cheese. A laser beam can cut through cheese; but in the hands of a skilled practitioner, who knows the wider possibilities of the instrument, it can perform delicate surgical operations. We have in our hands the key to the fiftieth gate, but we often lack the courage to ask the questions necessary to broaden our horizon.

Take, for example, the narrow view many people have of the Bible. We like simple meanings and easy answers. What would some lovers of the Bible make of the ancient story of a rabbi in Alexandria who likened the scriptures to a large mansion with many rooms? Outside each room there is a key . . . only it's the wrong key! Or the view that each letter (let alone each word) of the Torah has one hundred thousand layers of meaning, each layer corresponding to one of the Israelites who waited for the giving of Law at the foot of Mount Sinai? Or the image of the Torah as a beautiful woman hidden in a room at the top of a tall tower? Sometimes she appears at the window and the seeker after truth has to circle the tower day after day with love and devotion in order to get a fleeting look at her.

There don't seem to be many today who would be willing to treat the Bible as a strange book that is both full of ambiguities and open and life-giving. Many of its treasures are lost to those who bring to it only small questions. Charles Williams, in one of his letters, writes:

On how many subjects do you really allow you may be wrong—serious subjects? On Christianity? . . . There must be . . . something of that intellectual willingness to be wrong in order that words may be heard? Thus people can never read the Bible for either they believe it or they do not believe it, but either way, they do not notice what the words are.[16]

If we treat the Bible like a railway timetable and ask of it questions suited to such a document, we will get the response or revelation suited to our question. Faith requires the willingness to be wrong and to be found to be in the wrong. Ever-deepening questions are its lifeblood.

As we approach the fiftieth gate, the questions get harder and harder because they not only stretch the mind, they also call us to obedience. The truth has not only to be appropriated, but also to be served. The more we question, the more we are faced with questions of our identity. We come face to face with the person we have become. Think how carelessly and ignorantly we use and abuse each other because of our shrunken horizons and our fear of asking deeper questions. Eventually, the questions bring us to the point of the Rebbe's disciple who found himself alone, afraid, and in the dark.

When we have finally come to end of our rope, there comes faith's deepest opportunity. But, as Auden writes:

> We would rather be ruined than changed.
> We would rather die in our dread than
> Climb the cross of the moment
> And see our illusions die.

In the face of the rise of a virulent, ultraconservative form of believing that is all answers and absolutely no questions, it is very hard to "climb the cross of the moment and see our illusions die." The most popular way of believing has neither tolerance of nor appreciation for ambiguity or contradiction. Walker Percy writes:

Christ should leave us. He is too much with us and I don't like his friends. We have no hope of recovering Christ until Christ leaves us. There is after all something worse than being God-forsaken. It is when God overstays his welcome and takes up with the wrong people.[17]

The many fake Christs available to us, who give God a bad name, are unmasked and exposed for what they are only by painful probing and questioning.

What makes the intolerable tolerable, and the terrible process of questioning the fruitful exploding of illusions? What turns the Insatiable and Indefatigable Being Francis met during his three days in the cave into the Love that made the sun and stars? Our questioning, which we do *together*, can be transfigured at the fiftieth gate into a way of believing characterized by awe and wonder. There is revealed to us the fact that there is always more to us than even our most searching questions. It affirms that a human being is unfinished business. This way of believing stretches our imagination; we gradually discover that we are not defined or confined by the pathetically inadequate questions by which we reduce and shrivel reality to our own narrow specifications.

A friend of mine wrote a poem about her journey to the fiftieth gate, through which she was hurled, and found that she was not dead but more truly alive than ever:

I will show you the skins I have shed
Left in the grass as I crept away
They are proof that I have lived.
Skin one: docile child
Skin two: obedient adolescent
Skin three: scholar masked in niceness
Skin four: stunning career girl
Skin five: charming child-mistress
Skin six: loving wife
Skin seven: marvelous mother
Skin eight: admirable Christian
Skin nine: heroic savior of abandoned children
Skin ten: nervous breakdown
Skinned alive!

It is at the fiftieth gate that our questioning is turned into Good News; because beyond that gate there is not only the abyss of darkness and isolation, there is also the abyss of faith. I cannot *argue* anyone into it, but I can invite people into the community that is committed to gathering around its dazzling darkness. Some people seem to have the gift of being able to plunge right into its center. Others wait at its edge in hope. I have come to the end of my rope. I've questioned. I've probed. And I end up here at the fiftieth gate with you, and without you I cannot find my way home. That's why I belong to that strange human community called the Church. The Church, like the Rebbe in the story, brings me back to my people and to myself. Without you, I cannot be myself. Without you, the questions are unbearable. Without you, I cannot know Love's wild impossibility.

The fact is that we live only in communion—not only with our present but with the past and future as well. We are haunted by a whole poetry of living, by lullabies half remembered and the sound of train whistles in the night and the scent of lavender in the summer garden. We are haunted by grief too, and fear, and the images of childhood terror, and the macabre dissolutions of age . . . But I am sure that it is in this domain of our daily dreaming that the Holy Spirit establishes his own communion with us. This is how the gift is given which we call grace: the sudden illumination, the sharp regret that leads to penitence or forgiveness, the opening of the heart to the risk of love . . . [18]

6. Love: God's Wild Card

I'm mooring my rowboat
at the dock of the island called God.
This dock is made in the shape of a fish
and there are many different boats moored
at many different docks . . .

"On with it!" He says and thus
we squat on the rocks by the sea
and play—can it be true—
a game of poker.
He calls me.
I win because I hold a royal straight flush.
He wins because He holds five aces.
A wild card had been announced
but I had not heard it
being in such a state of awe
when He took out the cards and dealt.
As he plunks down His five aces
and I sit grinning at my royal flush,
He starts to laugh,
the laughter rolling like a hoop out of His mouth
and into mine,
and such laughter that He doubles right over me
laughing a Rejoice-Chorus at our two triumphs.
Then I laugh, the fishy dock laughs
the sea laughs. The island laughs.
The Absurd laughs.

Dearest dealer,
I with my royal straight flush,
love you so for your wild card,
that untamable, eternal, gut-driven *ha-ha*
and lucky love.[1]

ANNE SEXTON, *The Awful Rowing Toward God*

CHEERFULNESS BREAKS IN

Some people manage to maintain an unabashedly cheerful demeanor in the face of all obstacles. Such cheerfulness often makes me uncomfortable. If I sense that the cheerfulness is

genuine, I am made uneasy by my envy and longing. If I detect
a naive or even fraudulent bonhomie, I become suspicious and
critical. I think of myself as a cheerful enough person, and I
know something of the exuberant joy in discovering the wild
card of being loved without reservation. Love of this kind,
however, always takes me by surprise. Perhaps that's why some
of my friends find my way of believing rather dark, even gloomy.
I am often caught off balance by the surprise of love. In a world
like this I don't expect it and yet it's there, calling me out of
myself and into communion.

But I don't want to be cheerful at the expense of being
honest. One of Dr. Samuel Johnson's acquaintances, Oliver Edwards, confessed to trying, for a while, to be a philosopher. But
he gave up because he found that "cheerfulness was always
breaking in"! Cheerfulness does break into my thoughts about
the world and its glorious craziness, but it comes to me, like
love, as a surprise, as a gift.

In his preface to *Brighton Rock*, Graham Greene writes:

Some critics have referred to a strange violent "seedy" region of the
mind . . . which they call Greeneland, and I have sometimes wondered
if they go around the world blinkered. "This is Indo-China," I want to
exclaim, "this is Mexico, this is Sierra Leone carefully and accurately
described. I have been a newspaper correspondent as well as a novelist.
I assure you the dead child lay in the ditch in just that attitude. In the
canal of Phat Diem the bodies stuck out of the water . . . " But I know
the argument is useless. They won't believe the world they haven't
noticed is like that.[2]

I do not, indeed I cannot, affirm the unannounced wild card
of unconditional love and not dare look at the dead child lying
in the ditch or the bodies sticking out of the water. I don't have
to go as far as Mexico or Indochina, to Lebanon or Central
America, to see such things. Such atrocities happen in the world
in which I live, and I am puzzled by the fact that many people
do not seem to have noticed that the world is like that. The
trouble is that believers are often tempted not to "tell it like it
is." In Samuel Beckett's play, *All That Fall*, a baby falls under
the wheels of a train. When an attempt is made to soften the
blow, the refrain is, "But that's not the whole story! Tell the
whole story . . . Tell all! Tell all!" The title of Beckett's play is

taken from Psalm 154:14: "The Lord upholdeth all that fall."
He doesn't, does he? Or if he does, it is not in a way that we
can understand. And the world is like that.

THE "ISNESS" OF THINGS AND THE CALL TO BE

The world is like that, but this does not mean that nothing
can be done to change it. The intractable "isness" of things can
be either a source of delight or the occasion of despair. Some
believers want to emphasize the reality of God and what he does
in a very clear and objective way in order to pull us away from
what is regarded as a damaging and unhealthy indulgence in
introspection. Such an emphasis on "objectivity" can, as often
as not, be yet another form of escape from the "isness" of the
world. Yet it can also be a means by which I become anchored
in that which is other than myself. It all depends on the way
one *looks* at things. A sense of the "isness" of things could make
one want to give up.

Wilfred Barclay, the hero of William Golding's *The Paper Men*,
caught a vision of the "isness" of things and was convinced that
he was damned. A kind of exhilaration possessed him. He could
do anything and it wouldn't make a *damn* bit of difference. He
had nothing to lose, since everything was already lost.

I knew in one destroying instant that all my adult life I had believed
in God and this knowledge was a vision of God. Fright entered the
very marrow of my bones. Surrounded, swamped, confounded, all but
destroyed, adrift in the universal intolerance, mouth open, screaming,
bepissed and beshitten, I knew my maker and fell down.[3]

If one gives Wilfred Barclay's terrifying vision of damnation a
slight twist, the promise of hope comes into focus. One is moved
from being "damned" to being "saved." In Walker Percy's words,
one becomes an "ex-suicide."

The difference between a non-suicide and an ex-suicide leaving the
house for work, at eight o'clock on an ordinary morning:
    The non-suicide is a little travelling suck of care, sucking care with
him from the past and being sucked toward care in the future. His
breath is high in his chest.
    The ex-suicide opens his front door, sits on the steps, and laughs.

Since he has the option of being dead, he has nothing to lose by being alive. It is good to be alive. He goes to work because he doesn't have to.[4]

The "isness" that drives one to the brink of the abyss pushes one through it into faith. I must confess that I don't know how it's done or why it happens to some and not to others. Theologians use code words like "grace" and "eschatology" to talk about it, and psychologists provide interesting maps to help us understand why one person ends up at one particular place and not another. But the "why" of it all continues to elude me, although I haven't given up the exploration and cannot imagine my doing so. All I know is that love of some kind has got hold of me and will not let me go. That is why I describe myself as a believer and put up with the embarrassment of being seen in some dreadful company. And I am grateful for the many people (both friends and strangers) who don't mind being seen with me!

THE OPEN WOUND

I want to affirm *this* world in such a way that I do not turn a blind eye to tragedy, suffering, and failure. As Hans Urs von Balthasar has observed: "Great tragedy . . . compels the spectator to include even the most terrible and excruciating elements in that affirmation. There is no "classical" art without this open wound in the heart of Being, and in the heart of the man in whom Being is transparent."[5] In the light of this, we might say that believing is another way of saying Being. To believe is, in part, not only to acknowledge but also to bear the wound in the heart. Willingness to bear the wound comes when we begin to realize that we are loved. I am, however, not very good at knowing exactly how much and on what grounds I am loved. I do know that my usual line of enquiry (about the "who," the "what," and the "how much" of things) won't get me anywhere. I know that someone is looking for me. Someone wants me to come "home." Is it "the Hound of Heaven"? I think it is. At least that seems to me to be a good metaphor for what is happening to me. But the feeling that one is being pursued doesn't bring much comfort. In fact, in one sense there is no escape from love. Dante points out that the very gates of Hell were made by love and justice, and T. S. Eliot wrote:

> Who then devised the torment?
> Love. Love is the unfamiliar name
> Behind the hands that wove
> The intolerable shirt of flame . . .
> We only live, only suspire
> Consumed by either fire or fire.[16]

Love seems to be a terrible thing, bringing fire and torment. The old notion of love was simply that which drew one to one's true self, a gravitational pull in the soul that brought people "home." The "hell, fire, and torment" are there because of the peculiar nature of human freedom. It is the distinguishing mark of human identity that we can go against the grain of our own nature; we can defy gravity and, if we so choose, find ourselves in "hell." For mystics life is concerned with the joy of moving in the right direction and the experience of freedom in being released from loving the wrong things too much or the right things too little.

It all sounds very simple. The problem is, who can say what is the right direction? There are plenty of "madmen and ass-holes" who will tell us where we should be going and, if given half the chance, would force us to march with them. Learning to find the right way means going through "hell" and "purga-tory." Dante began his search for his true self in the middle of a dark wood where the right way was lost. In order to find his way home to love, he had to explore all his attempts to go against the gravitational pull of his own being. That's the mystery of "hell"—the fact that we have the power to choose to go against our own selves. We are free to wage civil war in and against ourselves.

Doesn't this sound familiar? In the language of psychoanaly-sis, we are in conflict with ourselves, in the grip of neurotic patterns. How wonderful it would be if we could be rescued from the pain of such conflicts! Well, there is help at hand . . . fanaticism, drugs, religion, sex, power: all these will help relieve the pain of inner conflict and save us the trouble of striving for a mature way of being in the world. They will also enable us to elude love, and will prevent us from finding our way "home."

Some people want religion or therapy to anesthetize them so that the civil war within can go on without their conscious knowledge. The casualities from the war keep surfacing in fits of temper, depression, or vindictiveness; but the blame for such outbursts is projected onto others. Part of what it means to love—to begin to come home—is learning to withdraw such projections and be attentive to the conflict within. Dysart, the psychiatrist in Peter Schaffer's play *Equus*, is dismayed by his so-called healing task. Is the job of psychiatry to help make people "normal"?

The Normal is the good smile in a child's eyes—all right. It is also the dead stare in a million adults. It both sustains and kills—like a God. It is the Ordinary made beautiful: it is also the Average made lethal. The Normal is the indispensable, murderous God of Health, and I am his Priest. My tools are very delicate. My compassion is honest. I have honestly assisted children in this room. I have talked away terrors and relieved many agonies. But also—beyond question—I have cut from them parts of individuality repugnant to this God, in both his aspects. Parts sacred to rarer and more wonderful Gods. And at what length . . . Sacrifices to Zeus took at the most, surely, sixty seconds each. Sacrifices to the Normal can take as long as sixty months.[7]

Both religion and therapy are in danger of idolatrous devotion to the God of the Normal. The Normal is defined by custom and fashion, by the views of a dominant or powerful group. It is the enemy of love because love is unpredictable. Love crosses boundaries and continually calls in question that which the majority defines as normal . . . and, as Robert Frost said,

> Society can never think things out:
> It has to see them
> acted out by actors,
> Devoted actors at a sacrifice.

The believer is one of the actors who plays his or her part in a drama of the *ways things are* so that others may live. The desert believer is an actor at a sacrifice. The soul comes into being through the unfolding of a plot of a play. Just what the drama is about and what is to be sacrificed is the concern of these final chapters. Anne Sexton, whose poem began this chapter, was such an actor. She was so engaged in the passion of believing that the drama overwhelmed her and she took her own life. I believe that she felt things and saw things that were too hard for "normal" people to bear. She felt them and looked at them and then wrote about them in such a way that more timid souls could read and understand. In the end, she was burned by the intolerable shirt of flame.

THE WILD CARD: LEARNING WHAT LOVE IS

The making of a soul, which is another way of talking about learning what love is, requires what the poet John Keats called "Negative Capability . . . that is, when a man is capable of being in uncertainties, mysteries, doubts, without any irritable reaching after fact and reason."[8] Playing cards with God requires the grace of negative capability. Without it, there would be no room for the unpredictable, the unexpected. There would be no room for love (the wild card); no room for the soul. The development of the gift of negative capability is difficult and painful. Yet without the nourishment provided by the ability to rest in uncertainties, mysteries, and doubts, the soul begins to starve. "It cannot live on fun alone. If the soul gets no other food, it will first tear apart other creatures . . . then itself."[9]

I cannot live on fun alone . . . not that I ever seriously believed that I could. But I often entertain the hope that love will come to me with ease and without the pain and the element of sacrifice that invariably accompany it. Love is often treated as a commodity—one should try to accumulate as much as possible. It will heal wounds, feed the soul, and come in handy as a bargaining chip when things get tough. But love is more like Anne Sexton's game of poker into which has been slipped the wild card of the unconditional. Love, for most of us, is often a scarcely veiled reciprocal trade treaty. Love is the name we sometimes give to a kind of spiritual cannibalism where two people devour each other. It can be another name for a parasitic or smothering relationship. When the real thing is unavailable, we look for terrible substitutes.

Such devouring and possessive forms of human relationship are, of course, not love at all. We need each other. Without the help of others, my soul cannot come into being. I do not "happen" without assistance. Geoge McDonald wrote in *The Last Farthing*:

Without the correction, the reflection, the support of other presences, being is not merely unsafe, it is a horror — for anyone but God . . . It is the lovely creatures God has made around us, in them giving us Himself, that, until we know Him, save us from the frenzy of aloneness.[10]

I need other presences, and I will do almost anything to acquire them. I have to learn, however, that the support and love I crave can come to me only as a gift. Love is a gift or it is nothing. Insofar as we are able to reject strategies of possessiveness and manipulation, the conditions are already being set for the development of real soul making, real loving.

As we have seen, the desert provides the environment for soul making. It is there we learn the lessons of the gift of tears and the fiftieth gate. They teach us that love requires freedom, spontaneity, and the grace to stand back and allow another simply to be. The desert teaches us that love can often mean the willingness to stand guard over another's solitude. Here is the basic paradox of soul making: in order for me to be myself, I need to be able to be alone; in order to be myself, I need to be with others. The question is, how can I be at one with another and yet remain myself? How can we be truly formed into a community without our swallowing or dominating one another? All questions concerning the making of a soul revolve around issues of identity (that's *me*) and unity (that's *you*).

When we begin working on our own souls, we discover that we are not self-made. Our identity depends on Another. We cannot make ourselves . . . but fortunately a wild card has been announced, only we were too preoccupied to notice it. In the end, the making of a soul, like love, requires a miracle, and the appropriation of miracles requires faith; and faith leads us back into the muddy question of "God" and the nonsense that often surrounds that word. But I am ahead of myself. Let us look more closely at the "wild card."

Most of us have something of the romantic in us. As we grow older, skepticism and even cynicism take over; but it must be a mean and dried-up spirit who has not at least the dregs of some romance in his or her soul. We long for love. No one seems to be able to get enough of it. We are all deprived to some degree, and when we cannot get what we need we try/neurotic solutions to the soul's craving.

Religion is often made into a comprehensive neurotic solution. There are those who think that they love God because they don't love anyone else. This seems to be an occupational hazard for religious people. Loving is hard and perilous, and there are many counterfeits. Part of soulmaking involves the willingness to sort out the true from the false and to face those inner cravings for control, security, and affection, that masquerade as love.

LOVE, DEATH, POWER, AND TIME

Carol Bly, in *Letters from the Country*, highlights four concerns that have to do with the theme of soul making. They are love (which speaks to our desire for union); death (which raises questions with regard to our destiny); power (which challenges us with issues of vulnerability); and time (which forces us to see our lives in terms of a play, a drama, or a story). We have come across all four in our travels through the desert.

Time is one of the most neglected topics in discussions of human relations. It takes a long time to make a soul. It takes a long time to make love. Intimacy takes time. Marriage takes time. After nearly twenty years I still haven't got the hang of it. Time gives our loving and our mutual soul making clarity and resilience by providing them with a narrative thread. This is a theme we shall have to come back to when we look at the question of conversion. Suffice it to say now that a narrative thread is vital for the making of a soul because we are all actors, "devoted actors at a sacrifice." The marriage vows speak to this need for dramatic continuity . . . "for better, for worse, for richer, for poorer, in sickness and in health, till death us do part." And these vows speak not only to those of us who are married, but to those who are not. True loving requires the kind of commitment that assumes a future where things might get better or they might get worse, but the loving will go on.

There's an old joke about how the various nationalities make love. Like all jokes of this genre, there is something to offend everyone. In each case it is taken for granted that love-making is an isolated act related only to the present moment and only concerned with personal gratification. The German woman looks up at the man after making love and says, "Hans, that was great. Where do we eat?" The French woman says, "C'est magnifique! Encore! encore!" The Russian responds, "Ivan, that was fantastic. You have raised my production level by 100 percent!" The American says, "Gee, honey, that was terrific. What didya say your name was?" Finally, the English woman turns to the man and says, "There, Hubert, feeling better?" It is only a joke, and admittedly not a very good one; but it hits close to home in pointing out some of the ways in which we use each other (sexually or otherwise) and call it love. We use each other as a means to something else: food, narcissistic gratification, power, to scratch an itch, or as a means of diminishing another person. In short, we use others in our efforts to be close or in our attempts to solve internal problems or meet personal needs. The idea of failure or of negative capability appals us.

Carol Bly suggests that we have two kinds of receptivity to life. The first has to do with our being touched by beauty, pain, or the unknown; the second with our will and capacity to solve problems. She writes:

Our gritty society wants and therefore deliberately trains problem solvers, however and not mystics. We teach human beings to keep themselves conscious only of problems that *can* conceivably be solved. There must be no hopeless causes. Now this means that some subjects of which death and sexual love come to mind straight off, should be kept at as low a level of consciousness as possible. Both resist problem solving . . . For example, a physician who has that mentality [i.e., that of a problem solver] does not wish to be near dying patients very much. They are definitely not a solvable problem.

The making of the soul as well as the making of a lover

requires the receptivity to life of the mystic rather than that of the problem solver. The latter are more common in our society, and we need them. But the shortage of mystics, desert believers, explorers of the inner world is the reason why we are undergoing a crisis of soul in our society, why we do not know how to love. Love is transformed into psychic poison when it is used as a means to an end, as a way of "solving a problem." I, for one, am not a solvable problem, and I don't want to be treated like one. I begin to happen in a new way (my soul comes to life) when someone says, "Alan, sometimes you're a mess, often you're infuriating, and I love you!" The soul cannot breathe when a person says, "There are some problems we have to iron out—in fact, you're the major one—before I can tell whether I love you or not."

This does not mean, of course, that there are problems that should not be faced and sorted out. It is just that we need to understand that our basic relationship to reality (we might even say to God) is one of gift, the wild card. The soul flourishes in the light of the spontaneous and the unconditional. We have, therefore, to learn to operate on two levels at the same time. We have "to keep both streams going—the problem-solving, which seems to be the mental genius of our species, and the fearless contemplation of gigantic things, the spiritual genius of our species." Souls come into being when they are willing to contemplate gigantic things, when they are willing to allow the wildness of the wild card to enter their systems.

We live, however, in a world for the most part mesmerized by its real problems; and, subsequently, we find ourselves in the thrall of the problem-solvers. "Gigantic things" cannot be solved. And what a threat they are to the ego! We would rather tackle small problems, problems that we know are solvable. We are very good at setting goals and gaining objectives. Such skill at coping with problems is very important. But if that is *all* we do, we gradually deny ourselves the possibility of playing poker on a beach with God. Love is denied because we spend a great deal of our energy building up our frail egos by "setting before it dozens and dozens of small situations." Thus the soul is aborted. When it is fed only on the small and solvable it shrivels and begins to die. Gigantic questions about love, death, power, and time feed the soul. They do not confront us as problems to be solved, but as mysteries to be wondered at, or intractable darknesses to be raged at or endured. "Playing poker with God" is a wonderful image for those who have come to the end of their rope with trying to solve their problems. The bag of tricks is exhausted, the repertoire of strategies is spent. There is nothing left.

This does not mean that we give up. There are problems to be solved and we must go on trying to solve them. But we need to learn that there is power in surrender, in contemplation of the gigantic things. Such contemplation is the very ground of our acting in the world. Without the willingness to be still on the beach and play poker, we won't have the energy or the resources that laughter and simple exhilaration in being alive brings. Carol Bly asks that the English teachers in our schools

help our children preserve pity, happiness and grief inside themselves . . . Adults . . . should make it clear that we expect this of English teachers and that we don't give a damn if Leroy and Merv never in their lives get the sentence balance of past conditional and perfect subjunctive clauses right. We need to protect some of the Things Invisible inside LeRoy and Merv and the rest of us.[11]

I would like to substitute the word joy for the word happiness in the quotation above, and add the word passion. We might, then, extend this request to preserve pity, joy, grief, and passion to clergy, counselors, and therapists. And why not engineers, politicians and deep-sea divers? Why not all of us? The soul is born when pity, joy, grief, and passion are preserved.

PAYING ATTENTION TO THE THINGS INVISIBLE

Soul making, then, has something to do with paying attention to the Things Invisible, things which do not lend themselves to manipulation and control. Things which contribute to the making of a soul will not succumb to being treated as problems to be solved. If we are concerned about those neurotic and destructive forces that try to abort the soul (often associated with mere problem solving), we will have to switch our whole style of thinking away from an overdeveloped analytical one to one that is more contemplative, more concerned for the Invisible Things. Soul making requires a move away from the need and desire to control to a waiting on the mystery at the heart of things. Negative capability is the key. It means cultivating a readiness for wonder and being ready for the special kind of pain that contemplative availability to reality always brings.

The kind of special wisdom for soul making is not "out there" to be had. The wisdom of the saints and mystics comes to us only after we have placed ourselves in a position of waiting and receptivity. This wisdom is what the medieval theologians called "connatural knowledge": a kind of knowing that is not so much intellectual as interior and intuitive. For example, to know what holiness really is, one must (in some small sense) *be* holy. To know what love really is one must have some experience of it.

This isn't to say that one must be completely holy or loving in order to know about these things. The seeds of holiness and love have to be there; or, better, the longing for them must be acknowledged if the soul is to grow. Longing and desire play a great part in soul making. It is as if God has deliberately put unfulfilled desires into our hearts so that our hearts may be stretched beyond their present capacity. Soul making requires this kind of stretching. It not enough to know *about* soul making, although there are some who like to dabble in a kind of psychic horticulture. It should be clear by now that such dabbling is merely a device to avoid the genuine birth of the soul. It is an invidious form of resistance to the very life for which the soul longs.

We become more and more who we are (that, after all, is another way of talking about soul making) when we struggle with the "four last things," the Things Invisible: love, death, power, and time. To be a soul (to be fully mature and alive as a person) is to struggle in hope with love, because we know that at our deepest we are loved. To be a soul is to know what it is to be a terminal case—to have come to terms, however minimally, with the fact that we are going to die. To be a soul means to know what it is to struggle for, to achieve, and to be denied power. To be a soul is to live in time, with all its opportunities and limitations. Our life is a story that slowly unfolds in time. The believer understands that the great wild card promises that we are to be understood, recognized, and known in terms of our future, which is secure in God, rather than our past. This means that, no matter how painful the memories are of a past in which there is much to regret, that past does not determine who and what we are. We are in God's hands. This does not mean that our past does not affect our present and our future. It simply means that the past does not have the last word. The wild card of God's unconditional love has seen to that.

One of the most damaging things about the popular view of love is that it requires being nice all the time. I don't think that I am a particularly nice person. In fact, one of the reasons that I count myself among the believers is that I cannot rely on my being nice to pull me through. Being nice is closely allied, of course, to being liked. The two go together. If I'm not nice you won't like me, and if you don't like me then there is no chance of love springing up between us. This kind of reasoning breeds dishonesty because it means that "love" becomes a code word for avoiding confrontation or disagreement. True love requires a strict and accurate regard for truth. We live in an age that would prefer the smooth lie to the hard truth. The result is that we are very poor at honoring genuine feelings and hard-won convictions. In the name of caring for each other we often do everything we can to diffuse one another's passion. We are embarrassed by strong expressions of emotion.

LOVE IS A KIND OF PAIN FOR WHICH WE ARE STARVED

Love, therefore, can easily become a device for avoiding unpleasantness and denying tragedy. In the name of love we tend to deny "pity, joy, grief, and passion" and all for the sake of an egocentric "peace." Carol Bly writes of the dire consequences in ordinary human life when these great Invisible Things are denied. Love is reduced to niceness and the passion and the grief are driven underground. Imagine a frustrated and angry man finding his way to the local bar. He wants to get away from the lie he's been living by trying to be nice all the time. He's about to explode because of all the energy and passion that's been building up inside him. His energy has no outlet. And so, the hell with it: he's going to do some serious drinking; that is, he is going to recover, somehow, feelings he has repressed . . . [in the bar] there is a very common expression of true cunning and a will to see straight; the men's eyes stare and look bald. . . .they have come to recover repressed knowledge which their wives or their town won't let them uncover elsewhere, not for a moment. They have come to say the damned things . . . [about politics, big business, religion]

The man has had a pretty good drunk and, in the process, has recovered an important part of himself. Getting drunk is certainly not the best way to achieve this. In fact, it is dangerous and destructive. But for some in our repressed and repressive society it is the only way. The man returns home and his wife is angry and terrified.

She snaps at him. And he is so vulnerable because his spirit is freed and has climbed outward nearly to his skin—in fact, it is nearly on his surface . . . So, when his wife snaps at him in her pain, she attacks part of his spiritual life.

She has no idea what a stunning blow it is. All his quiet judgments leak back down through the great crack in him . . . as water drops with lightning speed into a fissure of the earth, and then the crack itself closes, and he is locked out of his soul again for a while.

It is in such daily incidents when pity, joy, grief, and passion are denied that the soul is aborted. Our neuroses are God-given signals to us of these denials. Life will not be denied. If we cannot or will not live it out creatively then life erupts in "a good drunk," a fit of meanness, or uncharacteristic behavior. We often hear someone say, "I don't know what came over me." What "comes over us" is those parts of us that are denied and unlived. They need air. Without it they smell, and the odor of those repressed and unlived parts of us eventually finds its way to the surface.

A friend of mine once gave a lecture entitled "Your Neuroses as a low-grade Form of Religion." This title expresses an important truth; namely, that even our weaknesses are signs of life trying to get out. Love without a strict regard for the truth of what lies under the surface of things is not love at all. Souls are not made by lies, denials, or avoidances. Some believers (and I among them) are repelled by certain forms of religion that avoid the difficult or the unpleasant. Carol Bly quotes the old Christian camp-fire song:

> The Lord of Love
> Has come to me—
> I want to pass it on.

The problem is that for the desert believer, this is true—but it is not the whole truth.

> The experience is simply not complete because *contentment*, as such, which American churches teach without teaching *discontent* with it, simply doesn't explain our crimes, our fears, our horrible inaccuracy in reading each other's feelings, the sheer hauntedness of our dreams— all the things the unconscious, the thousand natural shocks to which Shakespeare knew we were "heir."
> The churches teach contentment even though Jesus lectured against it. He said he would divide man from man, and that he came with a sword. That suggests that Christians are supposed to have some pain. We are starved of this pain.[12]

Love is a kind of pain for which we are starved. The pain comes when all that we have tried to deny will be denied no longer. The soul suffocates when it is walled up. No wonder it resorts to violence when the pressure gets too much. Love, the wild card, comes to such a soul by first puncturing the hardened shell in which it has encased itself. Love, therefore, often comes as a terror—a threat to the self-protecting carapace under which we shelter. A friend explains to William Golding's hero Wilfred the dire consequences to the soul that constructs for itself a protective shell.

> You see, you are what biologists used to call exoskeletal. Most people are . . . endoskeletal, have their bones inside. But you, my dear, for some reason known only to God . . . have spent your life inventing a skeleton on the outside. Like crabs and lobsters. That's terrible, you see, because the worms get inside, and . . . they have the place to themselves. So my advice . . . is to get rid of the armour, the exoskeleton, the carapace, before it's too late.[13]

The task of love is to help us rid ourselves of the exoskeleton, to lay us bare, to set us free. But we love the prison-house. The place of bondage is, at least, familiar. Love, then, comes as an unwelcome shock. The very thing we think we want, we dread. Witness George Herbert:

> Love bade me welcome; yet I drew back,
>   Guilty of dust and sin.
> But quick-ey'd Love, observing me grown slack
>   From my first entrance in,
> Drew nearer to me, sweetly questioning
>   If I lack'd anything . . .
>
> "You must sit down," says Love, "and taste My meat."
>   So I did sit and eat.

Love invites us to that game of poker on the beach. Who would not hesitate? Who does not long to play?

III. THE CALL TO JOY

7. Love and the Making of a Soul

> The point is, one will never get to the end of it, never get to the bottom of it, never, never, never. And never, never, never, is what you must take for your shield and your most glorious promise.[1]
>
> IRIS MURDOCH

Love is that which lies beyond the fiftieth gate. Its infinite power is bound up with the "never, never, never" of limitless possibilities. Accepting the fact that one will never get to the bottom of it is like falling into the abyss where souls are made. Human beings take a long time to come to maturity. We are not made overnight. Or, to change the metaphor, playing poker requires patience and skill and even to attempt to play poker with God is surely self-defeating. Were it not for the fifth ace, the wild card, we would end up in a state of despair, impotence, and rage.

The card game and the "never, never, never" of the abyss of love, of course, are only metaphors; and what I have tried to say about desert believing and the making of souls has been simply playing with such images. To those who are "problem solvers" and "thinking types," this way of approach is at best unsatisfactory. I respect the problem solvers and the thinkers. They are needed. But I believe that when we want to keep alive important mysteries, another approach to reality is called for. If we would learn about love and the making of the soul we have to enter the world of myth, metaphor, and image. We have to be content with hints and gestures towards meaning. We have to surrender our desire to control reality by analysis and system building. These are vital skills for human growth and flourishing; but love (and therefore soulmaking) requires surrender. We have to come out from behind the protective carapace provided by analysis and system and expose ourselves to the elements.

SOUL MAKING REQUIRES PRECISION, FEAR, AND DELIGHT

Soul making involves the willingness to cultivate a certain disposition towards the world and to other people; an attitude of receptivity and openness. The question is: "Are we so wrapped up in ourselves that we have lost the capacity to be touched at our deepest?" If we can still be reached by the world and what is in it, there is hope. The soul is alive. Love is a possibility. There is hope even for the intellectual, a much-despised creature in our culture! George Steiner writes:

A man who has read Book XXIV of the Iliad—the night meeting of Priam and Achilles—or the chapter in which Alyosha Karamazov kneels to the stars, who has read Montaigne's chapter XX (*Que philosopher c'est apprendre l'art de mourir*/to philosophize is to learn the art of dying) and Hamlet's use of it—and who is not altered, whose apprehension of his own life is unchanged, who does not, in some subtle yet radical manner, look on the room in which he moves, or those that knock at the door, differently—has read only with the blindness of physical sight. Can one read *Anna Karenina* or Proust without experiencing a new infirmity or occasion in the very core of one's sexual feelings? It is the task of literary criticism to help us read as total human beings, by example of precision, fear and delight.[2]

At first sight, this somewhat erudite and elitist view of literature may appear to have nothing to do with either love or soul-making. Steiner is writing for those few who have read Homer, Dostoyevski, Montaigne, Shakespeare, Tolstoy, and Proust. In spite of the fact that Steiner's examples exclude the unlettered and undereducated, his main point is applicable to all of us. Our souls do not grow or move when we are so caught up in ourselves that we are unable to be touched. If we are incapable of being changed, altered, turned around by what we see and hear, then we are reading the story of our own life and that of others "with the blindness of physical sight."

How are we to read the story of our own life? There are patterns and cycles to be discerned in the inner life as in the outer. We follow a pattern of finding and losing, of dying and rising, of diminishment and increase. It is not unrelated to the cycle of the seasons of nature. Spring gives way to summer, and then the earth dies away through fall into winter. The story of the human soul does not unfold on automatic or fatalistic lines; but it has its own laws and the story needs to be read accurately if we want to share actively in its telling.

Steiner's description of the work of the literary critic might well be applied to that of desert believer, soul maker, lover. Believing, soul making, and loving require the three ingredients Steiner identifies as necessary to appreciating books: precision, fear, and delight. We have encountered these under various guises in the preceding chapters: precision in exploring the attentiveness and accuracy required in psychoanalysis and desert believing; fear in journeying to the fiftieth gate and facing death; delight in finding the wild card of unconditional love. Delight is an important word in the art of soul making. The Latin version of "God so loved the world" (John 3:16) reads *Sic Deus dilexit mundum*, which we might translate as "God so delighted in the world . . . " The Psalmist puts it this way: "He brought me out into an open place; he rescued me because he delighted in me" (Psalm 18:20). The hardest part of moving into mature believing is to allow oneself to be the object of God's delight. One of the priests who helped me to "make my soul" in my early twenties used to say that God made the world out of sheer *joie de vivre*, sheer joy of living, sheer delight.

Thus the making of a soul requires precision, fear, and delight; precision for the sake of clarity and honesty, and fear and delight because they are precise and accurate responses to the world as it really is. The question remains, however, as to the identity of the One who has been pursuing me, loving me, delighting in me. *Who* is this Lover who wants to bring me home? Unless I know the one who loves me, I have no way of responding, no way of learning how to love in return. I need a model of love. I need an example, a paradigm. A paradigm is simply a key pattern through which minor patterns are interpreted and coordinated. We all need them, including the unbelievers and half-believers among us.

THE NEED FOR A LENS THROUGH WHICH TO SEE THE WORLD

Morris West has created an interesting non-believer in his novel *The Clowns of God*. Annelein Meissner is a professor of clinical psychology. She worships at the shrine of precision. At one point in the story, she is thinking aloud with a friend about the need for models, paradigms, key images. She confesses:

the idea of salvation begins to make sense. We all experience pain, injustice, confusion, death. We struggle to stay whole through the experience. Even when we fail, we try to salvage ourselves out of the wreckage. We can't do it alone. We need support. We need more—a module or exemplar to show us what a whole human being looks like . . .

Yes . . . But the important question is, which module do you choose and why?[3]

Love always leaves me with the question of choice. I find myself scared to step out into the world where my choices matter. Much better to be a victim of circumstances. Victims bear no responsibility. They live in a world where blame and fault can be laid elsewhere. It is true that we are all victims in certain areas of our life. But most of us in the West have little conception of what it is like to be victimized by grinding poverty, gnawing hunger, and brutal injustice. We are mainly "victimized" by the trivial and the inconvenient. We have plenty of leisure time to concentrate on inner tyrannies and addictions: the tyranny of our egocentricity, our addiction to safety and security.

Soul making is a matter of choosing a certain paradigm or model. And the choice makes all the difference. Psychoanalysis is one method by which the soul is slowly freed to make a choice. It is one of the disciplines that help us choose *not* to be victim to our addictions and inner tyrannies. But how do we choose a "module or exemplar to show us what a whole human being looks like"? And can we count on any help once we have found and chosen the paradigm? Believers would affirm that while they *thought* they were choosing the paradigm, the paradigm was actually choosing them.

There is no way round the issue of the need to surrender to a "model" or exemplar if we are to move towards psychological and spiritual maturity. We will inevitably come to the question of conversion. Being in love is a key metaphor for understanding this process. The lover is mesmerized, besotted by the vision of the beloved. It is the prism through which the whole world is viewed. Anyone who has been in love (even if only for a short time) knows what it is to see the world through a particular lens. The lover is swept away and carried along by the passion for the beloved. It is a kind of conversion experience and, like all conversion experiences, can be lived into or betrayed.

We *see* someone, and suddenly the world changes. Dante saw the young girl Beatrice, and even though he was only nine years old, his world changed irrevocably. He saw the glory of God in a little girl and he did not understand the vision. To betray the vision would be to betray his very soul. Betrayal of Beatrice would mean the unraveling of his very self, the un-making of his soul. It took Dante a lifetime to work out the meaning of the vision. He had to plumb the depths of Hell and climb the heights of Purgatory in order to enjoy the heavenly fullness of the vision.

For those who profess and call themselves Christians, the lens through which everything else is interpreted is a person: Jesus Christ and his death and resurrection. Just as the lover never plumbs the mystery of the beloved, so we do not exhaust the mystery of Jesus. This, at first, seems a strange claim. But it is no less extraordinary that contemporary "messiahs, saviors, and gurus" possess the consciousness of modern men and women. For some the model is the Ayatollah Khomeini, for others it is Michael Jackson. A walk on a Saturday evening through the streets of a busy city reveals what models, exemplars, paradigms are operating in the lives of the people.

We cannot do without a paradigm to help us live. As a believer, I keep bumping into Jesus. I wander away, and there he is, perhaps in the eyes of someone on the street. There is no escape for me. Nor do I want there to be.

Sophisticated people are often unconscious of the models they have chosen (or which have chosen them). They are often looking for a way out of the prison of the ordinary. Human beings need a ritual, an icon, a holy place that will lift them out of the terrifying grip of a deadly everydayness. David Tracy writes, "Only the paradigmatic will heal what has happened to the ordinary in our lives—the wasted, distracted lives in society, our ambivalent recognitions of the terror in our willful history."[4]

The question remains: which model, which paradigm, which exemplar? The choice will make all the difference. That is why the last two chapters will be concerned with the twin lenses through which the desert believer looks at the world; conversion to Christ, and life in the Holy and Undivided Trinity. For believers, it is nothing less than the probing of the first and great love which first made us see. If not Jesus, then who or what?

"Choose and be chosen" is a law of the psychological and spiritual life. No one can avoid choosing or being chosen by a "paradigm." It is where we locate our sense of identity, where we find ourselves, our place. Human beings have found their sense of identity in such diverse models and paradigms as celibacy, sex, war, reason, equality, buffaloes, snakes, tea, peyote, alcohol, tranquility, money, ecology, psychoanalysis, Mao, and Christ. Choosing, therefore, is very important, because who we are and where we stand will depend on our choice.[5]

What happens when the soul is possessed of an evil and destructive paradigm? Two disturbing phrases from the teenage subculture have struck me forcibly with the power of negative images to capture the imagination: "Here's a dime, go and call someone who cares." The second is, "I think you must be mistaking me for someone who gives a shit."

Once the imagination has been infected by the interpretive key of self-hatred, where no positive paradigm can do its healing work, it is very difficult to shake it off. We become possessed by resentment, depression, and vindictiveness. The key makes all the difference. A thick, unpolished, and dirty lens seriously restricts our view. And souls are made by seeing and seeing clearly. Some days the visibility is good; on other occasions poor.

EVERYONE FINDS A CENTER

In order to be formed into a person, a human being has to be organized around a center. Christians center themselves on Jesus, Jews on the Torah, followers of Islam on the Koran,

Marxists on Marx, Freudians on Freud, the selfish on themselves. There are, of course, backsliders, revisionists, and heretics. But we all find a center, a love, and order our lives within the circle of our allegiance. Circles have the habit of getting smaller and smaller in order to keep their devotees centered and loyal. Thus there springs up a contrary need for disorganization. We need to break out of the tight little circles we get ourselves into so that they can be enlarged and reforged.

The desert believer's soul is formed through his double process of the making and breaking of circles. That is why the unbeliever is important. The unbeliever is a sign of this contrary iconoclastic need. What we are looking for is a paradigm that can bear both holding and breaking at its heart. Lovers understand this because they have to learn what it is to hold another without chaining up the other's soul. An unidentified person gave the following poem to someone who has done a great deal of work in the area of care for the terminally ill. It speaks of the need to let go, to be one's own person in simplicity.

> After a while you learn the subtle difference
> Between holding and chaining a soul,
> And you learn that love doesn't mean leaning
> And company doesn't mean security,
> And you begin to learn that kisses aren't
> contracts
> And presents aren't promises,
> And you begin to accept your defeats
> With your head up and your eyes open,
> And learn to build all your roads
> On today because tomorrow's ground
> Is too uncertain for plans, and futures have
> A way of falling down in mid-flight.
> After a while you learn that even sunshine
> Burns if you get too much.
> So you plant your own garden and decorate
> Your own soul, instead of waiting
> For someone to bring you flowers,
> And you learn that you really can endure . . .
> That you really are strong
> And you really do have worth.
> And you learn and learn . . .
> With every good-bye you learn.

John Drury describes a similar pattern of "letting go" when he tries to find a paradigm that corresponds to the experience of lovers.

It needs to be something more than religion as so far achieved and organized. It will even have to be something opposed to the confidence mixed with possessive restlessness of such religion, if it is to save religious people from the tight circles their religions get themselves into. If it posits a centre, as religions apparently have to do, it will have to be not just majestically clear and hospitable but also a *self-denying centre*. It will have to be a centre in which breaking and giving away is at least as permanently at work as joining and holding. There is an image of it in the central Christian rite of Holy Communion: the focal "body" of Christ broken and given.[6]

I do not expect unbelievers to make this connection between the need for such a paradigm and the central act of Christian worship, but I think they may understand why believers do so. For the believer, Jesus is the breaker of the charmed and throttling circle that holds us in its spell.

The God of our Savior Jesus Christ is the center of a faith that is as much concerned with breaking and letting go as with holding and binding. It is a faith for lovers. The believer claims that this double action of holding and breaking is characteristic of the life of God himself. Love is God's name. Genuine lovers and true believers know how far they are from being able, in any consistent way, to hold and let go at the same time. I tend to define myself, not in the light of a model or paradigm, but rather by a process of elimination or exclusion. I often measure myself against others, in the hope that I will come out just a little ahead. When I do this, love escapes me and my soul begins to dry up. I dislike people who excel. I resent those who surpass me.

The inability of human beings to reach out and touch each other causes many of us to suffer from a deformed and crippled sense of self. Where, then, is help to be found? A paradigm alone won't do. I need more than an example. I need help. Love requires a miracle because everything conspires to encourage me to define myself at your expense. If I am to grow and be fulfilled, then some of you will have to make do with less. This, after all, is the law under which our society lives and works: the law of *libido dominandi* (the desire to dominate). Is it not naive, even irresponsible, to think otherwise? We live in a competitive society, and there is only so much wealth to go round. Any fool knows that the things of this world are diminished by sharing. What we must do, therefore, is to get as large a slice of life as we can. My secret hope is that my slice will be substantially larger than my neighbor's. Love and the making of souls, however, follows a different logic. Love is the one "commodity" that is not diminished by sharing. In fact, it is increased. But that takes a lot of believing.

Why should one expect people to believe in a principle of sharing contrary to the principles that operate in the everyday world? The kind of work many people have to do in our society is often demoralizing. Its only reward is financial. In the long run, such work diminishes and mutilates human souls. For many it is an act of determination and courage simply to get up in the morning and survive the day. It is surely too much to ask that they be outgoing and altruistic as well.

There is, however, one other factor that militates our taking seriously the law of love and the realities of soul making. The social and political implications of men and women taking the law of love seriously are far-reaching. Love would radically upset existing structures. Love of this kind tends to bring with it change and upheaval. That is why most of us are resistant to it. In everyday life we make do with anything that might look like love. We settle for anything when the real thing eludes us. The experience of "everydayness," when today is very much the same as yesterday and tomorrow will be more of the same, makes me want to cry out in my loneliness, curl up in someone's arms, close my eyes and suck my thumb until I drop off to sleep. In short, I want my mommy! This desire, of course, is a commonplace of psychology. Since my mother is no longer available, I have to make the best of what I have. I make do. I have to admit that I am not looking for love in any mature sense; I am looking for safety and security. I need to be held safe and warm against the abyss, the darkness. So where does my eye rove when I realize that I can no longer curl up in my mother's lap? I turn to religion and to romance. Others may turn to money or to power. Love becomes a way into oblivion. Soul making is exchanged for soul stupor.

I am a believer; but when I turn to religion, I often find a religious universe in which I feel a stranger. The mainstream of religion in our culture is, to me, unattractive. I labored this point at the beginning of the book because I wanted to disassociate myself from its crass and crude appeal to the lowest of human emotions and its tendency to exploit human beings when they are at their most vulnerable. There seems to be little love and certainly not much soul. I have come to think that my judgment in this matter is not fair. It is understandable, but it is not just. For me to reject the popular religionists would be for me to succumb to the very disease I abhor. If I am to grow in love, if my soul is to continue to be made, if Jesus really is *the* paradigm for me, then I will have to surrender this judgmental attitude. I can no more reject my fellow believers than I can reject my blood relations. I may not like them, but the ties of blood are indissoluble. So it is when the soul is stretched into loving. It binds us together in such a way that to reject another is to reject one's own flesh. Those whose religion repels and appals me are my brothers and sisters. Those whose irreligion saddens and hurts me are my brothers and sisters.

CONVERSION TO JESUS CHRIST: ISSUES OF LOVE AND KNOWLEDGE

Conversion to Jesus Christ, for me, has been a struggle about love and knowledge. The point is that I do not know what I know and I do not know who I am without a paradigm. I cannot do without some means of self-recognition. While I do not want to reduce Jesus Christ to a mere paradigm, he is at least that for me. He is the means by which I interpret myself and my experience. In more theological language, Jesus is God's Word to me about myself. He imparts saving knowledge, in that he illuminates and enlivens my present experience of the world. For example, when I read the Bible within the community of faith I am able to say, "Ah! so that's what's been happening to me!" I am given an interpretive framework in which to set my life.

The paradigm or interpretive framework inevitably comes to me in story form. That is why Bible stories are important. Cohn, the lonely survivor with some apes in Bernard Malamud's *God's Grace,* tries to explain to Buz (a chimpanzee) the origin of stories. "Somebody spoke a metaphor and that broke into a story. Man began to tell them to keep his life from washing away."[7] I need stories to keep my life from washing away. And the story of Jesus is, for me, the key to all other stories. Stories, however, are not enough. Paradigms are everywhere; but Jesus is not only *a* or even *the* paradigm, but Savior. A savior is someone who comes to the rescue. Jesus is the One who comes to me. He is the One to whom I am accountable and responsible (which means that I am free to say "no," I am free to blow it and mess up my own life). I am loved so much that damnation is a possibility. He is the One who calls me and brings me home.

It is likely that any unbelievers who have stayed with me this far have, on reading the previous paragraph, been put off by what appears to be an illogical affirmation of faith. What I have done is simply *name* that which has been luring, goading, and drawing me through all the desert experiences. I name him Jesus, because that which has been drawing me is intensely personal. I name him Jesus because I know of no other name that so adequately fits the wide range of human experience (from the tragic to the glorious). When I am honest, I experience myself as a mass of contradictions (at least in my imagination). I am an artist, an authoritarian, a bigot. I am rich. I am poor. I am gifted. I am useless. I am cruel. I am loving. In Christ, nothing has to be left out, or sanitized. All my many "me's" meet in him, and with him I do not have to lie about any of them. I bring them for love, for healing, for acceptance. Carl Sandburg expresses something of this idea in his poem "Wilderness."

"There is a wolf in me . . . fangs pointed for tearing gashes . . . a red tongue for raw meat . . . and the hot lapping of blood—I keep this wolf because the wilderness gave it to me and the wilderness will not let it go.

Sandburg continues with his inner animals (the fox, the hog, the fish, the baboon, and the eagle) and concludes,

O, I got a zoo, I got a menagerie, inside my ribs, under my bony head, under my red-valve heart—and I got something else: it is a man-child heart, a woman-child heart: it is a father and mother and lover: it came from God-Knows-Where: it is going to God-Knows-Where—For I am a pal of the world: I came from the wilderness.[8]

Jesus came from the wilderness. And no other name does justice to all that we human beings are. I am, therefore, making exclusivist claims for Jesus. There is something irreducibly exclusivist about the Christian faith, but the exclusivity is turned on its head by its very subject matter. How are we to be exclusive about an all-inclusive, self-denying love? For a believer to urge the exclusive claims of Christ in a bullying, offensive, and triumphalist manner is to deny the very Spirit of the Christ one is proclaiming. Christ bullies no one. The Cross coerces no one. The believer longs for all to share in the knowledge and the love he or she has received. The believer is not content to be the member of an exclusive club. Believers know about the wilderness, the desert. The two great characteristics of the desert believer are joy and gratitude. These are the marks of the converted life.

COMING HOME AND FINDING LOVE

What is it, then, which unites us all—believers and unbelievers alike? The double desire to love and be loved is common to everyone. It is the ancient drive of *eros* that unites us one with another. *Eros* is not simply the drive towards sexual fulfillment; it is the impulse towards any satisfaction and completion. Believers, like the poet Dante, affirm that this basic drive of ours is good and is directed, in the end, to and by *the* Good who is God. God is the One who attracts, lures, draws us to himself. Thus the word "God" begins to acquire some kind of meaning when it becomes a codeword for the object and reason for our longing and our hoping. This by no means begins to exhaust the meaning of the word "God"; but it is helpful to see it related to that to which every human being is drawn.

All our desires spring basically from the same source. All our "erotic" impulses, even when misdirected, destructive, and erratic, relate in the end to the "Love of God." Love in this sense is much more than a romantic urge. It is the desire of every creature to find its proper place, to find its true home. It is like the force of gravity, which pulls things to their rightful place in the scheme of things. Water finds its own level. Smoke from a flame naturally rises upwards. So it was believed that everything spontaneously tended towards its own place. It is love that draws everything to its own unique home—for Dante, it is that which, literally, makes the world go round. It is this love/impulse that we all share in common.

When we talk about love, therefore, we are talking about our proper place in the pattern of things. We are talking about home. We are talking about the limitations and possibilities set by a particular time and a particular place. Souls are made and unmade in time and space. The unmaking of a soul depends on how far it refuses to follow its own homing instinct. In the Christian tradition this homing instinct is closely related to "God's Will." The most famous line in Dante's Paradiso is, "In his will is our peace" (III:85), which means that our true home is in the heart of God. To be a lover is, by definition, to be someone who is on his way home.

Psychoanalysis is one of the many paradigms or models for our struggle to find home, to find love. It begins with the arduous process of dismantling the false self which has tried, through various neurotic strategies, to make itself at home in the wrong place. These neurotic patterns, as we have seen, have to be disentangled if our "homing device" is to function properly. The neuroses are the result of a damaged compass that consistently and perversely sends us off in the wrong direction. The Jungian analyst, Robert Johnson, says that for every step forward he takes three steps back. It happens to be all right, because he was going in the wrong direction in any case!

Perhaps our internal compass knows more than we do. We used to call it our "conscience," a word that needs some rehabilitation. It has often been identified not with our homing instinct, but with the neurotic demands of our superego. Some of us are so confused about what we really want out of life that we often mistake a neurotic demand for a genuine desire to find our way home. We find ourselves on a treadmill looking for love: the treadmill of compulsiveness masquerades as duty; the treadmill of self-absorption is under the cloak of self-expression; the treadmill of moral confusion is done up to look like newness of life.

The process of uncovering such patterns of self-deception brings us into a place of psychological and spiritual openness that can be frightening. The will seems to have lost its power. Having given up following paths that lead nowhere, it dawns on us that perhaps there is nowhere to go. There is no love, no home, no place for us to be. We belong nowhere. It is at this point, where we are most vulnerable, that the second and more important stage of psychological development begins.

There is no shortcut to the second stage. We must reach this point of extreme vulnerability before we can move on to responsibility and maturity. The life of the will (which is the homing instinct) is repaired, and we slowly find the road to our true self. Now we are ready for love and the moral bite it puts into our everyday living.

Yes, love has teeth! It asks us one terrible and demanding question; "What are you going to *do* now? Now that you've stopped blaming your mother, your husband, your wife, your environment, the communists, the capitalists, the atheists, the fundamentalists . . . What are you going to do?" Being a lover, becoming a soul, means making choices. The key choice is, which paradigm? Who or what is *the* One for you? Who is the One who is calling you home? For me, the one is Jesus, inescapably Jesus.

The wild longing associated with adolescence has much to teach the so-called adult world. We often mistake maturity for a dampened ardor or a dried-up enthusiasm. True spiritual maturity is the serious honoring of the validity of our deepest longings. The soul of the maturing adult knows that love has to do with binding and with letting go; with the "never, never, never" of its boundless possibilities; and with "accepting the universe." We need to recapture the romantic impulse in its mature form. This means refusing to lapse into bitterness and cynicism when the romantic longing leads us into the wilderness of hurt, disappointment, and rejection. Being "romantic" in a mature way is a means of keeping important things alive in us,

things that would die without it. We have already looked at some
of these things: pity, grief, and happiness. We might now add
longing, hope, and the capacity to be touched.

The adolescent in me wants either an easy romanticism or a
special kind of suffering, of which I am the center. I am rescued
time and time again from the vicious narrowness of my own
projects and schemes precisely by the agency I both dread and
long for. That agency is other people, not least the unattractive
and despised among them. Jesus calls me, but I don't like some
of his friends. I am beginning to realize that my likes and
dislikes have very little to do with the case. Sometimes I feel like
the young woman who was supposed to have said in Thomas
Carlyle's hearing, "I accept the universe." Carlyle replied, "Gad!
She'd better!" Whenever I hear myself saying, in one form or
another, "I accept my fellow human beings," I hear another
voice thunder back, "Gad! He'd better!"

How can I relate to these others without wanting either to
merge with them or to put up barriers to keep them out? We
get tired of being alone, and we are fatigued by trying to keep
others at a distance. That is why some of us would rather give
up our individuality in order to belong to a group than be
alone. As a desert believer, I seek to be one with others, and yet
uniquely and unrepeatably my own person. To do this I need a
Savior. To do this I need to be loved by One who is Love. To do
this I need to be born again.

> Oh, Mary,
> Gentle Mother,
> open the door and let me in.
> A bee has stung your belly with faith.
> Let me float in it like a fish.
> Let me in! Let me in!
> I have been born many times, a false Messiah,
> but let me be born again
> into something true.[9]

The appeal to the mother is not accidental. Explortion of the
models of human development through the lenses of psychoanalysis and the desert leads us to the point of death and rebirth.
To be born again is to go back into the womb in order to re-

emerge with a new heart. Anne Sexton's imagery is very powerful. We are to float in the belly of the Mother like a fish. This belly is swollen with faith. It would be a rare human being indeed who has not, at one time or another, been brought to the edge of this abyss, to the womb of faith where the only rule is trust and surrender.

Both the desert way and that of psychoanalysis bring us to the issue of surrender. Why is surrender essential? If I refuse to respond to the invitation to surrender, I am then burdened over and over again to be born a false Messiah. I have to become my own savior, and that is exhausting. There is a desire in me to let go. There is a growing conviction that all of us are on the edge of great pain and great joy. W. H. Auden expresses the mood of the desert believer:

> Beloved, we are always in the wrong,
> Handling so clumsily our stupid lives,
> Suffering too little or too long.
> Too careful in our selfish loves:
> The decorative manias we obey
> Die in grimaces round us every day.
> Yet through their tohu-bohu comes a voice
> Which utters an absurd command—Rejoice.[10]

8. The Three Conversions

Contemplate Christ in three stages, as it were, planned by his wonderful kindness, not for his benefit but for ours. First he was baptized, then he was transfigured, finally he was glorified. He was baptized in the Jordan, transfigured on the mountain, and glorified at length in heaven. At Christ's baptism the Holy Spirit was shown as a dove, at his transfiguration as a cloud, but after his glorification as fire. Take these three stages to represent three stages in the soul's progress: purification, probation, and rewarding. Christ's baptism represents our purification, his transfiguration our probation, and his glorification our rewarding. We are purified by confession, we are proved by temptation, and we are rewarded by the fulness of charity.

AELRED OF RIEVAULX, Second Sermon for Pentecost

There must always be two kinds of art, escape art, for man needs escape as he needs food and deep sleep, and parable art, the art which shall teach man to unlearn hatred and learn love . . . [1]

W. H. AUDEN

I want to unlearn hatred and learn love. The tradition of which I am a part points to a threefold way of learning how to love by responding to a love that takes the initiative. Aelred relates the pattern to the life of Jesus and in turn finds a point of contact with that life in our own experience of failing, struggling, and loving. In this chapter we will look at this traditional threefold pattern of soul making and relate it to the question of conversion.

Where do I find that I am loved, known, and accepted without reservation? Where do I experience reconciliation, healing, and forgiveness? At what point do I give up my need to justify myself and allow a new heart to form itself in me? This is the point in the book where I have to come out with my own statement of faith. I believe in God, the Father Almighty, and in his Son, Jesus Christ, Our Lord. I know something of an answer to the three questions posed at the beginning of this paragraph in my encounter with Jesus and with the community of which he is the head. It is not easy to talk about conversion in this culture. The word suggests wild emotional experiences, a committed anti-intellectualism, and often bigoted opinions.

TWO KINDS OF CONVERSION AND MY MANY SELVES

How, then, are we to talk about the phenomenon of conversion? Morton Kelsey writes,

There are basically two quite different kinds of conversion. In one kind the rejected aspects of our inner being emerge and are integrated into what we are and have been. In the other . . . there is simply a turning upside down of the personality, with the former life being buried securely in the unconscious and the unconscious coming to the surface. People who experience this second kind are then likely to become as rigidly "righteous" as they were thoroughly dissipated and angry and destructive before.[2]

Both kinds of conversion are present in our culture, and it isn't always easy to distinguish one from the other. The second type of conversion leds to rigidity and to a destructive kind of exclusivity. Some people only *believe* that they believe in God. There is no passion, no doubt, and no real movement in their lives. They embrace a rigid moralism. For example, "In Plano, Texas, teachers no longer ask students their opinion because to do so, they have been told, is to deny absolute right and wrong."[3] Conversion, in this sense, involves the closing down of the mind. Often such "converts" seem devoid of all mythical and poetical imagination. They look at life with a peculiar literalistic squint. Edmund Gosse wrote of his mother as one who

had formed a definite conception of the absolute, unmodified and historical veracity, in its direct and obvious sense, of every statement contained within the covers of the Bible. For her, and for my father, nothing was symbolic, nothing allegorical or allusive in any part of Scripture . . . my parents read injunctions to the Corinthian converts without any suspicion that what was apposite in dealing with half-breed Achaian colonists of the first century might not exactly apply to respectable English men and women of the nineteenth. But my parents, I think, were devoid of sympathetic imagination . . . Hence there was no mysticism about them. They went rather to the opposite extreme, to the cultivation of a rigid and iconoclastic literalness.[4]

Conversion, in the sense of a movement to a fully integrated and maturing life directed towards its true end and home, requires a "sympathetic imagination," an intuitive appreciation of the mythical and the mystical. The mythical emphasizes the importance of telling stories. The mystical shows the way to the inner appropriation of their meaning for us. The story of Jesus is rooted in events that really happened, "wrought out grimly and murderously in one Man's flesh and blood on a few square yards of hillock outside a gate *epi Pontiou Pilatou.*" [under Pontius Pilate][5]

We live, however, in a society that naturally favors the second and easier form of conversion. We like our ideas to be attractively packaged and easily digestible. Evangelism has been infected by the desire to package things for easy consumption. Consumerism is now part of the "packaging" of religion. It hits us where we are most needy and vulnerable. But you can't sell Christ the way you can sell a car, a deodorant, or a bottle of scotch. Jesus doesn't sell well except as a narcotic that will take away all your pain and make you intensely happy all the time. The question for the desert believer is how to tell the truth in faith so that what we are and what we present is both genuinely hopeful and uncompromisingly realistic. How, asks Virginia Owens in her book *Total Image*, do we speak to the growing number in our society who simply aren't making it on this particular society's terms, and to the nagging doubt in each one of us that makes us wonder how much longer we'll go on "making it?"

The Gospel is grotesque. We have got to give in to that idea, no matter how repulsive, no matter how—and especially because—it goes against every culturally conditioned notion of "significant issues" we have. The Gospel is ludicrously incongruous in our world. It is *not* headline material. It cannot make it onto the C.B.S. News.[6]

THE THREE PAIRS OF EYES

Conversion, for the desert believer, is about soul making. It is not material for the ten o'clock news. It takes a long time to make a human being, and conversion is that continual process of being made and re-made. In one sense, it is never complete. To be human, from the believer's point of view, is to be in a continual process of conversion. St. Paul writes, "I am in travail with you . . . until you take the shape of Christ." (Gal. 4:19) To try to approach the fulness of the stature of Christ in one short lifetime seems presumptuous.

As we have seen, there are as many crises, betrayals, and false starts as there are new births and resurrections for those who would follow the desert way of believing. Many believers can, with legitimate gratitude and pride, point to a particular moment when they said "Yes" to Christ—and from that moment their lives were never the same again. I can remember making such a momentous decision at the early age of seven. I was captivated by the gentle and compassionate Walker by the Sea of Galilee and I stuck many a picture of Jesus in my Sunday school book: Jesus teaching the people in parables, Jesus healing the sick, Jesus feeding the five thousand, Jesus in the Garden of Gethsemane. This man, I knew, was for *me*.

What can be said about this conversion of a seven-year-old boy? First, this conversion was the real thing. God was present in it. Second, it was an unfinished and incomplete conversion. It was the initial, significant step on a long and exciting, if difficult, road. It was, then, only the first step and not the second or third. Still less was it the last.

No one has an experience of Jesus without it being filtered somehow through the medium of another person; and the Jesus to whom I was converted was seen through three sets of peculiar spectacles. The first set of eyes through which I saw Christ was that of my Sunday school teacher. She was an English spinster, very tall and thin, of sterling quality and gentleness of spirit. She was a bit like a character from one of the novels of Barbara Pym. Hers was "gentle Jesus meek and mild," although he was not weak. He could be as stern as the occasion demanded, but he was always a gentleman and very wise. He was also very English, in spite of his long robes and soft brown beard.

The second pair of eyes belonged to the fiercely evangelical minister of our church. His Jesus was the Judge, the scourge of wrongdoers and the bane of heretics (especially of Roman Catholics, who weren't considered even to be real Christians). I believed in his Jesus as strongly as I believed in the gentle preacher of my Sunday school teacher. I could not, however, reconcile the two pictures.

The third pair of eyes were my own. My Jesus was more of a cosmic force, a wilderness man bearing an energy of love that permeated the whole universe. His love held trees, mountains, and rivers in being. His love exploded and burst inside me and made me feel, for a while, at one with all that is. Of course, the seven-year-old boy never thought of it in these terms or put it into words. But the memory is very strong. The passion of that vision never completely died out, even though the institutional church did nothing to encourage or nurture it.

All believers who profess and call themselves Christians come to Jesus Christ through this wonderful yet flawed human way. First, we meet someone who is attractively or compellingly Christian—like my Sunday school teacher. I looked at her and said to myself, "I want to be like her. She has something I want." She was a model, but she was more than that. She had power to nurture, to teach, and to love.

Second, we encounter Christianity in a particular form or tradition. It is filtered through a historically conditioned community—Protestant or Catholic, liberal or conservative, narrow or open. A particular tradition is often represented by a person, the minister or priest. Sometimes the tradition is mediated to us through a particular form of worship or through a body of writings.

Third, we come to Jesus in our own unique and idiosyncratic way. Temperament and timing have a lot to do with it. Our neuroses also push us into a particular style of believing or into a particular tradition. For example, I treasure and value my evangelical roots, but I now find myself at home in a sacramentally centered form of Christianity that has a broad catholic vision.

These labels are, at best, unsatisfactory; and my prejudices are continually undermined when I meet and like people from different traditions—traditions which hitherto I had been conditioned to reject as bigoted or false. Nowadays I find allies and friends in all the traditions. Where there are healing, reconciliation, and love, I find myself gratefully at home. Desert believers know that however we have come to acknowledge Christ as Lord, there is always more of him to know and more of ourselves to know and surrender to him. There are also opportunities for repentance—not only for the pains and hurts of the world, but on account of the countless numbers of people who have rejected Christ because of the lazy, careless, bigoted, and fragmented witness of Christians.

The various traditions need to learn to listen to one another if the Christian witness in the world is to grow in unity and integrity. Desert believers have a great deal to offer in the work of reconciliation. They tend to have a wider view of conversion than many of their Christian companions. Conversion is not a once and for all event, but a way of psychological and spiritual formation that takes a lifetime. Often the great and first step is confused with the whole lifelong process. Conversion experiences, life-changing though they may be, are but the first step on a long journey.

EVERYTHING THAT HAPPENS TO CHRIST HAPPENS TO US

There are two biblically based ways of understanding this continuing conversion to Christ. They are found in the ancient writers on prayer who asked the basic question, "How do I become and remain a Christian?" They suggested a process of imitation, participation, and discipline by first insisting that to walk in the Way of Christ involved a radical identification with him and with all that happened and happens to him.

Everything that happens to Christ also happens to us. This means, among other things, that we don't all have to experience the same things at the same time. This saves us from the bullying attitude of some believers, who insist that to be a true Christian one has to duplicate their experience exactly. If they are happy, then we must be happy. If they are gloomy, we must share their gloom.

If we follow the life of Christ as set out in the Gospels, however, we find a wide range of possible experiences. There is a birth, and a growing up. He is driven by the Spirit into the wilderness to be tempted. He engages in an active ministry of teaching and healing. And he sets his face towards Jerusalem to suffer and endure a shameful death. He is raised on the third day and now reigns in glory and in the hearts of his faithful people. So runs the story. And so for the believer there are Bethlehems, times of growing up, wildernesses, and bursts of compassionate activity. There are also Good Fridays and Easter Days. If we take as our maxim, "Everything that happens to Christ happens to us," the Christian life won't always take away our suffering and our hurt; but it will place them within the context of meaning and hope.

We are actors in a great drama. Some believers, for example, might enjoy an active and worthwhile ministry, while others struggle in the wilderness. Some might experience a great and terrible suffering, while others feel as if they have just been raised from the dead. Some are so exhausted that they feel that they are as good as dead. They are waiting to be raised from the tomb. But it is all one drama. This basic rhythm is not confined to the individual believers. It shapes the believing community as well. This drama is also played out in some form in every human life. Christ is honored or despised, loved or rejected, in every one—believer and unbeliever. The cycle of the Church's year spells out this inner drama and helps us to understand ourselves and the great love that holds us in being.

WE "REPEAT" THE EXPERIENCE OF THE FIRST APOSTLES

The second way of understanding our continuing conversion to Christ is related to the first. The early writers asked, "What was it like for the first disciples to walk with Jesus through all those wonderful and terrible events? What was their experience of Jesus?" They attempted to discern a pattern of apostolic experience that would help the newly converted interpret what was happening to them. Thus two patterns are simultaneously working themselves out in the believer and in the community of which he or she is a member. We share in the life of Christ, *and* the experience of the first disciples helps us interpret our own.

That is why the Bible is important for the believing community—not as an oracle or magic formula, but as the document that bears witness to fundamental experiences without which its members cannot understand themselves and their world. Everyone has such a document or collection of texts. They are often an unacknowledged anthology of readings, experiences, and events that have been stuck together with scissors and paste. The point is that everyone lives from some sort of "text" or "script." The Bible is the major "text" of Christians. It provides, in the words of Bishop Stephen Bayne, "the architecture of our thoughts."[7]

Let us look more closely at this second pattern of our ongoing conversion in which we are invited to "repeat" the expeience of the first disciples. Indeed, we are more than invited to do so. We are told, in no uncertain terms, that this is how it is going to be for those who follow in the Way. The apostles' experience of Jesus was not static. There were times of growth and development, times of setback and suffering. There were also key moments; and these crucial turning points have been of particular interest to the writers of the desert or mystical way. Three major crises shaped the apostolic experience of Jesus, and these three crises provide us with a way of understanding our movement through the process of conversion.

THE THREE CRISES

The first crisis is one of meaning. "What shall I do with my life? To whom should I surrender my obedience?" The twelve apostles "forsook all and followed him" because in Jesus they found new meaning and direction in their lives.

The second crisis is one of betrayal. "The one whom I am following is making his way to meaninglessness and destruction. Does he know what he's doing? Where is a way of escape?" It is easy to follow Jesus while all is going well; but when he sets his face steadfastly towards Jerusalem, the disciples are gripped by fear and they all abandon him.

The third crisis is one of absence or emptiness. "We have experienced new life in the Risen Lord, and now he is going to forsake us again." The disciples meet the Risen Lord and he tells them that he is going to leave them, and this time for good (in both senses of the word).

From this perspective, conversion has to pass through three critical moments concerned with meaning, betrayal, and absence. Each crisis is followed by a new insight that invites commitment. Thus we read of the initial call of the disciples to follow Christ. After following him in his active ministry, they have to learn the cost and the glory of the call. They become witnesses of his death and resurrection. Finally, in mature faith, the believers have to do without the direct presence of Christ and learn to live in the stretching, demanding experience of Christ's hidden yet pervasive presence through the gift of the Holy Spirit.

At each stage or crisis of conversion, the drama or Gospel has to be reinterpreted. An open view of conversion will take into account all the stages in the journey home. In classical Christian mysticism, this journey has three distinct phases. These phases, which exactly correspond to the three critical moments in the experience of the first disciples, have intimidating names: purgation, illumination, and union. The early writers were quick to apply the pattern they discerned in the Bible to their own experiences of meaning and its loss, of faith and its betrayal, of hope and a sense of emptiness. At each step of the way they were purged of a false sense of self, they received new insight, and experienced the love of God in a deeper way. In modern terms, we can say that the three critical moments speak to our battle with a false sense of self and the quest for a new center.

My quarrel with popular evangelism and its love of easily digestible solutions is that it concentrates not on the dismantling of the false self, but on the baptism of its neuroses and pathologies. The idea is that the convert is to hand everything over to God with the naive understanding that that is the end of the matter. There is not enough emphasis on the need to reorder the personality and redirect the character. Instead, our weaknesses and fears often get redirected in the service of a newfound but false faith. Thus a weak and timid person is converted into a narrow-minded fanatic, when what was demanded of true conversion was a way of dealing with and transforming the weakness and timidity. But it takes a long time for a life to be totally converted, and most of us want instant conversions and overnight transformations.

The triple way that is at the heart of all Western models of spiritual development[8] has its origins in traditions that precede Christianity—for example, in Plato and in his later followers. Christian writers took up the way of purgation, illumination, and union and made it their own. This triple way, grounded in the biblical witness, served as a powerful model by which individual believers could interpret and understand themselves and their community.

The trouble comes when people take this threefold model and use it as a yardstick by which to measure themselves. Following Christ then becomes a *work* that is never finished, rather than a life that is never ending. The Christian life becomes burdensome and exhausting. The simple way of following Christ easily becomes overlaid and embellished with degrees, gradations, and steps. The way to God degenerates into a struggle up a ladder or progress by degrees. At each stage of the way we stop to take our spiritual temperature.

It was these later developments, complications, and rigidities that made the classic threefold way so repellent to many generations of believers that they identified all spiritual disciplines and talk of distinctions and gradations as fundamentally un-Christian and incompatible with true evengelical commitment. Spirituality degenerated into work and was, therefore, the enemy of grace. This was the basic heresy of Catholicism, from the Protestant point of view. That is why many Protestants still find it hard to deal with questions of spirituality. Historically, they have good reasons to be hesitant. While the Protestant tradition has almost lost the fullness of the scriptural vision of conversion, the Catholic has tended (until recently, at least) to tangle the believer up in rules and regulations.

David Lodge, in his novel *Souls and Bodies*, satirizes with compassion and humor pre-Vatican II Catholic spirituality. It was a religion of intricate law. *How Far Can You Go?* the title of the novel in the original edition in England, captures the feel of that spirituality more accurately. Catholicism is caricatured as a game of snakes and ladders:

Up there was Heaven; down there was Hell. The name of the game was Salvation, the object to get to Heaven and avoid Hell. It was like Snakes and Ladders; sin sent you plummeting towards the Pit; the sacraments, good deeds, acts of self-mortification, enabled you to climb back towards the light. Everything you did or thought was subject to spiritual accounting. It was either good, bad or indifferent.[9]

This is not an entirely inaccurate picture of popular Catholic spirituality as it was practiced by many a few years ago. As we have seen, religion is (in part) what we do with our craziness; and it should come as no surprise that Catholics at times play snakes and ladders.

Protestants have their own games. A favorite Protestant game has been one mis-named "Justification by Faith." The doctrine behind the game is a very beautiful one: We are in the hands of God who made us and who loves us unconditionally. There is nothing we can do or are required to do to earn his love. It is a free gift. Protestants have played themselves into a state of paralysis by making faith itself a work, something to earn. If things don't go well, then it is because of a lack of faith; and so in the Protestant game we are to work as hard as we can to acquire more of it. A great deal of psychological harm has been done by the perversion of this central Christian doctrine, which was recovered and emphasized at the Reformation.

The making of a soul is hard work, and yet it is also a free gift. God's wild card of unconditional love is secure and sure, but we are found or lost in our choosing. We are free to get lost and stay lost. It is, therefore, legitimate to understand soul making and conversion in terms of progression and growth. We are free to slip back. We are free to fail. We are free to say "No." Perdition—which means being lost—is always a possibility, and rescue is always near at hand. The choice is ours. Let us now look at the threefold pattern of conversion and soul making and then see how it reflects the experience of the first apostles.

THE THREEFOLD PATH

The threefold path always begins with some kind of an awakening. This awakening is sometimes painful. It is an invitation to self-knowledge, and part of self-knowledge is the acknowl-

edgment of our soul-sickness. We are broken open and threatened with the invasion of the genuinely new in our lives. Some
people are put right off balance. They hear "voices" and see
"visions." They are overcome by a deep longing that remains
unsatisfied.

This first way is called the *Via Purgativa* or Purgative Way. It
is a commitment to self-knowledge, which is an essential preparation for serious Good News. It is often precipitated by a
crisis of meaning in a person's life. Purgation (or self-simplification) is a way of "clearing the decks for action." The house is
swept and polished and the garbage is collected and burned.
The purpose of purgation is always remedial and never puni-
tive. It is meant to help and not to punish. St. Catherine of
Genoa (1447–1510) in her *Purgation and Purgatory* likened the
process to the burning off the rust which covers, disfigures, and
therefore obscures the soul. In Dante's *Purgatorio*, the souls are
not being punished for their wickedness; rather, the souls there
are freely working their way to that clarity and focus which true
love requires. Purgatory is the place where freedom begins to
come alive in us. Dante's sinners go to Purgatory of their own
free will and know instinctively when they can move up the
Mountain towards Paradise. Thus the work of purgation is to
release the soul's energies of loving. The way through the crisis
of meaning is to respond to the call of love. Julian of Norwich
(c. 1342—after 1413) put it this way: "I saw fully surely that it
behoveth needs to be that we should be in longing and penance
until the time that we be lead so deep into God that we verily
and truly know our own soul."

THE FIRST CONVERSION

The first stage of conversion involves the first step on the
road to self-knowledge, because knowledge of God and knowledge of self cannot be separated. One feeds the other. An
essential ingredient of proper self-knowledge is proper self-
love. As we saw right at the beginning, the most basic and true
thing about each one of us is our unique and inalienable dignity.
The sinner knows that he or she is loved, and weeps. Who would
not weep when we realize just how far we have trivialized and
trampled on our own true worth? Appreciation of our true

dignity and worth initiates the process of purgation because true self-knowledge brings with it an awareness of the discrepancy between what we are now and what we are meant to be.

We explored much of the process of purgation in the chapter on the gift of tears. These tears help believers to be who we are called to be. Purgation is the beginning of hope. It assumes that this life is a rite of passage into an ever deepening and more permanent relationship with God. It does not in any way deny the value of this life; it merely tries to have an accurate picture of what it is about. Purgation, then, as it relates to the making of a soul, is about self-simplification. It teaches us to accept discipline, travel as lightly as possible, and remember that "here we have no abiding city."

The purgation of the soul provides an opportunity for growth and for the integration of the warring elements inside us. Believers are always on the road, always under canvas. They are always leaving the known and moving out into the unknown. They live in the desert of untried things. "The Lord said to Abraham, 'Leave your own country, your kinsmen and your father's house and go to a country I will show you" (Gen. 12:1–3). Jesus simply says, "Come. Follow me." And we follow him into an unpredictable future.

This is a recurring pattern for the believer. It was a pattern that the first disciples had to learn. They followed Jesus. They were willing to be on the move with him, but they had no idea of the pain and the cost and the glory of their discipleship. In our own day it is fatal to interpret Christianity as a program for self-improvement or self-fulfillment. It is now, as it was then, a response in obedience to the God who calls us out of our lostness and pain into the light of his future. Believers are people who are always making new beginnings. Their souls are being made and re-made all the time. Yet it is not a matter of tedious repetition, because each new beginning is an invitation to enter a genuinely new situation. The making of souls is neither linear nor circular; rather, it is spiral. We seem to repeat our lives, but at different levels and in new ways.

The major problem with this first stage of conversion (as with the popular view of evangelism) is that it tends to be highly individualistic and private. The newly converted often attach their egos to the new experiences of self-knowledge and self-acceptance that an encounter with the transcendent often brings. The first stage can easily become simply another occasion for self-centeredness, with an exclusive focus on *my* conversion, *my* Savior, and *my* faith. The disciples "forsook all and followed him"; and instead of finding that this was the end of the matter, they found themselves caught up in a drama that led to a shameful death and unhoped-for resurrection.

They had to learn that soul making or conversion had to include others. They had to move from saying "I" to "we," from saying "me" to "us." Things of the Spirit operate by different laws than those of the material world. Material goods are diminished by sharing. Spiritual things (like love, joy, and peace) are increased, not diminished, when they are shared. Everyone can enjoy the same gift simultaneously and uniquely. Life in the Spirit cannot be possessive and individualistic and still be true to itself. Yet it is precisely the opposite that is more often than not inculcated in popular evangelism, with its emphasis on "Jesus as my personal Lord and Savior." Nothing could be more wonderful than a living encounter of saving power between the believer and God; but when it is made private and exclusive, it can be a terrible thing. It can be used to judge and hurt others. When this happens, conversion is made a mockery and the soul is aborted. Father Garrigou-Lagrange wrote many years ago, " . . . if we desired only one soul to be deprived of Him, if we excluded only one soul—even the soul of one who persecutes and caluminiates us—from our own love, then God Himself would be lost to us."

There is little doubt that some of what passes for evangelism today is scarcely veiled vindictiveness. How marvelous to be numbered among the favored few, to be a member of the elect! How splendid to belong to God's "us" to the exclusion of his rejected "them." I am puzzled why the doctrine of eternal punishment is still revered by so many Christians. It cannot be explained simply as a desire to preserve human freedom, although I suppose it must be logically possible for a person to go on saying "No" to God forever. Christian orthodoxy requires that I believe in the logical possibility of hell (or utter lostness or damnation). It does not require that I believe that anyone is there. There is nothing to prevent my *hoping* that hell is empty.

The first conversion is but the first step on the hard but glorious road to the recovery of a view of reality in which no one is excluded and the fact that people are free to choose to be excluded is the occasion of deep pain in the heart of the believer. Our first conversion is but a beginning that will prepare us for deeper, harder, and yet more glorious conversions. The importance of the first conversion cannot be denied, because it is the first of many steps.

The saints found it difficult to put all this into words. St. Bernard (1090–1153) suggested that the making of the soul (what we might here call the converted life) was like entering into a love affair, with all the pains, joys, and risk that implies. Falling in love is not something we do. It is, rather, something which is done to us. All we can do is respond.

St. Bernard loved the *Song of Songs*, and he writes on the text, "Let him kiss me with the kisses of his mouth." The first kiss is one of adoration, wonder and repentance, when the believer prostrates herself in sorrow for her sins and in joy that she is loved. And so she kisses the feet of Christ. This kiss gives her courage and hope, and thus she is lifted up by love and begins to live more openly as a disciple of the Risen Lord. At this point she is bold enough to kiss Christ's hand. This strengthens her even further and she stands upright, lifting up her eyes not only to gaze on the glory of God, but also to kiss it. This is the third and final kiss on the mouth.

The threefold way of St. Bonaventure (1221–1274) is not at all like that of St. Bernard. The Franciscan leads us from the immediacy of the sensual world to the very presence of God. We begin where we are with the world of the senses, with all the things we can hear, see, smell, taste, touch, and enjoy. We then move to the enjoyment of the things unseen, to the life of the mind. Finally, in an act of love, we go beyond both sense and mind (or feeling and thought). We are taken out of ourselves in order to live from a new center, which is God. For Bonaventure, soul making can be summed up as the working of the Holy Spirit in the soul to recreate it after the image of the Holy and Undivided Trinity. For both Bernard and Bonaventure, the threefold path is for the sake of unlearning hatred and learning love. Love requires purgation so that we can see clearly. It requires illumination so that we can love unequivocally.

Learning what love is, is simply another way of talking about conversion. This is, after all, what the early apostles were learning. They had to be converted three times. And, as we have seen, each conversion was preceded by some sort of crisis. It is easy to make connections between this ancient tradition of the threefold way and our own progression through childhood to youth and on to adulthood. The crisis of puberty, for example, is not unlike the crisis associated with the first conversion. It is a transition period of changing and developing identities. It is a time of dying to the old and waiting for the new to be born.

THE SECOND CONVERSION: FALLING APART

We are now ready to look at the second conversion (or, in terms of the traditional scheme, our entrance into the illuminative way). How did the first disciples experience this second conversion? Their first encounter with Christ is marked by joy and enthusiasm. Jesus is the one for whom they longed, the fulfillment of their hopes, prophecies, and dreams. They were lost and they met Jesus and their lives were changed. They followed Jesus and listened to him preach and tell stories to the people. They saw him heal the sick and feed the hungry. Everything was wonderful. The new life with Jesus couldn't go wrong. But then he "set his face towards Jerusalem." Thus the coming passion of Jesus was the crisis that occasioned the second conversion of the apostles. The first crisis was one of meaning. The second was one of meaning betrayed. Father Garrigou-Lagrange writes,

. . . beginners in the spiritual life must, after a certain period undergo a second conversion, similar to the second conversion of the Apostles at the end of our Lord's Passion, and that, still later, before entering the life of perfect union, there must be a third conversion or transformation of the soul, similar to that which took place in the souls of the Apostles on the day of Pentecost.[10]

The second conversion provides new occasions for stretching and temptation and one of the key texts for this is Luke 22:31, "Simon, Simon, behold Satan asked to have you that he might sift you as wheat."

At this critical moment, everything seems to fall apart. Imagine what it must have been like for the disciples. The new life they had experienced with Jesus is about to be snatched away from them. Jesus is taken away to be crucified. Meaning, purpose, and hope are all draining away. Centuries later, St. John of the Cross was to describe what the disciples went through as "the Dark Night of the Senses." The second conversion has none of the warm and liberating feelings associated with the first. In the terms of St. John of the Cross, the believer enters into a dark place and becomes numb. The first conversion was full of light and inspired devotion. The second becomes a desert place of waiting that invites naked surrender. It is this second conversion that is of most interest to believers today, because only a glimpse is given of the third conversion and they would like to get beyond the regressive, infantile, and often repeated cycle of the first.

The strong evangelical tradition of the United States tends to preach only the first conversion. Lives are turned around and relationships healed. People are hungry for some good news. They want to follow Christ and acknowledge him as Lord. Like the first disciples, they follow, listen to the stories, see miracles, and share in the fellowship of a lively community. There are even moments of transfiguration when a person is given a new heart.

All goes well until the Yellow Brick Road turns into the Via Dolorosa (the Way of Sorrow). The newly converted are suddenly threatened with betrayal. Like Peter, they are being sifted as wheat. They sense that something terrible is going to happen; and it is at that point that new disciples have a wild longing to go back to the beginning again, to the first encounter with Jesus. Wouldn't it be better to get as far away from these terrible events as soon as possible and go back to the beginning?

When we refuse the opportunity for the second conversion, we stop growing. Religion tends to function like a drug for those who have shrunk back from the second conversion. Jesus becomes their "fix," and each time they go to church they expect a new "high." Don Cupitt writes of this critical moment in *The World to Come*:

The Christian declares that if we avail ourselves of the disciplines and practices of religion and are willing to pass through the fire of nihilism, it will burn out our natural egoism and bring us through on the far side to a new kind of human reality and a new basis for social life. I have no wish to conceal the arduousness of the spiritual journey. I did not undertake it willingly, and I only venture to recommend it now because we have come to a time when it is the only recourse left to us.[11]

The second conversion comes as a terrible shock to believers of long standing and wide experience. The burning out of our normal egoism takes a long time. It is peculiarly painful when we realize that even our "faith" has been, in part, enslaved to the ego. St. Teresa of Avila experienced the second conversion when she was thirty-nine years old. She had tried for years to be an exemplary Christian, a model to others. While she was reading St. Augustine's *Confessions*, her heart broke at the vision of the wounded Christ. "I threw myself down before him with the greatest outpouring of tears."[12]

The second conversion is marked by tears and begins immediately after the denial of Christ by St. Peter. "And the Lord turned and looked upon Peter. And Peter remembered the word of the Lord, how that he had said unto him, Before the cock crow this day, thou shalt deny me thrice. And he went out and wept bitterly" (Luke 22:61–62).

The second conversion is also preceded by tears of repentance. Like St. Teresa, the believer is shown the extent and the cost of God's love. As we follow in the steps of the first disciples, this critical second conversion stage lasts until the day of Pentecost, which in its turn marks the beginning of the third and final conversion. It not only marks the occasion of the great outpouring of the Holy Spirit, but is also the prelude to the disciples learning to live in the presence of the Christ who will soon be "absent."

Why is the second conversion necessary? Why is the way of the desert an important part of the experience of the believer? One of the hardest transitions to make in the life of faith is that from loving someone for our own sake and loving someone for his or her own. One of the fundamental questions posed by the tradition of the mystics is, "How far do I love God for my own sake and how far for his?" This is a hard transition to go through in human relationships. Is any of our loving disinterested? Is it possible to love with both passion and detachment?

The history of religion provides a great deal of evidence of people who, albeit unconsciously, love and serve God out of sheer self-interest. They are not bad or malicious people. They simply are attached to the consolations and comforts of religion. It is not uncommon for religious people to whine when they are deprived of these consolations. There are people who think that they love God because they love nobody else. On this side of the grave, our loves are a mixture of genuine reaching out to others for their own sake and a spontaneous reflex action of self-interest and self-preservation. St. Catherine of Siena (1347–1380) put these words into the mouth of God, "What they seek in My service is their own profit, their own satisfaction, or the pleasure that they find in me."[13]

The question is, do I worship God or do I worship my experience of God? Do I worship God or do I worship my idea of him? If I am to avoid a narcotic approach to religion that forces me to stagger from experience to experience hoping for bigger and better things, I must *know* what I believe apart from the nice or nasty feelings that may or may not accompany such a belief. The second conversion has to do with learning to cope and flourish when the warm feelings, consolations, and props that accompany the first conversion are withdrawn. Does faith evaporate when the initial feelings dissolve? In psychological terms, the ego has to break; and this breaking is like our entering into a great darkness. Without such a struggle and affliction, there can be no movement in love.

It is easy to see how such an approach to soul making might easily slip into a kind of spiritual sadomasochism. The second conversion does not exult in suffering for its own sake. The tradition affirms that hardship and difficulty will come to those who follow Jesus Christ, but that what suffering and tribulation there is is for the sake of love and for no other reason. Forms of evangelism that preach the Gospel as a sort of divinely inspired problem-solving device have nothing to say with regard to the Christian life when the going gets rough and we have to enter the desert. "Accept Jesus Christ as Lord and everything will be all right" is a cruel half-truth. Accepting Jesus Christ as

Lord *does* have power to renew and make a new heart; but after acceptance in faith comes cost, pilgrimage, and growth in love.

THE SECOND CONVERSION: LETTING GO

From time to time we fall flat on our faces! This is routine in soul making. Father Garrigou-Lagrange puts it more gracefully. "Not infrequently Providence allows us . . . at this stage to commit some very palpable fault, in order to humiliate us and cause us to take a true measure of ourselves."[14] And St. Catherine of Siena says, "I withdraw from it [the soul], not in grace but in feeling."[15]

We make mistakes, and thank God we do! In these "mistakes" lie our greatest hope for movement and change. We tend to believe that when we no longer feel the presence and consolations of God, he is no longer there. Remember the word of the older priest in Iris Murdoch's *Henry and Cato*: "the ego had to break, something absolutely natural and seemingly good, seemingly perhaps the only good, has to be given up. After that there's darkness and silence and space. And God is there."

This, in effect, sums up the theology of St. John of the Cross, who writes that there are three signs of the second conversion.[16] The first sign of the second conversion is that we no longer have any pleasure or consolation either in God or in creation. Nothing pleases us. Nothing touches us. Everything and everyone seems dull and uninteresting. Life is dust and ashes in the mouth. The second sign is the abiding and biting sense of failure, even though the believer conscientiously tries to center her life on God. There is a sense of never having done enough and of needing to atone for something that has no name.

The third sign, and the one that is most threatening to us today, is that it is no longer possible to pray or meditate with the imagination. Images, pictures, and metaphors no longer seem to reach us. God (if he is there) no longer communicates with us through the senses. In more modern terms, it is a matter of living from a center other than the ego. Even to begin to do this is to enter a great darkness. The saints say that, after waiting in this darkness, a new kind of light or illumination comes; and through it our relationship to God, although more hidden than before, becomes deeper and more direct.

If more of us knew about these three stages we might save ourselves a great deal of needless pain and anxiety and thus use our energy for the real work of soul making. It might help to know that, when things are hard and we feel abandoned, we are going through a well-documented process and traveling a path that many have covered before us. Soul making has its solitary side, but it is not a totally solitary thing. We stand in a great tradition. We have companions. The testimony of the survivors of spiritual conflict are there to assure us that there is glory through struggle; and this gives hope to those who are waiting in the dark on the edge of the second conversion.

After the crisis of betrayal comes illumination. The mystical tradition talks of contemplation, which is a sort of simple waiting for light. Gerald May writes, "In traditional religious usage, the term *contemplation* implies a totally uncluttered appreciation of existence, a state of mind or a condition of the soul that is simultaneously wide-awake and free from all preoccupation, preconception and interpretation. It is a wonder-filled yet utterly simple experience."[17]

To get to that place where our loves and lives are so uncluttered that we are free of preoccupation, preconception, and interpretation is a costly and painful process. Often the light of illumination is harder to bear than the dark. "And Jesus turned and looked on Peter." Imagine what the impact of that look had on Peter. In the eyes of Jesus there was light. One glance brought Peter's whole life into question. Light brings tears. The look of Jesus gave Peter "an experimental knowledge of his poverty" (to use a phrase from St. Catherine of Siena).

The pattern is simple. Peter heard the call of Jesus and followed him without delay. The period of the first conversion was full of joy and possibility. Later, when things got tough, Peter felt betrayed and frightened and denied Jesus. He received illumination when their eyes met. Peter remembered and then he wept. This look of Jesus cuts at the root of self-love—particularly at that form of self-love which darkens and perverts our sense of judgment and twists our perceptions. The second conversion or way of illumination is seeing what it might mean to love God with all our powers of mind and heart (Luke 10:27). Thus we find ourselves pupils in what the mystics call the school of love, where we learn how to love another for his or her own sake and not from self-interest or for our own personal satisfaction.

The purpose of the second conversion, however, is not to frighten us and render us immobile and impotent. The light we receive, as we weep, enables us to move on because we are not only made aware of our poverty before God, we are also made aware of how much we are loved, and of the lengths to which God is willing to go because he loves us. Because of this we are moved to turn away from our self-preoccupation and love and serve others. The second conversion brings not only a new awareness, but also a new energy and power. The light warms and heals and makes strong as well as shines in the darkness. It is thus that souls are made. It is thus that we grow in discipleship. We move from an initial burst of enthusiasm, through a period of humbling, to a bracing yet relaxing enjoyment of grace. We become less victims of mood and emotion. We learn that feelings come and go. We move in the light from a vague and unfocused faith to a living conviction. But the desert believer knows that this is not the end of the story. There is a third conversion, deeper and more devastating and more wonderful than the second. We have to be born again and again.

Walker Percy's comment in *The Second Coming*, "If the born-again are the twice born I'm going to wait for the third go round," is a sobering one. Christians, particularly noisy and vociferous ones, do not always impress others with their living of the life of faith. There is always room for further conversions and new births. Don Cupitt has harsh words for those who rest in and are complacent about their having been "born again." "Thinking he is bearing witness to Christ, the twice-born believer in fact merely exhibits the strange and sinister power of the group over him, a group which puts him under such a very great psychological pressure to testify that he is enjoying certain experiences and to speak of them in certain authorized formulae."

I think Cupitt is being a bit harsh here; but there is no doubt that there is in our culture a popular brand of religion "which is anti-intellectual, and has no self-criticism and no saving sense of its own absurdity, is all too often arrogant, bigoted, self-deceived and self-regarding."[18] Cupitt writes of Christianity as primarily a way or a path rather than a system of doctrines and rules. For the desert believer, it is *the* Way. The point is that the center of Christianity is "a moment of dereliction, loss, tragedy, emptiness and meaninglessness." Christ did *not* go into The Void so that we could bypass it altogether. We have to go through it too.[19]

No wonder we want over and over again to go back to the first conversion. The third conversion, like all the others, is preceded by a crisis, this time by one of absence and abandonment. We have followed Christ even to the foot of the Cross. We have been witnesses of his resurrection. Now he is going to leave us for good.

THE THIRD CONVERSION

For the apostles, the third conversion occurs during the period between Pentecost and the Ascension. They have been through the first conversion and enjoyed the experience of new life. They have watched with horror and awe the humiliation and crucifixion of Christ. They have experienced his risen presence. They are now ready for the third conversion. In the language of the mystical tradition, they are to enter even more deeply into the life of contemplation—that life uncluttered and free from preoccupations and preconceptions. The spiritual principle is that action and service in the world proceed from a fulness of soul that is the result of contemplation. Contemplation is receptivity and availability in love to whatever life has to offer.

Jesus ascends into heaven. He is present to the disciples, yet he is beyond sense and feeling. In the terms of St. John of the Cross, the disciples are going to enter the Dark Night of the Soul, after which comes a deepened faith that is not dependent on mood, emotion, sense, or feeling. Father Garrigou-Lagrange writes,

Such was their third conversion; it was a complete transformation of their souls. Their first conversion had made them disciples of the Master . . . the second, at the end of the Passion, had enabled them to divine the fecundity of the mystery of the Cross, enlightened as it was by the Resurrection which followed it; the third conversion fills them with the profound conviction of this mystery, a mystery which they will constantly live until their martyrdom.[20]

This may be an antique and uncritical way of putting it for contemporary ears, but the pattern he describes is accurate and loyal to the tradition. The last word in the quotation above should be noted: martyrdom. This is the potential consequence of the third conversion.

The great danger of soul making as a progression through various stages is that it is easy to do it all in the service of the ego and to take a special and possessive interest in *our* progress. We may be tempted to check up on ourselves to see whether we are special or advanced, to be sure that we are at least sweating it out in the second conversion! Of course, it doesn't work out as a neat and logical progression. The pattern recapitulates itself over and over again in our lives. The point is that this ancient pattern points to a fullness of human experience, so that there is nothing which needs to be edited or left out. There is no need to lie about anything. There is joy, betrayal, dereliction, abandonment, hope and new life patterned for those who are following in the Way. Much of religion seems to be a tired pattern of cosmetic surgery performed on the ravaged face of human experience. It is often the denial of pain and tragedy rather than the promise of their transformation. We tend to make religion only of our better moments. The desert path opens us up in such a way that nothing has to be "laundered" before we can enter the expanding and ever-breaking circle of God's love.

EVANGELISM AND THE THREE CONVERSIONS

All of this has some serious implications for the way in which believers spread the good news. It requires a rigorous honesty in the way human beings experience the world. The first conversion is important as the first step on a long journey, and the different churches can help each other to emphasize this first step. It may well be that those churches which understand themselves as catholic and sacramentally oriented have neglected the first conversion too much. They tend to take it for granted and hope that people will want to walk in the Way by a sort of osmosis. The evangelical churches, alas, know of little else but the first conversion. We need all three. The first calls on us to be born again, the second and third invite us to grow up into "the fullness of the stature of Christ."

Unless there is a change and renewal from within that takes into account the hurts and tragedies of human life the second and third conversions seek to address, millions will be left without much spiritual sustenance. I am convinced that many who ache for the Gospel are so repelled by popular methods of evangelism that they cannot hear the Good News. I am reminded of the theologian Schleiermacher's heroic attempt to address the cultured despisers of Christianity. Human longings and human needs are much the same everywhere, regardless of class or education. The street-corner preachers in the ghettos and corrupt areas of our cities have only one thing in mind and that is rescue and they are right. I have enormous respect for these unconventional street-corner evangelists. Something powerful could happen if those who know how to preach the First Conversion with love and power could get together with those who know something about the Second and Third. Each group of believers has a great deal to teach the other.

Harry Williams writes of his own second conversion, which is in tune with the experience of St. Teresa and a host of others:

Christ crucified said now to me that in order to create the universe in all its infinitely varied loveliness and splendour, God himself was prepared to suffer to the uttermost . . . I saw that I was called upon to accept my own personal sufferings, in so far as they were unavoidable, as my particular share in the cost to God of his creative work, and that this was true even of the terror from which I was rightly doing in all my power to liberate myself.[21]

The second and third conversions are necessary precisely because they reach those painful depths of personal suffering and terror that routine religion simply cannot touch. Without the second and third possibilities, the first conversion can easily become a masquerade that keeps us infantile (rather than childlike) and prevents us from moving into a maturing faith.

"Nothing is as apt to mask the face of God as religion," wrote Martin Buber. Soul making has to do with the removing of masks and with setting us free. We are called to enjoy the very life of God himself, and it is to that life that we must now turn.

9. The Soul Maker: The Holy and Undivided Trinity

Look at us! Four gaping mouths. What a perfect quartet! I'd love to write it—just this second of time, this *now*, as you are! Herr Chamberlain thinking: "Impertinent Mozart. I must speak to the Emperor at once!" Herr Prefect thinking: "Ignorant Mozart. Debasing opera with his vulgarity!" Herr Court Composer thinking: "German Mozart. What can he finally know about music?" And Mozart himself, in the middle, thinking: "I'm just a good fellow. Why do they all disapprove of me?" . . . That's why opera is so important . . . Because it's realer than any play! A dramatic poet would have to put all those thoughts down one after another to represent this second in time. The composer can put them all down at once—and still make us hear each one of them. Astonishing device—a vocal quartet . . . I tell you I want to write a finale lasting half an hour! A quartet becoming a quintet becoming a sextet. On and on, wider and wider—all sounds multiplying and rising together—and then together making a sound entirely new! . . . I bet you that's how God hears the world. Millions of sounds ascending at once and mixing in His ear to become an unending music, unimaginable to us! . . . That's our job! That's our *job*, we composers: to combine the inner minds of him and him and him, and her and her—the thoughts of chambermaids and Court Composers—and turn the audience into God.[1]

PETER SHAFFER, *Amadeus*

It has been said that heaven is complete unity in unimaginable diversity. Mozart understood the miracle of unity in diversity. The device of the vocal quartet, becoming a quintet, becoming a sextet, and on and on—until everyone is singing is a vivid metaphor for the truth that each of us sings our own unique melody, and all contribute to one great and glorious sound: all sounds mix and rise together to become unending music. It is thus that I find my "home" in harmony with all other creatures. Soul making, in the end, is not an individual affair. It is concerned with our all being one, and yet each remaining unrepeatable and distinctly unique.

The Christian understanding of "God" is concerned with

holding together unity and diversity. And the belief in God as the Holy and Undivided Trinity speaks directly to our desire to be at one with one another without being swallowed up. The doctrine of the Trinity is, of course, much more than this; but it is at least this. What follows is not an exposition of the doctrine of the Trinity. All I wish to do is look at some of the *vestigia* or traces left by the Trinity in ordinary human experience. The doctrine seems too tangled to bother with for most people, yet the believer finds traces of the trinitarian structure everywhere: in political and social arrangements, in intimate relationships, and in the depths of one's own heart. Thus my concern is not with God "as he is in himself." In theological language, my focus is "economic." I am interested in God's "housekeeping," how he arranges things and leaves around us and in us the signs of his presence.

THE ORIGINAL "WE"

Fritz Kunkel wrote some years ago of what he called "The Original We." By this he meant that sense of undifferentiated solidarity we experienced, first with our mothers and then with the world.

The small child is not yet conscious of his center; but he is closer to the real Self and therefore to real love and creativity than any other members of the group. The adults are conscious of their centers—but they have exchanged the group center (the Self) for the individual center (the Ego). Therefore they have to become like children again, discovering anew that their real center is the group and behind the group the whole, and finally God.

Soul making might be defined as the moving away from this original "We," through the painful process of separation, initiation, and growth, to a sense of identification with a new and maturing "We," which is the Real Self. In other words, solidarity with others is essential if the soul is to be made and re-made. I have to learn that my ego is not my real and best self. The ego is not the soul. I am, paradoxically, most myself when I can say "we."

Most of us, however, make do with simple group identification to satisfy our need to be part of something bigger than our- selves. This sham "we" makes us feel safe and at home for a while, but it often depends on excluding others and even per- secuting and killing them if our safety is threatened. A family can be the prison house of the soul. Each member must serve its honor and worship at its shrine. Freedom and spontaneity are crushed by the family group. A nation can wound the souls of its members by belligerent and exclusivist policies formulated in the name of "national security." That is why the making of a soul requires us to break out of the small groups in which we live and find our true Self in an ever-widening circle, first in the whole and then in God.

As believers we find that in identifying with the ever-widening circle of the whole, we have available immense and even infinite resources. Our puny egos have only their own individual wit and cunning to rely on. And, since it is going against the stream of life flowing towards that wholeness which is in God, the ego is always on the defensive, always at war with others and with itself. I (as ego) have to wage war on two fronts. There is battle against other egos and there is civil strife within, because my ego has conflicting and contradictory desires.

The dominant lure of life is towards the "We" and we may thank God for our neuroses in that they are, at least, signs that there are cracks and crevices in the egocentric shell we build around us. That is why our falling apart can be a sign of God's work in us. It is the beginning of the process of benign disin- tegration. As Kunkel puts it, "The unknown and despised We shows . . . its inescapable and irresistible power." Why? Because the "We" is the real frame of our life. To refuse it means entering into a terrible place of lostness, where the ego is all there is. This is hell: the ego is mistaken in the belief that it is the fount and origin of everything. Kunkel writes, "The Ego considered as a whole is a mistaken image of the Self." This false sense of self has to be undermined if the soul is to survive and flourish. We prevent our own healing when we misrepresent what is going on inside us, and lie to ourselves.

Soul making is fraught with difficulty; yet the basic thrust of life is on our side. Kunkel laments the fact that many people, nations, and institutions fail and perish because they do not dare expose themselves to the pains of suffering, crisis and rebirth. Only those who go through the crisis, only those who endure "the perils of the soul" and dare to brave the unknown dangers of the future find the way to new, mature and productive life. They attain the experience of the Maturing-We and they help this We even if they sacrifice their lives in joining it. They find themselves and they find the We—the We being their Self. Even if they lose their lives they will find them.[2]

I find that these insights point me inexorably in the direction of the Gospel, which is fundamentally about losing the ego to find the soul. It is about learning to live and to live abundantly. It is about finding identity with others in God.

From the point of view of human experience, the doctrine of God as the Holy and Undivided Trinity speaks to issues relating to unity and identity. This is not to say that God is the real Self or the Original-We. The real Self is not God, but finding ourselves in solidarity with others and working in and through the nurturing and sustaining presence of God for the good of the whole. We might, therefore, venture to say that the real Self in which we find our identity is an *image* of the Trinity. The Christian tradition affirms that we are made after the image of God, the Holy Trinity; and this is as true for us collectively as it is individually. We are formed and shaped by a trinitarian pattern, and this patterning of the soul is what we must now explore.

WE ARE WHO WE ARE WHEN WE ARE LOVINGLY INCLINED TOWARD ONE ANOTHER

Jürgen Moltmann, in his book *The Trinity and the Kingdom*, is concerned with the fact that the way we think about God determines the way we think about ourselves and vice versa. It is no accident that he prefaces his theological arguments with a traditional and arresting image of the Trinity. He uses the so-called "Old Testament Trinity" or Troika (also known as the Rublev Trinity) as a model or paradigm for the shape of human relations or soul making. The Christian believes that this "model" corresponds to reality itself, and thus we are most truly ourselves when we conform to the divine patterning.

The Rublev Trinity is based on an incident in the Old Testament. Genesis 18:1–5 tells the story of the visit of three young men to Abraham, and his preparation of a meal for them. This simple act of hospitality for the messengers of God became an icon of the Trinity of the Christian revelation and also a sign of the pattern of human relations for those who believe that they are made after the divine image. The three Persons are sitting round a table on which there is a chalice. Moltmann writes,

Through their tenderly intimate inclination towards one another, the three Persons show the profound unity joining them, in which they are one. The chalice on the table points to the surrender of the Son on Golgotha. Just as the chalice stands at the centre of the table around which the three Persons are sitting, so the Cross of the Son stands from eternity in the centre of the Trinity. Anyone who grasps the truth of this picture understands that it is only in the unity with one another which springs from the self-giving of the Son "for many" that men and women are in conformity with the triune God. He understands that people only arrive at their own truth in their free and loving inclination towards one another.[3]

Here we have a key paradigm for the nature of the human soul. We are who we are insofar as we are tenderly inclined towards each other and are thus in conformity with the God who is revealed as a self-giving and self-emptying center. We are called to live and be in conformity with the triune God. To discover the truth of this, we must be lovingly inclined towards each other—because the inner life of God is shown to be a deep communion of love.

From the perspective of soul making, the doctrine of the Trinity is one about how human beings are. We have a trinitarian form. A human being is, to use Raimundo Panikkar's phrase, "a theandric mystery."[4] That is to say, there is something irreducibly mysterious about a human being. There is something of a "god" about us. There is in me something more "me" than myself. There are many names for this "something more." The Christian tradition would call it "the image of God," Kunkel the real Self or the maturing "We." Others would identify it as the indwelling of the Holy Spirit. My resistance to the Spirit, to the maturing "We," is very strong. My ego tells me that I would be better off on my own.

Many of us try, from time to time, to go it alone. I discover, much to my discomfort, that I am not a monad. I am not meant to be alone. In fact, it is not good for anyone to be alone. This discovery is as much of a relief to me as it is a threat. I have to relearn that what I am in myself (memory, intellect, and will) cannot be separated from my relations with other selves. I often wish it were otherwise. I often wish I weren't "trinitarian" (that is, needing others to bring me to fullness of being). I wander far from my trinitarian and communal home, and this wandering can be very important because it is the only way I ever learn anything—by getting it wrong. The Trinity bursts in upon me in a disquieting way. I experience both my neighbor and my God as an intrusion into my boring, but comfortingly familiar monadic existence. Robert Jenson writes,

... personhood is intrinsically a communal phenomenon. I—and God— am the *person* that I am precisely in that *you* intrude into my life, opening me to be what I am not yet ... Personal presence and so personal knowledge occur always as an address, always as a word-event by which one person enters the reality of another. This entrance may be destructive, it may initiate a relation of dominance or subservience, and a struggle over who will have which.

The life of God, in which the Three Persons are always tenderly inclined towards each other in loving surrender, shows us how love really works: without either subservience or dominance. God not only shows us how to love (merely to be shown without being given the means would lead us to despair); he also loves us into being by his willingness to risk and be vulnerable. The openness of the life of the Trinity both commands and enables me to open myself up to others. Soul making becomes a movement from monism to trinitarianism. Jenson puts it this way: "I must appear in your world as a possible target for your intention ... as a reality about which you can make choices and upon whom you can act ... This is how God 'appears' in our world."[5]

God's "appearance" in the world shows us how we are to "appear" to one another. The pattern or paradigm of God's self-giving love is found in John 15:15: "I call you servants no longer; a servant does not know what his master is about. I have called you friends because I have disclosed to you everything that I have heard from my father."

God is willing to open himself up, to disclose himself to us. I can know myself only insofar as I am willilng to disclose myself to others and to allow others to disclose themselves to me. William Johnston writes,

> This self-revelation takes place slowly and quietly between two people who are attentive to one another, understand one another, know one another, love one another. In this way I become the mirror in which the other sees himself or herself; and the other becomes the mirror in which I see myself. Yet this takes time. For much dust . . . must be removed from that mirror.[6]

The point is very simple. I cannot be myself, be a "soul" apart from others or an other. At first, this causes me a great deal of pain, because it raises questions about my identity. How can I be truly myself and yet at one with others? I could surrender to a group, to a person, to a political party or to a religion, but that would be a form of slavery. Or I could remain aloof and keep myself in isolation with only my "sweating self" for company. That would be unbearable. God is not solitary, and neither am I. God is Trinity, and so am I. To be truly me I have to turn to you, and you open me up to what I am not yet. You make the future an issue for me. You and God push me into the unknown. Who I am is suddenly lifted out of the past and placed somewhere in the future. I am invited to define myself in terms of my future instead of my past. This is liberating because, as a believer, I trust that my future is in God.

This does not mean that the past is irrelevant. It means that my past is interpreted in terms of my future rather than the other way round. All the things I wish I hadn't done are not obliterated; rather, I see them in terms of the future, which is secure in the hands of the Love that brings me home and makes and re-makes my soul. If I love without that thrust towards the future that relationships with others always bring, I am stuck with my past—either as a wound that will never be healed, or as a golden age that will never come again. If I live in terms of my destination, then all that has gone before—the bad with the good—is understood in the light of the final outcome. And what is "the final outcome"? The final outcome is described, as we have seen, in a codeword for restoration and healing: the Reign of God. Which is another way of saying that there is a future, and the future is God's; the future is Trinitarian; the future is relationship; the future is for the making of souls.

THE TRINITY OPENS US UP FOR THE FUTURE

The main questions raised by the doctrine of Trinity are: "What does it mean to be a person?" "How are we to relate to one another?" and "Do we have a future?" I am convinced that if we allow the doctrine of the Holy and Undivided Trinity to enter as deeply into our minds and hearts as possible, it will eventually impinge upon and revolutionize our self-understanding.

This speaks to one of the most pressing needs of our time. Human beings are trivialized and reduced by hidden assumptions and definitions that render them of no consequence. In an age when nearly everything is disposable, human relationships are understood as just another item in a consumer society. We enjoy or abuse each other as long as we "get" something out of the relationship. Our friends, allies, and partners are disposable and interchangeable. We treat each other as if there was no tomorrow. Much of what we do betrays a hopelessness about the future. The vision of humanity provided by the doctrine of the Trinity wages war against any reductionist view of human beings. God wages war on our despair by loving us into the future and by opening us up to infinite possibilities. The person, from the believer's point of view, is a pilgrim, a sign of what is to come. Thus it is that we are invited to live not *in* the future, but *from* it. David Baily Harned writes of the invitation "to live against appearances and as though the earth were other than it is, to see others and ourselves from a perspective that nothing in the world can entirely legitimate, to act as though we were what we are not yet and other than we are, and to transform the present by living in relation to a future age when the power and the glory of God will be everywhere and every tongue will praise his name."[7]

Soul making is a matter of my living from God's future and finding my identity in him. When I do that my soul comes into being through a special kind of suffering and a new kind of joy. My allegiances are thus broadened and the circle in which I live my life is constantly expanding. I am challenged with the possibility of change from within and pressured towards wanting to make changes in the world.

In the social and political arenas, for example, there is a pressing need for us to see ourselves "no longer as sons of Manu or Israel or Ishmael alone, but children of Man." Panikkar claims that it is "the intuition of the threefold structure of reality, of the triadic oneness existing on all levels of consciousness" that holds us together. The Trinity is the meeting place between God and Humanity.

A non-trinitarian God cannot "mingle" and much less unite himself with Man without destroying himself. He would have to remain aloof and isolated. No incarnation, descent and real manifestation of any kind would be possible. He would cease to be God if he became Man. A non-trinitarian Man cannot jump outside his little self, cannot become what he wants and longs for without destroying himself. He would have to remain aloof, isolated. No divinisation, glorification, redemption of any kind would be possible. He would cease to be Man if he became God. Man would stifle within himself just as God would die of self-consumption if the trinitarian structure of reality were not the case.

Many human beings try to live non-trinitarian lives, because they fear both the suffering and the joy that the necessary reaching out to others entails. They refuse or are unable to reach out of themselves. They are not lovingly inclined one toward the other, and the results are disastrous. God, the Holy Trinity, as the maker of souls, calls us home to himself—who is absolute identity in absolute unity, in absolute freedom. These are the three ingredients for the making of a soul: identity, unity, and freedom.

How, then, do I experience this threefold divine structure of my being? Human language gives us a clue. Panikkar invites us to look at the personal pronouns.

No known language lacks "I," "Thou," "He/She/It" and "We," "You," and "They." It is in this ultimate and universal structure that the Trinity is reflected or, to speak theologically, because the Trinity is "I, Thou, He/She/It, We, You, They," human experience presents this character. The Trinity appears, then, as the ultimate paradigm of human relationships.[8]

Behind this statement is the conviction (based on rigorous observation) that everything is radically interrelated and that everything is ultimately one. The evidence for this is right under my nose. My experience as a person gives me a clue to the mystery. I experience myself as neither a monolithic oneness nor as a disconnected plurality. When I am lonely and isolated, I cease to be myself. I begin to die. For me to be me there has to be you. An "I" implies a "Thou."

Why are these pronouns and their interrelatedness important? Because these modest, everyday words help structure my sense of identity. The collective pronouns are no less important than the individual ones. I am reluctant to give up the word "Man" as a single simple noun that includes us all, because God relates himself in Jesus Christ to the whole human race. "Humanity" won't quite fit the bill, as it sounds to me as impersonal as the word "herd." A friend suggests that we use the old term "Adam," which is both a personal name and a word that denotes collective identity. Vernon Eller rightly points out that

... the God/race relationship is just as truly person to person as is the God/individual one. In fact the God/race relationship is the prior, paradigmatic model of what 'personhood' means. ["God created *Man* in his own image."] ... It is not said that God created a bunch of individuals who got together and formed a corporation named MAN. And notice that it is this person, *man*, who was created in the image of God. ....Scripture does not say that each individual human being is in the image of God; no, man [or Adam] as a whole is ... the only hope of an individual's becoming a true "person" is through his participation in the fuller personhood of "man."[9]

Our mistake, and it is a tragic one, is our finding "normative personhood only in the human individual." We make the individual instead of the community the norm. In Kunkel's terms we choose the isolated ego over the real Self.

I CANNOT BE ME WITHOUT YOU

Imagine an enormous apple pie marked Man, or Adam, or Humanity. In our modern understanding, each individual has a slice of this pie. The enormous Adamic pie is thus dished up until everyone has a piece, large or small, depending on his or her lot. In a competitive society we hustle as much as we can for as large a slice of that pie as we can get hold of. All are in competition with one another to become isolated slices or "individuals" of what was once more pie.

But that isn't the way God constructed reality. The Christian vision—based on the revelation of God as Trinity and the understanding that I cannot, therefore, dispense with others when I seek to become my true self—turns this picture of the divided pie upside down. We violate the substance of Man/Adam when we seek to divide him/her/us/they up into little pieces and parcel them out. Each one of us is the whole pie in a unique and unrepeatable way. Each one of us is Adam. It is thus that we are called to be persons, sharing in one reality. We are not called to be individuals warring with one another over a divided and fragmented substance. To be a soul is to be a person. If I am a unique instance of Adam then I no longer need regard you as a rival. Nor do I need stand guard defensively over my slice. I am no longer pressed to define myself as someone over against you. The doctrine of the Trinity in which all the Persons are utterly distinct and yet fundamentally One is a model for Man/Adam: for women and men, for you and me, for them and us. This is the fundamental truth about soul making. And once this simple truth has been grasped, one's way of being with others and oneself in the world changes.

Soul making can therefore be described as the liberating movement from being individuals to becoming persons. The doctrine of the Trinity (or better, the very power of the Trinity) begins to come alive for us when we can say with all honesty, "I cannot be me without you, and we cannot be us without them. *Together* we have a future." When human beings begin to believe this fundamental truth and act on it, prejudices are undermined and injustices denounced. Action is taken against the proliferation of nuclear weapons, against the exploitation of our natural resources. The world becomes "ours," and all men and women "us." The believer is called upon to anticipate this trinitarian future as much as possible. The doctrine of the Trinity is, when properly understood, political dynamite. Politically, the world sways between the extremes of a totalitarian collectivism (which tends to obliterate human uniqueness and identity) and an atomizing individualism that leaves some lonely, afraid, and exploitable and others greedy, ruthless, and selfish. Communism and Capitalism come to mind in the political realm, with their twin sins of envy and greed. Both are enemies, in their extreme form, of the development of persons. Both are soul destroyers rather than soul makers. Catholicism and Protestantism come to mind in matters of religion. Historically, one side has emphasized the "We" at the expense of the "I"; the other the "I" at the expense of the "We." In terms of the Christian vision of our common life, each one of us is called to say "I am" precisely because of the receptive and open nature of the "We."

W. H. Auden writes of the two complementary movements of Catholicism and Protestantism.

The Christian doctrine which Protestantism emphasizes is that every human being, irrespective of family, class and occupation, is unique before God; the complementary and equally Christian doctrine emphasized by Catholicism is that we are all members, one with another, both in the Earthly and in the Heavenly City . . . Thus Protestantism is correct in affirming that the *We are* of society expresses a false identity unless each of its members can say *I am*; Catholicism is correct in affirming that the individual who will not or cannot join with others in saying *We* does not know the meaning of *I*.[10]

The doctrine of the Trinity speaks to our basic human need to be able to say I and We at the same time. It points to an ever new way for us to understand and interpret ourselves. Each of us is able to say "We" without being swallowed up into the collective because the unique, unrepeatable person is not an individual self, but a complete representation of the whole.

This truth is expressed in the central act of Christian worship, the Eucharist. There is only one bread. Thus each bit of consecrated bread is not a piece or part of the Body of Christ (as if we had to gather all the bits together in order to make up the whole Christ). No—each piece of bread is the bearer, sacramentally, of the whole Christ. In the same way the Church is not a federation or consortium of isolated congregations, the fullness of which is only expressed in great gatherings of the World Council of Churches or at the Vatican Council. The fullness of the Church as the Body of Christ is present where two or three are gathered together.

When it comes to more intimate personal relations, the Trinity speaks to the structure of love itself. Love, to be love, requires both union and identity. The lovers seek to be united, but in such a way that each remains his or her unique person. Indeed there is a tenderness and deference in true love concerning the separateness and uniqueness of the other. The question is, "How can you and I be totally one, and at the same time honor the special and glorious differences between us—those things which make you you and me me?" The doctrine of the Holy and Undivided Trinity (as tortuous as it seems to some) is a paradigm of loving. It shows us first that we are loved; and second, how to love in such a way that unity and identity are perfectly balanced.

There is a phrase in the tradition of soul making which speaks of "unmerging friendship." That is what we are after. St. Thomas Aquinas put it this way: "How true it is that mutual help and delight are without prejudice to distinctness."[11] A romantic way of saying this would be, "When I am with you, I not only feel more alive; I become more me."

TRACES OF THE TRINITY IN HUMAN EXPERIENCE

Let us now look a little more closely at the Christian teaching about love as it is grounded in the doctrine of the Trinity. We need still to bear in mind that this is not a treatise on the doctrine as such. We are merely looking for traces. St. Augustine found the *vestigia* of the Trinity in the pattern of human loving. He made an identification between will and love, which he likens to that which gives us a sense of weight or gravity. It is that which centers us and holds us, not down, but in our proper place. We become what we love because it is that which makes us who we are and is our center. He wrote, "My weight [*pondus*] is my love."[12] This sense of weight or identity that we enjoy is, first and foremost, grounded in the being or the *isness* of God. That is to say, a thing *is* insofar as it participates by grace in the being of God. We *are* insofar as we are in harmony with God.

Some things share in the life of God more than others. One might say that some things have more "soul" than others. Stones, for example, simply participte in being; whereas plants not only are, they are also alive. Animals are higher up the scale because they not only participate in being and living, but in sensing as well. Human beings (along with the angels) share in all of these with the addition of reasoning. Because of our ability to reason (this should not be understood as cold rationality), we share in the life of God more fully and comprehensively than any other created thing. Reason here is more akin to intuition, to discretion (which is the ability to see exactly how one thing is related to another), than to the ability to calculate and work things out. Reason, in this sense, plays a large part in the life of prayer. It is that which enables us to know and understand what we have seen. And because prayer is concerned with both wonder and amazement, we are led into a way of knowing and understanding that is radically different from the popular view. Knowledge ceases to be a possession. It becomes a process of participation in the life of another.

Most of our knowledge is acquired by a process of domination or manipulation. Moltmann describes the believer's way of knowing in this way.

. . . knowing does not transform the counterpart into property of the knower; the knower does not appropriate what he knows. On the contrary, he is transformed, through sympathy, becoming a participator in what he perceives. Knowledge confers fellowship. That is why knowing . . . only goes as far as love, sympathy and participation reach.

In other words, meditating on God in history as the God of Passion (in both senses of the word—as sufferer and lover) will alter the way we think. There will be "a change from lordship to fellowship, from conquest to participation, from production to receptivity." This could free our reasoning processes in such a way that we will be capable of being more and more receptive to others. Our reason would be freed for fellowship; and thus trinitarian thinking will prepare "the way for a liberating and healing concern for the reality that has been destroyed."[13] That reality is our solidarity with one another in God. It is the reality of complete union in unimaginable diversity.

We are created *ad imaginem Dei*, after the image of God, the Blessed Trinity; we are most truly ourselves when we are "trinitarian" in our loving, when we can say "We" in such a way that the "I" is set free. We are, of course, free to fall away from our true selves because love could not survive without the freedom to say "No." We are free to wander far away from our proper place. We are free to become eccentric—that is, off center. The work of Redemption is to restore the pattern of the Trinity in us so that we love in a way that is not disordered or out of tune.

Augustine found traces of the Trinity in his own inner being, in his own psychological and spiritual constitution. He was convinced that love worked in us from the inside through the trinitarian shape of our reasoning in memory, intellect, and will. We should note that the intellect is only one part of the reasoning process for Augustine. The motivating force is love (or the sense of gravity that brings us to our desired place). It is like a magnet that draws us to the spot where we truly belong. Augustine believed that something had gone drastically wrong with our gravitational system. Sin is the loss or damage of our homing device. It is the wounding of the homing instinct. Our memory is faulty, our intellect cloudy, and our will unruly. We then have to endure our own lack of being in emptiness and boredom. If we want to find our way home, the trinity of memory, intellect, and will have to be healed and restored. Traces of the Trinity can, therefore, be seen in the various ways in which we try to understand what it is to be a person. They can also be discerned in our attempts to relate to each other in love.

William of St. Thierry (1085–1148) says, "The art of arts is the art of love."[14] God is the great teacher of love, and love must have a trinitarian structure to be true to itself. The lover, the loved one, and the love make three. Or, the love between the lover and the loved one always seeks to open itself up to include others in its embrace. In Augustine's words, "You see the Trinity when you see Love . . . For the lover, the beloved and the love are three/ *Ecce tria sunt, amans et quod amatur, et amor.*"[15] Love doesn't stand still. It always desires another. It must always be outgoing in creation.

ACCURACY, LIBERTY, AND OPENNESS: MARKS OF SOUND DOCTRINE

Why is "sound doctrine" about the love of God (or better, about the God who is our Lover) important? It is important because what we think about God determines what we think about ourselves. The structure of human identity is dependent on how we view ultimate reality. You could reconstruct my practical "doctrine of God" from watching what I do, how I behave, how and what I love. I *say* that I believe in God, the Holy and Undivided Trinity, but I am often hard-pressed to say what that means for the making of my soul.

One of the places where the connection between what I *say* and what I *do* is celebrated and tested is in the life of prayer. Prayer often provides the occasion when false connections are broken and new starts are made. Prayer is the process by which we become the friend of God the Father, through the Son, in the power of the Holy Spirit. Soul making is, in part, a process of living into this mystery. It is a process of struggle and obedience, of integration and harmonization in the light of the love of the God to whom we owe allegiance and by whom we are made. My soul is made and re-made as I am brought back to my true center, as I am drawn towards "home." Soul making, therefore, is a matter of "sound doctrine" about God, since what I think matters as much as what I feel.

Jürgen Moltmann lays out some ground rules for doing theology or discovering "sound doctrine." His rules might well be applied to the art of soul making. The making of the soul, no less than theology, requires "a critical dissolution of naive, self-centered thinking." It further requires that I have the right to the liberty of my own personal conviction and my own free assent. Soul making and the doing of theology require a "free community of men and women, without privilege or discrimination." Moltmann insists that a proper sense of my own identity and destiny requires a threefold commitment; to accuracy, to freedom, and to openness. All this before we are ready to face the issue of actual content.

We can put this threefold commitment in question form. We

must ask of any statement three questions: Is it true? If it is true, is the truth asserted in such a way that its proclamation is liberating and not imprisoning? and, Does the truth and its formulations liberate men and women both to think their own thoughts and, at the same time, reveal the incompleteness and provisional nature of any human and historical concept or formulation? This last question is very important in the making of a soul. It involves a nimbleness of spirit that allows the believer to assert what he or she believes with utter sincerity and conviction and, at the same time, allow for the possibility of error. My mind must be free enough to formulate its own ideas, and yet be humble enough to abandon its own formulations in the face of the new and unexpected.

Whatever I believe or say about the Trinity must be in tune with the threefold commitment to accuracy, liberty, and openness. Moltmann makes a startling suggestion to move us forward in our search for the traces of the Trinity. He suggests that the doctrine of the triune God is bound up with the question of suffering. When the issue of suffering is probed, the doctrine of the Trinity emerges. To bring us to this point of understanding, Moltmann suggests that we not only ask, "How do I experience God? What does God mean for me? How am I determined by him?"; but also ask these questions in reverse. "How does God experience me? What do I mean for God? How is God determined by me?" This is not to say that the relationship between God and us is a reciprocal one between equals; rather that for a relationship to be a relationship at all, it must be a two-way affair.

The question, "How does God experience me?" suggests a fresh way to look at ourselves and our way of being in the world. What is God's experience of me? God's experience of me must seem strange, disappointing, amusing, hurtful, and occasionally delightful. Once the initial question has been entertained by the believer, its effects go on reverberating in the soul. Because I am capable of reflection and self-transcendence (I can go beyond myself), I can also experience God's experience of me. I can "see" what I am like from God's point of view. I can learn to know myself in the mirror of God's love, suffering, and joy. When I reflect on how God experiences me I begin to learn more about myself; and the more I understand God's experience of me and my world, the more deeply the mystery of God's passion comes home to me. The making of my soul has something to do with suffering and not just mine and my world's, but God's too. The making of my soul is bound up with the passion of God. As Moltmann points out, the person who is willing to probe the question of God's "experience" of us and our world begins to see

that the history of the world is the history of God's suffering. At the moment of God's profoundest revelation there is always suffering: the cry of the captives in Egypt; Jesus' death cry on the cross; the sighing of the whole enslaved creation for liberty. If a person once feels the infinite passion of God's love which finds expression here, then he understands the mystery of the triune God. God suffers with us—God suffers from us—God suffers for us: it is this experience of God that reveals the triune God . . . From time immemorial, experience has been bound up with wonder or with pain.

Wonder is the joy of identification and union: pain, the sense of isolation, conflict, and contradiction. As we have seen, our understanding of what it is to be a person always involves him or her in a relationship with someone or something which is "other." We experience wonder when we seek to open ourselves to others. We experience pain when we discover differences, contradictions, and the threat and promise of change. If we are not open to wonder and to pain, then we deny ourselves any true interaction with another—this is the very stuff of soul making. We suffer the terrible boredom of experiencing only ourselves. When we are frightened of experiencing others, something in the soul begins to die. A capacity for wonder and a readiness for pain are essential for the life of the soul. And the place where such capacity and readiness are fostered is in prayer.

Prayer, gratitude, joy, and adoration provide the ground from which I can begin to move out of my self and the tight little circles I get myself into. Prayer is the means by which I open myself up to that which is not me. Prayer is the most important activity in the desert. Prayer moves me towards accuracy, liberty, and openness. And these three bring me into the life of the

Holy and Undivided Trinity. Why? Because my passion is taken up into God's Passion; and where there is passion there is love and suffering, and where there is love and suffering a trinitarian patterning is evident. "To know God is to suffer God," runs an old theological saying, and Moltmann comments,

> To suffer God means experiencing in oneself the death pangs of the old . . . and the birth pangs of the new . . . The closer people come to the divine reality, the more deeply they are drawn into this dying and rebirth. . . .Christian meditation and contemplation are therefore at their very heart *meditatio crucis*, meditation on the passion.

Souls are made when we help each other "suffer" God in this way. And when God is thus "suffered" as "the all transforming fact" (to take a phrase from Karl Bath), joy becomes a possibility.

THE TRINITY: GOD AS FELLOW-SUFFERER

What, then, has our pilgrimage to do with suffering? Is this not simply yet another instance of religion's morbid and masochistic fascination with the subject? The believer has always struggled with the issue of suffering, both with his own and with God's. Does God suffer or is he "apathetic," without suffering? The doctrinal tradition always insisted on God's "apathy" as a way of insisting that God was above human emotions and passions. God was unchangeable. Unfortunately, it came to be believed in such a way that God seemed uncaring and untouchable. The concern was for God's faithfulness. God is, indeed, unchangeable; but in the sense that his love and his faithfulness are constant and steadfast. Moltmann is one of the few modern theologians who insists on God's passion. The word "passion" has a useful double meaning here. There is suffering that is passion, and there is a passion for life. God's Passion is not the glorification of suffering, nor an admission of its terrible necessity. God's Passion shows us a passion that is "the voluntary laying oneself open to another and allowing oneself to be intimately affected by him; that is to say the suffering of passionate love."

The doctrine of the Trinity emerges, insists Moltmann, when we apprehend God as the fellow sufferer. As the early theologian Origen wrote in his notes on Ezekiel, "In his mercy God suffers with us; for he is not heartless." Moltmann notes: "It is significant that Origen has to talk about God in trinitarian terms at the moment when his text makes him begin to talk about God's suffering." Strict monotheism would not permit talk of God's suffering. The God of the desert believer makes himself vulnerable. He goes out of himself and makes a covenant with his people and "in the fellowship of his covenant with Israel, God becomes capable of suffering." God and his people suffer together because of their willingness to be open to each other in passionate participation with each other. Moltmann writes, "The eternal God takes men and women seriously to the point of suffering with them in their struggles of being wounded in his love because of their sins . . . The experience of the divine pathos throws a person open to the joy and the pain of life."

There is a cross in the heart of God. This is simply a way of talking about the extremity of God's love and his risk in loving us. A famous English priest, G. A. Studdert Kennedy, wrote doggerel verses about God's gracious availability to us in Jesus. He was known as "Woodbine Willie" because of the cigarettes— Woodbines—he distributed to the troops during World War I. The verses he wrote are not very good poetry, but they are emotionally charged.

> The sorrows of God mun be 'ard to bear,
> if 'e really 'as Love in 'is 'eart,
> And the 'ardest part i' the world to play
> Mun surely be God's Part.

The believer is convinced that God longs for him, God aches for him, God loves him. This is the way he can live through the pain of the world and the sorrow of God. We live with what Moltmann calls "an open wound" because of this pain and this sorrow. Indeed, "the more a person believes, the more deeply he experiences pain over the suffering of the world."

Moltmann writes,

What happens in Jesus' passion is the giving up of the Son through the Father. In giving up his own Son, God cuts himself off from himself and sacrifices his own self. The giving up of the Son reveals a pain in God which can only be understood in trinitarian terms, or not at all.[16]

In the mystical tradition of Judaism, it was believed that the Shekinah, which represented God's gracious and over-arching presence in the world, suffered a series of self-humiliations by which the history of the world developed. God "suffered" in creating the world, choosing the patriarchs, making the various covenants, enduring the slavery and the exodus from Egypt, and going with his people into exile. The Almighty thus will "humiliate" himself until the end of the world.

This is a wonder. God freely limits himself for the sake of love. He reigns in heaven, yet he dwells with widows and orphans. It is out of this tradition that the doctrine of the Trinity was formulated. The humiliation of God for the sake of his love for his people means that there is a rift in the heart of God. There is, therefore, no human heartbreak, no alienation, which cannot find its home in the broken heart of God. God's own trinitarian brokenness is the place where I am always welcome. Nothing can separate me from this love. And, since this love has gone to the very depths of brokenness (when the Son was forsaken on the Cross) for me, there is nothing of which I need be afraid. There is no longer any need for me to lie to myself about anything ever again, because there is a cross in the heart of God. God on the cross was cut off from God, and that cross in the heart of God abides forever. Soul making means entering into the mystery of the cross, into the mystery of God's passion.

The desert way of believing is a hard way, but not so hard as one might imagine. His yoke is easy and his burden is light. All we have are traces of the Trinity, patterns in the sand. They are enough for those who see themselves in the School of Love. I learned something of which I write in the Egyptian desert, where flowers bloom and fountains of water sustain life. I may not yet be a Christian, a trinitarian; but I want to be one and I believe I am becoming one. I have seen them and I want to be among their number. God aches for us in his Son and his Spirit cries out to us.

Epilogue

Is any of the desert story, as I have outlined it, true? There is no way I can prove it. All I can do is challenge any reader with the issue of choice. A German proverb says, "The person who chooses has the torment of choice." The challenge has to do with this torment. Once a person moves out of the realm of mere necessity and admits to only a mustard seed of freedom, he or she is immediately tormented by the question of choice. What should I do? Which path should I take? The desert is the symbol of the struggle of choice in the human heart. The desert question is, "Choose this day whom you will serve."

There's a great deal of talk about "reality." We wonder what is real. The answer is that everything is real. The question is, a real what? The vinyl couch that is advertised as "simulated leather" isn't leather, but it is real vinyl. The pleasure, power, and robust sexuality that is promised in the advertising of everything from cigarettes to automobiles is also real. But a real what? A real seduction? A real romance? A real fraud? Every human being has to decide not so much what is real, but rather the true nature of the reality in which we find ourselves.

CHOOSING REALITY

"Reality" is, in a sense, a matter of choice. Some people with the precious freedom to choose, choose a nightmare for reality. Other who have lost that freedom have to live out the nightmare. I have been struck by the way in which we (particularly when we are young) try on different personalities and live in different "realities" until we find one we want to be. Sometimes a way of being chooses us rather than our choosing it. We fall into a way of being and then we are stuck with it.

Anne Carlisle, a talented modern actress and star of the science fiction movie *Liquid Sky* (a euphemism for heroin), has apparently made certain choices about what is real. In the movie she plays two roles, that of the misogynist junkie Jimmy, and that of the androgynous and promiscuous Margaret. A tiny alien, landing on the earth in search of a special chemical that is present in the human body at the point of orgasm or after the injection of heroin, finds that Margaret and her friends offer a steady supply. So far this sounds like the scenario for a bizarre movie which would appeal to an escapist society. What is extraordinary is that Anne Carlisle claims that the movie, which promises nothing and proposes nothing, is simply a reflection of the way things are. "In some weird way, it shows how we're all behaving like animals . . . It was time for a film that didn't promise anything . . . I have no feeling for the past at all. I just don't care about it. I have no desire to do classic roles or Shakespeare."[1]

Art, particularly the best of modern art, has a way of showing us our own patterns of alienation. *Liquid Sky* may have something of the prophetic in it. And, insofar as it is prophetic, it is a work of art. It shows our lostness and alienation. Anne Carlisle is right. We *are* all behaving like animals in some respects. If we go on doing so, human lives will be diminished and destroyed. I cannot, however, be sure that the makers of the movie have understood that somewhere in the middle of creating the film they made a choice about what reality is. Some people believe that art should be "uplifting" and "wholesome." But there is the terrible art of prophecy that holds up a mirror to us to show the true condition of things. The artist is called to show us glory. He or she is also called to show us how far we have fallen from it. Art that is only "uplifting" easily degenerates into sentiment and hypocrisy. Art not only ennobles the soul, it also judges it. It is said that after a performance of Shakespeare's *Antony and Cleopatra* in London during the reign of Queen Victoria, a member of the audience asked his neighbor what he thought of the play. "Very interesting," he replied, "but so unlike the family life of our own dear Queen!" There are two "realities" to contend with: the wildly irresponsible love affair on Cleopatra's royal barge, and the stuffy formalism of the Victorian court! They are both "real"; both represent aspects of reality that have to be attended to.

Art is always presenting us with issues of choice. "Reality," up to a point, is a matter of our own choosing. I can choose some destructive behavior, or I can choose to telephone a friend. I can choose to give in to a mood of self-pity, or I can choose a mood of expectancy and hope. The area of freedom is, in fact, very small; but it is enough to make a difference. Is *Liquid Sky* prophetic art or is it merely another indication of a lost society? Choose. Perhaps it is both. But the choice is ours. "Only the paradigmatic is real": which pattern or model have you chosen?

Graham Greene, in his novel *Monsignor Quixote*, challenges the reader to choose between life and death, between conflicting views concerning the nature of reality. At the end of the book Father Quixote suffers a fatal accident. His death, however, isn't immediate. Before he dies he wants to celebrate the Mass one last time. His misadventures with his unbelieving friend, the communist ex-mayor of his village, have so alarmed and annoyed his bishop that Quixote has been inhibited from exercising his priestly duties. In the middle of the night, in the monastery that has offered him hospitality after his accident, Father Quixote sleepwalks his way to the chapel, followed by his unbelieving friend and other concerned people.

Father Quixote led them down into the shadows of the great church lit only by the half moon which shone through the east window. He walked firmly to the altar and began to say the words of the old Latin Mass, but it was in an oddly truncated form . . . The Mass went rapidly on— no epistle, no gospel: it was as though Father Quixote were racing towards the consecration . . . The Mayor moved a few steps nearer to the altar. He was afraid that, when the moment of waking came, Father Quixote might fall, and he wanted to be near enough to catch him in his arms.

"Who on the day before He suffered took bread . . . " Father Quixote seemed totally unaware that there was no Host . . . He raised his empty hands, *"Hoc est enim corpus meum,"* and he went on steadily without hesitation to the consecretion of the non-existent wine in the non-existent chalice . . .

The Mayor took another step forward ready to catch him, but then he spoke again: *"Corpus Domini nostri,"* and with no hestiation at all he took . . . the invisible Host and his fingers laid the nothing on his tongue.

And so Father Quixote said his last mass. He turned, the non-existent bread between his fingers, and offered it to his nonbelieving friend. The Mayor knelt. "The fingers came closer. The Mayor opened his mouth and felt the fingers, like a Host, on his tongue." At which point the old priest died.

The question is, how would one describe the *reality* of Father Quixote's last mass? The Mayor, the non-believer, may have received communion. His love for his friend the old priest may have made him available to the power of love in "the Body of Christ." Could he have received Christ then? Did he? At least it raised a question in the Mayor's mind:

... an idea quite strange to him had lodged in his brain. Why is it that the hate of a man—even of a man like Franco—dies with his death, and yet love, the love which he had begun to feel for Father Quixote, seemed now to live and grow in spite of the final separation and the final silence—for how long, he wondered with a kind of fear, was it possible for that love of his to continue? And to what end.[2]

The Mayor, in the simple act of friendship, chose love. The desert believer chooses Jesus and is chosen by him. And this choosing becomes a way of knowing, loving, and living that knows no end. Soul making is a matter of choosing the reality of love against which all other realities are tested as if by fire. The choice is ours.

Notes

Preface

1. Kingsley Amis, *Collected Short Stories* (London: Penguin Books, 1983), 12.

Introduction

1. Walker Percy, *The Second Coming* (New York: Farrar, Straus and Giroux, 1980), 189–90.
2. John Mortimer, *Clinging to the Wreckage* (London: Penguin Books, 1982), 62.
3. Don Cupitt, *The World to Come* (London: SCM Press, 1982), 6; 20.
4. Karl Rahner, *The Practice of Faith: A Handbook of Contemporary Spirituality* (New York: Crossroad, 1983), 3; 6–7.
5. See Colin Thompson's review of Patrick Grant's *Literature of Mysticism in Western Tradition*, *Times Literary Supplement*, 13 January 1984, 42.
6. J. Christian Beker, *Paul's Apocalyptic Gospel* (Philadelphia: Fortress Press, 1982), 21.
7. Rahner, *Practice of Faith*, 7.

1. Children of the Desert

1. Colin Thompson, *Times Literary Supplement*, 19 January 1984, 42.
2. J. D. Salinger, *Franny and Zooey* (New York: Bantam Books, 1964), 115.
3. See Edward Schillebeeckx, *God is New Each Moment* (Edinburgh: T. and T. Clark, 1983).
4. See Don Cupitt, *The World to Come* (London: SCM Press, 1982), 7.
5. See Janet Malcolm, *Psychoanalysis: The Impossible Profession* (New York: Vintage, 1982).
6. Morton Kelsey, *Companions on the Inner Way* (New York: Crossroad, 1983), 7–8.
7. Salinger, *Franny and Zooey*, 178–79.
8. E. Allison Peers, ed. and trans., *The Complete Works of St. John of the Cross* (Westminster, Maryland: Newman Press, 1953), 192–93.
9. Evagrius Ponticus, *The Praktikos and Chapters on Prayer*, trans. John Eudes Bamberger, no. 4 of the *Cistercian Studies Series* (Kalamazoo: Cistercian Publications, 1978), 65; 116; 117.
10. John Meyendorff, *St. Gregory Palamas and Orthodox Spirituality* (New York: St. Vladimir's Seminary Press, 1974), 98; 7.
11. John Updike's introduction to Henry Green, *Loving, Living, Party Going* (New York: Penguin Books, 1978), 7.
12. Nelson S. T. Thayer, "Merton and Freud: Beyond Oedipal Religion," *The Journal of Pastoral Care*, vol. XXV, no. 1 (March 1981): 37.
13. Quotations from Bruno Bettelheim are from his article "Freud and the Soul," *The New Yorker*, 1 March 1982, 52 ff. See also Bettelheim, *Freud and Man's Soul* (New York: Vintage Books, 1984).

2. The Christian Neurosis

1. John Osborne, *A Better Class of Person* (London: Penguin Books, 1982), 63.
2. Karen Horney, *Neurosis and Human Growth* (New York: Norton, 1950).
3. Pierre Solignac, *The Christian Neurosis* (New York: Crossroad, 1982), 14–15.
4. Horney, *Neurosis*, 23.
5. William Golding, *The Paper Men* (New York: Farrar, Straus and Giroux, 1984), 155.
6. John Mortimer, *Clinging to the Wreckage* (London: Penguin Books, 1982), 222.
7. Michael Holroyd, *Lytton Strachey* (New York: Holt, Rinehart and Winston, 1980), 91; 108; 233.
8. Arianna Stassinopoulos, *Maria Callas: The Woman Behind the Legend* (New York: Ballantine, 1981), 79; 83.
9. Robertson Davies, *The Rebel Angels* (New York: Viking Press, 1982), 56.
10. Bruno Bettelheim, "Freud and the Soul," *The New Yorker*, 1 March 1982, 64.
11. Erich Fromm, *Greatness and Limitation of Freud's Thought* (New York: New American Library, 1980), i; ii.
12. Jacob Needleman, *Consciousness and Tradition* (New York: Crossroad, 1982), 4.
13. William Golding, *A Moving Target* (New York: Farrar, Straus and Giroux, 1982), 186–87 (both quotes).
14. See Needleman, *Consciousness and Tradition*, 4 ff.
15. Ibid., 5; 6; 16.
16. Morton Kelsey, *Companions on the Inner Way* (New York: Crossroad, 1982), 42.
17. Andrew Porter, Metropolitan Opera *Stagebill*, vol. XI, no. 5, January 1984.
18. Janet Malcolm, *Psychoanalysis: The Impossible Profession* (New York: Vintage, 1982), 6.
19. Madeleine L'Engle, *Lines Scribbled on an Envelope* (New York: Farrar, Straus and Giroux, 1969), 49.
20. Peter Hawkins, *The Language of Grace* (Cambridge: Cowley, 1983), 3.
21. Malcolm, *Psychoanalysis*, 19. Quotations from Malcolm that follow are from *Psychoanalysis*; page numbers are cited in text.
22. J. D. Salinger, *Franny and Zooey* (New York: Bantam Books, 1964), 200–02.
23. Bobbie Gerber, *Shelter* (New York: Seabury Press, 1983), 8–9.
24. Malcolm, *Psychoanalysis*, 39. Quotations from Malcolm that follow are from *Psychoanalysis*; page numbers are cited in text.

3. Death in the Desert

1. Iris Murdoch, *Bruno's Dream* (London: Chatto and Windus, 1969), 216.
2. John Mortimer, *Clinging to the Wreckage* (London: Penguin Books, 1982), 145.
3. Quotations from Stephen A. Kurtz are from his article "Silence," *Commonweal*, March 1984: 137; 139; 138; 139; 140; 141.
4. Frank Kermode, *The Genesis of Secrecy* (Cambridge: Harvard University Press, 1979), 1.
5. See Urban T. Holmes, *Spirituality for Ministry* (San Francisco: Harper & Row, 1982).
6. Walker Percy, *The Message in the Bottle* (New York: Farrar, Straus and Giroux, 1975), 51.
7. Y. Nomura, *Desert Wisdom* (New York: Doubleday, 1982), 14.
8. W. H. Auden, *Forewords and Afterwords* (New York: Random House, 1973), 79.
9. Teilhard de Chardin, *Le Milieu Divin* (London: Fontana, 1964), 72.

10. Carlos Castaneda, *Journey to Ixtlan* (New York: Pocket Books, 1974), viii.
11. Donald Nicholl, *Holiness* (New York: Seabury Press, 1982), 27.
12. Castaneda, *Journey to Ixtlan*, 15. Quotations from Castaneda that follow are from *Journey to Ixtlan*; page numbers are cited in text.
13. Quoted by James W. Douglass, *Resistance and Contemplation* (New York: Delta, 1972), 55–88.
14. Castaneda, *Journey to Ixtlan*, 86–88.
15. Iris Murdoch, *The Nice and the Good* (New York: Penguin Books, 1978), 315.
16. See Karl Rahner, *Theological Investigations III* (New York: Seabury Press, 1974), 73–85.
17. W. H. Auden, *For the Time Being* (London: Faber and Faber, 1945), 66.

4. The Gift of Tears

1. *New York Times*, 22 February 1982.
2. Isaac of Ninive, quoted in Andre Louf, "Humility and Obedience in Monastic Tradition," *Cistercian Studies*, vol. XVIII, 1983:4, 272.
3. Ibid., 268.
4. See Ibid., 273.
5. See Jacob Needleman, *Lost Christianity* (New York: Bantam New Age Books, 1982), 158–59.
6. See Ibid., 118.
7. Harry Williams, *Some Day I'll Find You* (London: Mitchell Beazley, 1982), 213; 209.
8. Ibid.; 119–20.
9. Needleman, *Lost Christianity*, 123–24. Quotations from Needleman that follow are from *Lost Christianity*; page numbers are cited in text.
10. Flannery O'Connor, *The Complete Stories* (New York: Farrar, Straus and Giroux, 1974), 270.
11. For a discussion of Lewis's experiences, see Mary Warnock, *Imagination* (Berkeley: University of California Press, 1976), 208–209.
12. Rowan Williams, *The Truce of God* (London: Collins Fount Paperbacks, 1983), 85.
13. W. H. Auden, *Forewords and Afterwords* (New York: Random House, 1973), 37.
14. See Krister Stendahl's address at the 15th Trinity Institute National Conference 1984, as reported in *Trinity News*, vol. 31, no. 1, February 1984.
15. Irenee Hausherr, *Penthos: The Doctrine of Compunction in the Christian East*, trans. Anselm Hufstader (Kalamazoo: Cistercian Publications, 1982), vii.
16. T. S. Eliot, *The Cocktail Party* (New York: Harcourt Brace and Co., 1950), 126.
17. Hausherr, *Penthos*, 24. See also Evagrius Ponticus, *The Praktikos and Chapters on Prayer*, trans. John Eudes Bamberger (Kalamazoo: Cistercian Studies, 1978).
18. John Chrysostom, *De Compunctione* PG 47: 409F. Quoted in Hausherr, *Penthos*, 27; 28.
19. See Jürgen Moltmann, *The Trinity and the Kingdom* (San Francisco: Harper & Row, 1981), chapter 9.
20. Hausherr, *Penthos*, 29.
21. Abba Poeman, in Benedicta Ward, *The Desert Christian: Sayings of the Desert Fathers* (New York: Macmillan, 1975), 155.
22. Ibid., 35.
23. Robertson Davies, *The Rebel Angels* (New York: Viking Press, 1982), 114.
24. Ponticus, *The Praktikos*, 76:125.

25. Hausherr, *Penthos*, 53. See PG 35:1049C. Quotations from Hausherr that follow are from *Penthos*; page numbers are cited in text.
26. *Adv. Haer.* 4.25 and Ibid., 178.
27. *Adv. Haer.* 4.64 and Hausherr, *Penthos*, 158.
28. C. S. Lewis, *The Voyage of "The Dawn Treader"* (New York: Collier Books, Macmillan, 1971), 75–76; 90–91.

5. The Fiftieth Gate

1. Elie Weisel, *Four Hasidic Masters and Their Struggle Against Melancholy* (Notre Dame: University of Notre Dame Press, 1978), 29–31.
2. Iris Murdoch, *Henry and Cato* (New York: Viking, 1977), 370.
3. Nikos Katzantzakis, *St. Francis* (New York: Simon and Schuster, 1962), 118–19.
4. Father Bede Thomas Mudge, OHC, to whom I owe a debt of gratitude for what follows.
5. Weisel, *Four Hasidic Masters*, 21.
6. Weisel, *Four Hasidic Masters*, 60.
7. , Graham Greene, *Monsignor Quixote* (New York: Simon and Schuster, 1982), 55; 69–70.
8. Graham Greene, *The Portable Graham Greene*, ed. Philip Stratford (New York: Penguin Books, 1977), 586.
9. Ibid., 587.
10. Ibid., 588.
11. Shusako Endo, *The Samurai* (New York: Harper & Row, 1982), 175.
12. Greene, *The Portable Graham Greene*, 591.
13. Thomas Merton, *Raids on the Unspeakable* (New York: New Directions, 1970), 45.
14. Greene, *The Portable Graham Greene*, 594.
15. See Kingsly Amis, *Collected Short Stories* (London: Penguin Books, 1983), 12.
16. *Charles Williams: An Exploration of His Life and Works*, Alice Mary Hatfield (New York: Oxford University Press, 1983), 172.
17. Walker Percy, *The Last Gentleman* (New York: Farrar, Straus and Giroux, 1966), 372.
18. Morris West, *The Clowns of God* (New York: Farrar, Straus and Giroux, 1983), 270.

6. Love: God's Wild Card

1. Anne Sexton, *The Awful Rowing Toward God* (Boston: Houghton Mifflin, 1975), 85–86.
2. Graham Greene, *The Portable Graham Greene*, ed. Philip Stratford (New York: Penguin Books), 477.
3. William Golding, *The Paper Men* (New York: Farrar, Straus and Giroux, 1984), 123.
4. Walker Percy, *Lost in the Cosmos* (New York: Farrar Straus and Giroux, 1983), 78–79.
5. Hans Urs von Balthasar, "Transcendence and *Gestalt*," *Communio*, vol. IX, no. 1, Spring 1984:5.
6. T. S. Eliot, "Little Gidding," *The Four Quartets* (London: Faber and Faber, 1968), 53.
7. Peter Schaffer, *Equus: Shrivings* (New York: Atheneum, 1974), 34.
8. John Keats, *Letters* 32, 21 December 1817.

9. Selma Lagerlof, quoted in Carol Bly, *Letters from the Country* (New York: Harper & Row, 1981), vii.
10. George McDonald, "The Last Penny" in *George McDonald: Creation In Christ*, Rolland Hein, ed. (Wheaton, Ill.: Harold Shaw), 173.
11. Bly, *Letters from the Country*, 175–76; 176; 177; 184.
12. Ibid., 54–56; 80–81.
13. Golding, *The Paper Men*, 114.
14. *George Herbert: The Country Parson, The Temple*, John N. Wall Jr., ed. (Paulist Press: New York, 1981), 316.

7. Love and the Making of a Soul

1. Iris Murdoch, *Henry and Cato* (New York: Viking Press, 1977), 270.
2. George Steiner, *The Critical Moment* (London: Faber and Faber, 1964), 29–30.
3. Morris West, *The Clowns of God* (New York: Farrar, Straus and Giroux, 1983), 144.
4. David Tracy, *The Analogical Imagination* (New York: Crossroad, 1981), 382–83.
5. See Hans Mol, *Identity and the Sacred* (New York: Free Press, 1976); and Alan Jones, *Exploring Spiritual Direction* (New York: Seabury Press, 1982), chapter 6.
6. John Drury, *The Pot and the Knife* (London: SCM Press, 1979), 4–5.
7. Bernard Malamud, *God's Grace* (New York: Avon Books, 1982), 80.
8. Carl Sandburg, *Harvest Poems: 1910–1960* (New York: Harcourt, Brace and Jovanovich, 1960).
9. Anne Sexton, *The Awful Rowing Toward God* (Boston: Houghton Mifflin, 1975), 61.
10. W. H. Auden, "In Sickness and in Health," *The Collected Poetry of W. H. Auden* (New York: Random House, 1945), 31.

8. The Three Conversions

1. W. H. Auden, quoted from "Psychology and Art To-day," 1935, in Samuel Hynes, *The Auden Generation* (New York: Viking Press, 1979), 14.
2. Morton Kelsey, *Companions on the Inner Way* (New York: Crossroad, 1983), 192.
3. *New York Times*, 17 May 1981.
4. Edmund Gosse, *Father and Son*: (London: Penguin Books, [1907], 1970), 49–50.
5. Dom Gregory Dix, *The Shape of the Liturgy* (London: Dacre Press, Adam and Charles Black, 1945), 748.
6. Virginia Owens, *The Total Image* (Grand Rapids: Wm. B. Eerdmans, 1982), 44.
7. Bishop Stephen Bayne, "The Crisis of Spirituality in the Church," *The Quarterly Gazette of the Anglican Society*, Autumn 1971, vol. 2, second series no. 7.
8. For further reading, see Evelyn Underhill, *Mysticism* (New York: Meridian, New American Library, 1974), part II.
9. David Lodge, *Souls and Bodies* (New York: William Morrow, 1983), 6.
10. Father Réginald Garrigou-Lagrange, *The Three Ways of the Spiritual Life* (Westminster, Maryland: Newman Press, 1950), 2–3. 29
11. Don Cupitt, *The World to Come* (London: SCM Press, 1982), xv.
12. St. Teresa of Avila, *The Book of the Life* IX.8. See *The Collected Works of St. Teresa*

of Avila, Kieran Kavanaugh and Otilio Rodriguez, trans. Vol. 1 (Washington D.C. Institute of Carmelite Studies, 1976).
13. St. Catherine of Siena, *Dialogs* LX.37. See *Catherine of Siena: The Dialogue*, Suzanne Noffke, trans. (New York: Paulist Press, 1980).
14. Garrigou-Lagrange, *The Three Ways*, 39.
15. St. Catherine of Siena, *Dialogs* LXIII.
16. See St. John of the Cross, *Dark Night* I.9, from *The Complete Works of St. John of the Cross*, trans. and ed. E. A. Peers (Westminster, Maryland: Newman Press, 1953).
17. Gerald May, *Will and Spirit: A Contemplative Psychology* (San Francisco: Harper & Row, 1982), 25.
18. Cupitt, *The World to Come*, 74; 83.
19. See Ibid., 22.
20. Garrigou-Lagrange, *The Three Ways*, 55.
21. Harry Williams, *Some Day I'll Find You* (London: Mitchell Beazley, 1982), 192–93.

9. The Soul Maker: The Holy and Undivided Trinity

1. Peter Schaffer, *Amadeus* (New York: Harper & Row, 1981), 57–58.
2. Fritz Kunkel, *Selected Writings*, ed. and with an Introduction and Commentary by John A. Sanford (New York: Paulist Press, 1984), 56–57; 122; 140; 148.
3. Jürgen Moltmann, *The Trinity and the Kingdom* (San Francisco: Harper & Row, 1981), xvii.
4. See Raimundo Panikkar, *The Trinity and the Religious Experience of Man* (New York: Orbis Books, 1973), 82.
5. Robert Jenson, *The Triune Identity* (Philadelphia: Fortress Press, 1982), 145 (both quotes).
6. William Johnston, *The Mirror Mind* (San Francisco: Harper & Row, 1981), 159.
7. David Bailey Harned, *Creed and Personal Identity* (Philadelphia: Fortress, 1981), 116.
8. Panikkar, *The Trinity*, xi; xii; xv.
9. Vernon Eller, *The Language of Canaan and the Grammar of Feminism* (Grand Rapids: Eerdmans, 1982), 13–14.
10. W. H. Auden, *Forewords and Afterwords* (New York: Random House, 1973), 87.
11. In *De Divinis Nominibus*, IV. lect. 6.
12. *Confessions* XII, ix, 10.
13. Jürgen Moltmann, *The Trinity and the Kingdom* (San Francisco: Harper & Row, 1981), 9 (all quotes).
14. See William of St. Thierry, *On the Nature and Dignity of Love* (Kalamazoo: Cistercian Studies Vol. XXX), 1981.
15. *De Trinitate*, VII.12.14.
16. Moltmann, *The Trinity and the Kingdom*, pp. xii; xiii; 4; 4–5; 8; 23; 25; 25–27; 36; 49; 83.

Epilogue

1. Moviegoer, July 1984, 11.
2. Graham Greene, *Monsignor Quixote* (New York: Simon and Schuster, 1982), 215–221.

Index

Abgescheidenheit, 45
Abraham, 171
Abyss of faith, 109
Accidents, 49
A Christmas Carol (Dickens), 52
Adolescence, longings of, 156–157
Aelred of Rievaulx, 3, 159
Aesthetic, 28
Affirmative way, 30
Aletheia, 28
All That Falls (Beckett), 126
Aloneness, 189–190
Ambition, 37
Amis, Kinsley, viii–ix
Anatta, 64
Angels, 53-56
Anger at God, 113–114
Anglo-Saxon Chronicles, 117
Anorexia nervosa, 50
Antony and Cleopatra (Shakespeare), 207
Apatheia, 45
Apophatic way, 25-27; Freud and, 30
Apostles: experiences of, 165–166; third conversion of, 181–182
Appetite, victims of, 43–45
Art, 207–208
"The Artificial Nigger" (O'Connor), 91
Athanasius, St., 14
Atheism, 8–9; of Freud, 31; and God, 62
Attentiveness, way of, 56–58
Auden, W. H., 94, 122, 158, 159, 196
Augustine, St., 59, 176, 197, 199
Authority, issue of, 20–21

Bad news, 3
Balthasar, Hans Urs von, 127
Barukh, Rebbe, 107–109

Bauman, Lynn, ix
Bayne, Stephen F., viii–ix, 166
Beckett, Samuel, 126
Beker, J. Christiaan, 10
Believers, 3–5; three marks of, 118–120
Bellow, Saul, 68–69
Bernard of Clairvaux, St., 3
Bernard, St., 173
Betrayal, crisis of, 166
Bettelheim, Bruno, 31–32
The Bible, 121; as architecture of our thoughts, 166; importance of stories, 153
Bismarck, Otto, 67
Blake, William, 119
Bly, Carol, 132, 133–134, 135, 137, 139
Bonaventure, St., 173
Bottomless Abyss, 111
Brighton Rock (Greene), 125
The Brothers Karamazov (Dostoevsky), 118
Buber, Martin, 184

Callas, Maria, 40
Calvin, John, 59
Carlisle, Anne, 206–207
Carlyle, Thomas, 157
Castaneda, Carlos, 69, 74, 75–77
Catherine of Genoa, St., 170
Catherine of Siena, St., 177, 178
Catholicism vs. Protestantism, 196
Cell, sitting in one's, 64–67
Center, need for, 148–152
Chardin, Teilhard de, 68
Cheerfulness, 125–126
Childishness, 111–112
Christ. *See* Jesus Christ
Cistercian writers, 3
The Clowns of God (West), 146
The Cocktail Party (Eliot), 95–96

Companionship, 51–56, 110; and
    death, 73–75
Complementary pairs, 24–25
Confessions (St. Augustine), 176
Confession, sacrament of, 85
Connatural knowledge, 136
Conscience, 155
Contemplation, 28–29
Contemplative approach, 25
Contradiction: of opposites, 24–25;
    pain of, 89–90
Conversion, 159–184; to Christ,
    152–154; continuing conversion,
    164–165; evangelism and, 182–
    184; path to, 169–182;
    phenomenon of, 160–161;
    process of, 161–164
Coping mechanisms, 46
Crises of conversion, 177–179
Cults, 21
Cupitt, Don, 6, 7–8, 175–176,
    180–181

Dante, 56, 128, 147, 154, 155, 170
Dark Night of the Senses, 175
Darwin, Charles, 7, 27, 44
Davies, Robertson, 41, 98–99
Day, Dorothy, 54–55
Death in the desert, 60–72
Delight, 145
Desert tradition, 2, 5–6; and
    Freud, 31–34; psychoanalysis
    and, 23–24
Detachment, 45–49
Dickens, Charles, 52
Discontinuity, fear of, 58
Disloyalty, 118-119
Divine Comedy (Dante), 56
Dominate, desire to, 151
Don Juan, 69, 72, 73, 74, 75–77
Doubt of God, 113–114
Drury, John, 150
Dying to self, 71

Eckhart, Meister, 8–9, 45
Edwards, Oliver, 125
Eichmann, Adolf, 119
Eliot, T. S., 95–96, 128
Elisha, prophet, 14
Eller, Vernon, 194
Emptiness, 45; crisis of, 166–167
Endo, Shusako, 117–118

The Enlightenment, 20
Ephrem, St., 97
Equus (Schaffer), 129
Eros, 154
Eternal punishment doctrine,
    9–10; affection for, 39–40
Eucharist, 196
Evagrius, 96, 100, 102–103
Evangelism, 161, 167–168; and
    conversion, 182–184; and
    vindictiveness, 172
Ex-suicide, becoming of, 126–127

Fake Christs, 122
Fat Lady, 54–55
Fear and soul-making, 145
Feeling and understanding, 26
Fifth baptism, 103
Fiftieth gate, 107–123
Finished people, 2
First conversion, 170–174
Formulas and faith, 10–11
Forster, E. M., 23, 48
Francis de Sales, St., 104
Francis of Assisi, St., 67; of
    Katzantzakis, 109, 110–111
Franny and Zooey (Salinger), 26, 54
Freedom: limits of, 50; love
    requiring, 131
Friend: death as, 67–69; God as,
    22
Freud, Sigmund, 19, 27, 30, 44–
    45; atheism of, 31; and desert
    tradition, 31–34; on expectations
    of psychoanalysis, 49; on
    freedom, 50; midwife, analyst as,
    42–43; savior, need for, 58; on
    transference, 46; translations of,
    32
Fromm, Erich, 42–43
Frost, Robert, 129–130
Fundamentalism, 21
Fundamentalist literalists, 4
Future and the Trinity, 192–194

Gandhi, Mahatma, 46, 64
Garrigou-Lagrange, Father, 172,
    174, 178, 181–182
Gerber, Bobbie, 55
Gide, André, 67
Gifts: from monastery, 14–16; of
    tears, 22, 82–106

Gnosis, 86–87
Good news, 2–3
God: anger and doubt of, 113–
114; appearance of, 190–191; as
Bottomless Abyss, 111; as center,
150; darkness in, 26; doctrine of,
200–203; experience of me,
201–202; as fellow-sufferer, 203–
205; as Friend, 22; as good, 154;
humiliation of, 205; idea and
reality of, 70; as limitless
horizon, 120–123; and
perfectionism, 36–37; shock of,
84; tears as gift from, 100; word
as problem, 8
God's Grace (Malamud), 153
Golding, William, 38, 44, 126,
139–140
Gosse, Edmund, 160
Gosse, Philip, 7
Grace, miracle of, 59
Green, Aaron, 58
Greene, Graham, 115–116, 117,
118–119, 125, 208–209
Gregory of Nazianzen, St., 100,
103
Guilt of believers, 118

Happiness, 43
Harned, David Baily, 192
Healing oils, 15
Heart-work, 20
Hell, doctrine of. *See* Eternal
punishment doctrine
Henderson the Rain King (Bellow),
68–69
Henry and Cato (Murdoch), 109,
178
Herbert, George, 140
Hermes, 63–64
Herz-Werk (Rilke), 20
Holiness, 55
Holland, Henry Scott, 10
Holmes, Urban, 63
Holy and undivided Trinity, 185–
205
Home to ourselves, 103–104
Horney, Karen, 36, 37
Hospitality, 12, 14–15
Humor, 15–16, 63
Hunt in desert, 75–78
Hyperboreans, 6

Ideas, idolatry of, 27–30
Ignatian spirituality, 29–30;
inordinate affections, 102
Ignatius Loyola, St., 46
Illumination, light of, 179
Illusions, 65–66
Images, 24–27; of God, 199; and
Jung, 30–31
Imperatives of believing, 21–23
The Impossible Profession (Malcolm),
58
Indifference, 45
Insane believers, 3–5
Intolerable believers, 3–5
Invitation to change, 114–117
Involvement, 45–48
Isaac of Ninive, 82
Isness of things, 126–127

Jenson, Robert, 190
Jeremiah, Father, 13–16
Jesus Christ: acts in life of, 164–
165; conversion to, 152–154;
following of, 171; image of, 26–
27; laughter of, 99; mystery of,
147; and Peter, 176, 179; and
Truth, 7
John Chrysostom, St., 96, 104
John of the Cross, St., 25, 87, 175,
178
Johnson, Robert, 155
Johnson, Samuel, 125
Johnston, William, 191
John the Baptist, 14, 103
Jones, Edward A., viii–ix
Journey to Ixtlan (Castaneda), 69
Joy, 92–94
Julian of Norwich, 170
Julian the Apostate, 14
Jungian analysis, 29
Jung, Karl, 19, 27, 29–30; images
and, 30–31; and numinous, 47;
saintly man story of, 37; savior,
need for, 58
Justification by faith, 169

Kataphatic way, 30
Katzantzakis, Nikos, 109, 110–111
Keats, John, 1, 130
Kelsey, Morton, 24–25, 47, 160
Kennedy, G. A. Studdert, 204

Kermode, Frank, 63
Kierkegaard, Søren, 64
Kingdom of God: and tears, 85; understanding of, 94–95
Knowledge without love, 88
Krishnamurti, 90
Kunkel, Fritz, 186, 187–188, 194
Kurtz, Stephen A., 60–61

The Last Farthing (McDonald), 131
"The Last Pope" (Greene), 119–120
Learning and suffering, 86–92
L'Engle, Madeleine, 49
Leo, Brother, 109–111
Letters from the Country (Bly), 132
Letting go, 59, 149–150; in second conversion, 178–181
Lewis, C. S., 92, 105–106
Libido dominandi, 151
Life of virtue, 3
Liquid Sky, 206–207, 208
Live, as imperative, 22
Living death, 67
Lodge, David, 168–169
Longing, 156–157
Look, as imperative, 22
Lorenz, Konrad, 58
Louf, André, 83
Love, 124–140; and first conversion, 173–174; and soul-making, 143–158; and the Trinity, 199
Love-making, 133
Luther, Martin, 21

Macarius, Abba, 12
McDonald, George, 131
Malamud, Bernard, 153
Malcolm, Janet, 50, 52–53, 58
Man/Adam, 194–195
Marx, Karl, 27, 44
Mature believing, 21–23
May, Gerald, 179
Meaning, crisis of, 166
Medieval theology, 24
Meditation, 51
Mending the creation, 94–96
Mental illness, 46
Merton, Thomas, 75, 119
Metanoia, 95
Meyendorff, John, 27–28

Midwife, psychoanalyst as, 42–43
Moltmann, Jürgen, 97, 188–189, 198, 200–205
Monastery of St. Macarius, 12–16
Monastic life, 13–14
Monsignor Quixote (Greene), 115–116, 208–209
Mortification, 71
Mortimer, John, 4–5, 38, 60
Moses, 103
Moses, Abba, 64
Mozart, Wolfgang, 185
Murdoch, Iris, 60, 78, 109, 143, 178
Music, 47
Mystery of the Second Baptism, 85

Needleman, Jacob, 1, 44, 45–46, 88, 89, 90–91
Negative Capability, 130
Neurosis and Human Growth (Horney), 36
Neurosis, Christian, 35–59
The Nice and Good (Murdoch), 78
Nicholl, Donald, 72
Normalcy, 129
Not-self, 64, 65
Nuclear war, 69

O'Connor, Flannery, 91
Oedipal period, 58
Oils for healing, 15
Old Testament Trinity, 188–189
The Original We, 186–188
Osborne, John, 35
Owens, Virginia, 161

Pain of love, 139–140
Panikkar, Raimundo, 189, 193
The Paper Men (Golding), 38, 126
Paradigms, 148
Parturire, 51
Pascal, Blaise, 73
Passion, 78, 203–204
Penthos, 84–85, 95, 96, 104
Percy, Walker, 3–4, 8, 64, 114, 122, 126–127, 180
Perfectionism, 35–39
Peter and Christ, 176, 179
Phan, Peter, ix
Photismos, 104
Plato, 27, 168

Ponticus, Evagrius, 96, 100, 102–103
Porter, Andrew, 47
Potter, Beatrix, 92
The Practice of Faith (Rahner), 8
Prayer: and companionship, 73–74; process of, 200; and silence, 62
Precision in soul-making, 145
Problem-solving, 134–135
Protestantism vs. Catholicism, 196
Psychoanalysis, 23–24; and contemplation, 29; as cure through love, 32, as game-playing, 43; goal of, 65–66; midwife, analyst as, 42–43; as paradigm, 155; relationship with analyst, 52–53; and repression, 38–39
Purgation and Purgatory (St. Catherine of Genoa), 170
Purgative Way, 170
Purgatorio (Dante), 170

Quixote, Monsignor, 115–116, 208–209

Rabbit, death of, 75–77
Rahner, Karl, 6, 7–8, 77–78
Ramakrishna, 25
Reality, choice of, 206–209
Reason, 198
The Rebel Angels (Davies), 41, 98–99
Receptivity to life, 133–134
Reik, Theodore, 61–62
Rejection of images, 24–25
Remembering, pain of, 51
Repression, 38–39
Rilke, Rainer Maria, 20
Rise and Fall of the City of Mahagonny (Weil), 47
Romantic longing, 156–157
Rublev Trinity, 188–189
Ruminare, 51

St. Francis (Katzantzakis), 110–111
Saintly man story, 37
Salinger, J. D., 19, 54
The Samurai (Endo), 117–118
Sandburg, Carl, 153–154
Sayings of the Desert Fathers, 12

Scetis, 12
Schaffer, Peter, 129
Schillebeeckx, Edward, 20
Schleiermacher, Friedrich, 183
Schmemann, Alexander, 53–54, 55
The Second Coming (Percy), 3–4, 180
Second conversion, 174–181
Self-knowledge, fear of, 32–33
Self-simplification, 89–92; and conversion, 170
Sexton, Anne, 124, 130, 131, 157–158
Shaffer, Peter, 185
Shakespeare, William, 207
Shared silence, 62
Shekinah, 205
Shock: of Christianity, 84–85; of second conversion, 176
Silence, 60–63
Simeon, St., 104
Simplicity, 13–14
Sin, 199
Sister Death, 67, 69, 74
Smith, Stevie, 114
Sobriety, 45
Souls and Bodies (Lodge), 168–169
Sound doctrine of God, 200–203
The Spiritual Canticle (St. John of the Cross), 25
Spirituality, 23–24; of the desert, 27–28; see also Ignatian spirituality
Squirrel Nutkin (Potter), 92
Steiner, George, 144–145
Stopping the world, 69–73
Strachey, Lytton, 39
Struggling faith, 113–114
Suffering and learning, 86–88
Surprised by Joy (Lewis), 92
Survivalists, 68
Sylvan, Father, 90–91

Tears: gift of, 22, 82–106; and purgation, 171
Teresa of Avila, 19, 176
Terror, 72
Thanksgiving Day Parade, 44
Theandric mystery, 189
Things Invisible, 135–137
Third Conversion, 181–182
Thomas Aquinas, St., 197

Thompson, Colin, 19
Time, 132–133
The Torah, 121
Total Image (Owens), 161
Tracy, David, 148
Transference, 46–48; and love, 49
The Trinity, 185–205
The Trinity and the Kingdom
    (Moltmann), 97, 188–189
Troika, 188–189
The Truce of God (Williams), 93
Truth: *aletheia*, 28; and Jesus
    Christ, 7

Unbelievers, 60
Updike, John, 29

Via negativa. See Apophatic way
Via Purgativa, 170
Victims, 146
Vindictiveness, 39–41
The Voyage of the Dawn Treader
    (Lewis), 105–106

The Way of the Pilgrim, 26
Ways of believing, 9–11
Weakness, 58–59
Weep, as imperative, 22
Weil, Kurt, 47
Weil, Simone, 9, 28, 64
West, Morris, 146
We, the Original, 186–188
Whitehead, A. N., 22
"Wilderness" (Sandburg), 153–154
William of St. Thierry, 3, 199
Williams, Harry, 87–88, 183
Williams, Charles, 121
Williams, Rowan, 93
Winter, Henry, 38
Wisdom, 136
Wonder, 202
The World to Come (Cupitt), 6, 175–
    176